9

THE OXFORD UNION

CHRISTOPHER HOLLIS

THE OXFORD UNION

LONDON

EVANS BROTHERS LIMITED

Published by Evans Brothers Limited,
Montague House, Russell Square, London, W.C.1

Set in 11 on 13 point Baskerville and printed
in Great Britain by Richard Clay (The Chaucer Press), Ltd.,
Bungay, Suffolk

7/5491

PR2630

CONTENTS

ILLUSTRATIONS

TO ANTHONY GREENWOOD

My dear Tony,
You are so nearly 'the onlie begetter' of this volume that it is but just that in antique fashion I should offer you the dedication of it. The first plan was that you should write it and then, when the call to higher things made that impossible, you generously handed over your papers to me. I have made full use of them and among them made full use, with kind permission, of the notes which Mr. Anthony Howard collected for you. I am grateful to you both. I am indebted to Mr. Evelyn Waugh for permission to quote from his life of Monsignor Ronald Knox, to Lord Birkenhead for permission to quote from his father's obituary eulogy on Gladstone—also to Mr. Godfrey Smith for valuable information about Augustus Hare and to Mr. Victor Gollancz for permission to quote from his *My Dear Timothy*. I have received patient and invaluable assistance from the Steward of the Union, Mr. Crawte, and his staff and from the successive Presidents who have held office during the time that I was engaged on this work—Mr. Stephenson, Mr. McDonnell, Mr. Beloff, Mr. Karnad, Mr. Jowell, Mr. Hart, Mr. Pratt and Lord James Douglas Hamilton. To all of them I am deeply indebted.

CHRISTOPHER HOLLIS

CHAPTER ONE

THE UNITED DEBATING SOCIETY

Dr. Routh, the famous centenarian President of Magdalen, who was to preside over the College until 1854, first assumed the Presidency in 1789. He had become a Tutor there in 1775, and in his old age would entertain his guests by describing how in his early years as a don he had seen undergraduates hanged. They used to be hanged on what were known as Gownsmen's Gallows at Hollywell. In the strange Oxford of the eighteenth century, unless in the process one was either hanged or refused to sign the Thirty-nine Articles, an undergraduate eventually qualified for a degree by what was for all intents and purposes the mere effluxion of time. Examinations were but a formality. With the end of the century a certain spirit of reform began to stir. Gownsmen's Gallows were dismantled and a seat and up-to-date stocks put in their place. Public examinations were introduced and, although the fear of Jacobinism was still such as to prevent any radical reform of Oxford life, yet its very challenge stirred up a certain intellectual curiosity, if only in order to denounce the challenger.

The famous Dean Jackson of Christ Church, who began his reign of a quarter of a century in 1783, had an ambition, similar to that of a latter-day Jowett, to train his most promising pupils for subsequent success in public life. He had 'a wonderful tact,' records George Cox, Beadle of the University in his *Recollections* 'in managing that most unmanageable class of undergraduates, noblemen'. Yet he did not confine his attentions to the highly born. Plebeians, if they were likely to be successful, were to his mind of hardly less importance. First Canning and then Peel were among his favourite pupils. Canning had brought from Eton a liking for debates. He belonged at Christ Church to a small, intellectual, politically-minded set which kept itself somewhat ostentatiously apart from 'the emptiness and vanity of the generality of good folks' there, and the members of this set had the notion of forming among themselves a little debating society, known as the Speaking Society. They adopted a special crown coat with velvet cuffs and collars and buttons stamped with the initials of Demosthenes, Cicero, Fox and Pitt. A certain Whig proposed dangerously revolutionary toasts. Dean Jackson spoke a word of warning to Canning about the way that things were going, and Canning, who was well aware which side his bread was buttered, withdrew from the Club. His secession proved its death blow.

Canning's Speaking Society in Christ Church died in 1793. A similar Literary Society in Trinity, which experimented in debates under John Skinner, met with no better favour from the President of that College than Canning had met with from the Dean of Christ Church. Then a group of men from various colleges met together and formed the Society for Scientific and Literary Disquisitions. By their rules they agreed that religious and political subjects should be barred from their debates. They proposed only to discuss historical questions such as the character of Julius Caesar or of Queen Elizabeth. They applied to the Vice-Chancellor and Proctors for leave to hold their debates. The Vice-Chancellor replied that 'innovations of this sort and in these times' might have alarming consequences and forbade them any public debates. For some years they held private meetings in private rooms, but at these meetings it seems that papers were read and were followed rather by discussion than by debate.

In 1812 Augustus Hare of New College founded the Attic Society. The reason for its name is uncertain. The classical interpretation suggests itself, but the ribald traced it to the garret-like apartments in which it met. Augustus Hare, was then a young man imbued with an almost mystical belief that discussion was both the road to truth and the only justification of a university education. Such a claim today would not seem very surprising, whatever the reservations there might be in its application. The England and Oxford of 1812 saw matters very differently. The law still thought it right to reserve all posts of importance in the State to members of the Church of England and to treat those who were not of that faith as second-class citizens.

'The University of Oxford', Sir William Hamilton was to write in 1831 perhaps with some exaggeration, 'is distinguished at once for the extent to which the most important interests of the public have been sacrificed to private advantage—for the unhallowed disregard in its accomplishment of every moral and religious bond—for the sacred character of the agents through which the unholy treason was perpetrated —for the systematic perjury it has naturalised in this great seminary for religious education—for the apathy with which the injustice has been tolerated by the State, the impiety by the Church—nay even for the unacquaintance, so universally manifested with so flagrant a corruption.'

So when Augustus Hare proclaimed the virtues of free discussion as an essential part of a university education, there were those who agreed with him but agreement was by no means universal—particularly not among the University authorities. Many agreed with the opinion that Cardinal Manning was later to pronounce that debating was 'likely to lead young men to form premature ideas'. In the eyes of most dons of that day the business of the University was not to encourage speculation but to impose on its pupils the correct views about Church and State.

The Attic Society, to begin with, consisted of seven members. Hare was an iconoclast and an enemy of privilege. He delivered a vigorous attack on the privileges granted at New College to 'Founder's kin'. This earned him unpopularity among the authorities of the College, and, despairing of

Oxford as a home of lost causes, he moved over to Cambridge, where in the more Whiggish and Liberal atmosphere, he had hopes that the Cambridge Union, newly founded in 1815, would have freedom of life denied to such enterprises at Oxford. By 1817 the Cambridge Union had run into its own troubles with its own Vice-Chancellor, and indeed the panic measures which Lord Sidmouth, then Home Secretary, imposed on the nation after the failure of a supposed attempt on the life of the Prince Regent, left University authorities perhaps no alternative but to frown on undergraduate debates. The Habeas Corpus Act was repealed. The Home Secretary circularised all Lord Lieutenants, bidding them be vigilant to suppress all blasphemous and seditious meetings. Extreme restrictions were placed on the rights of public assembly. A magistrate refused to sanction a Mineralogical Society on the grounds that study of mineralogy leads inevitably to atheism.

Returning to Oxford from Cambridge, Hare attempted to collect some of his old friends of the Attic Society. 'A miniature Parliament,' as his biographer puts it, 'was the Elysium in which his imagination and that of his friends developed'. But the Vice-Chancellor was not in the temper of the times prepared to allow any such body, and the Attic Society, by then renamed the Academical Society, was only able to continue a shadowy existence as a sort of government in exile in London.

Most of the members were going forward to Holy Orders. Oxford at that time, of course, offered no attractions for those who were destined for industry or commerce. It prided itself that its curriculum was non-vocational and based on a contempt for trade. It was primarily the preserve of the Church of England. Holy Orders were the only profession for which it provided in any way a training, and its undergraduates were therefore either of independent means or destined for Orders. Politically minded aristocrats were not as a whole inclined to mix themselves in debating until debating was recognised as sufficiently respectable to be no

handicap in a subsequent career, and speechifying was a
sport mainly indulged in by those who wanted to acquire
practise for their subsequent exercises in the pulpit.

In 1822 Lord Castlereagh committed suicide. Though
only indirectly connected with Oxford's affairs, it was yet a
happy event in the University's history. Throughout all the
changes Lord Liverpool, an old House man, remained Prime
Minister, but Canning was substituted for Castlereagh as
the leader of the House of Commons and the effective architect of the Government's policy. Canning was opposed to
Parliamentary reform. But policy under him was not an
absurdity. He had his Oxford memories. He had his memories of debates in the Speaking Society and perhaps had
come a little to repent of the supineness with which he had
accepted Dean Jackson's hint that he should break with that
Society. He was not going to bring Government pressure to
bear to persuade University authorities to suppress reasonable undergraduate freedom.

Accordingly, full of hope, some twenty-five Oxford men,
most of whom had matriculated in about 1820, got together
towards the end of 1822 and started to prepare a code of
rules for an Oxford debating society—the United Debating
Society, as it was then called. They had learnt from experience that, if they wished for tolerance from authority,
they must be prepared to move cautiously. They made it
clear that their proposals were not revolutionary. The subjects to be discussed, according to their proposed rules, were
'the historical previous to the present century and the philosophical exclusive of religion'. By March 1823 all was ready.
On April 5, 1823, the first debate of the new Society was held.
The Society had as yet no premises. It met in rooms in
Christ Church. It was decided that the chairmanship should
be changed every fortnight. Vesey of the House, afterwards
Lord de Vesci, raised the question, 'Was the revolution
under Cromwell to be attributed to the tyrannical conduct
of Charles or to the democratic spirit of the time?' There was,
it seems, a little innocent mischief in the wording of the

question. Oxford was a High Tory place. The new debating society was an aristocratic club, consisting largely of titled members, with a high subscription of two guineas, exclusion of undesirable candidates by blackball and no pretence of democracy. The members nominated their friends as candidates and quite confessedly formed a clique. It was for Old Etonians and the like, who saw before them the career of cabinet ministers in an unreformed Parliament. In this first debate Vesey, was supported by the son of the Earl of Lichfield and by Vane, who was later to become Duke of Cleveland. All the members were at least of landed families. The Society neither pretended nor wished to be representative of all Oxford, even as Oxford then was. Poor servitors had no place there. Therefore it was amusing that such gilded company, if it wished to refute the charge of tyranny against Charles I, should be compelled instead to recognise 'the democratic spirit of the age'. Democracy in 1823 was by no means the platitudinous goddess to whom one gave a sort of automatic incantation, which she is today. It was rather then the ultimate evil, and the young men, careful to avoid a trap, proposed and carried an amendment which enabled them to deny that Charles was a tyrant without admitting that democracy had been triumphant.

The condition which forebade religious debate was truly observed since the members wished to observe it. With the ban on contemporary political subjects it was very different. At Oxford, as at Cambridge, they very easily got round that ban by discussing some political principle which had an obvious reference to their own day, in terms of past controversy. The burning issue of the reform of Parliament could easily be debated in terms of the controversies of the seventeenth century.

On April 12, 1823, Mr. Wildman of Christ Church raised the somewhat curious question; 'Has America been benefited by its intercourse with Europe?' The details of the argument are not clear, but they seem to have revolved round the contention that the Red Indians would have been better off had they never been discovered by Europe—a contention which, if it can hardly be very seriously maintained, at least throws light on what young English aristocrats of that time thought of Americans. The debate was interesting because among its speakers appears for the first time the name of Richard Durnford of Magdalen, who was afterwards, over a long life which led him eventually to the Bishop's Palace at Chichester, to be one of the Union's most faithful friends and to reply for the ex-officers at the banquet which was to celebrate its Jubilee fifty years later. It was he more perhaps than anyone else who was responsible for regulating the early proceedings of the Society and in particular for the suggestion that it should acquire a regular meeting place.

So long as its debates received no official recognition, the would-be politicians on the make tended to shun the Society. Its members tended to be either peers or aspirants to Holy Orders. As soon as it was recognised, politicians flocked to its debates. Of the eight men who occupied its rotating presidential chair during 1823, one, Bramston, was to become the Dean of Winchester, all the other seven found their way either into the House of Lords or into the House of Commons.

Durnford proposed that the Society acquire a regular home. The acquisition was not so simple. The authorities were prepared to tolerate debating in private rooms. A debating hall was another matter. 'We were a feeble people,' explained Durnford fifty years later at the Jubilee banquet. 'As numbers grew beyond the original eighty, largely owing to the admission of graduate members, private rooms were not big enough at any rate for some debates. The numbers attending varied a good deal from debate to debate and the last meeting of 1823 had to be dissolved because it did not attract the requisite quorum of twenty.' But a public room could only be acquired with the consent of the authorities. The easy-going Hall of Pembroke was Vice-Chancellor during 1823 and permission might perhaps have been wrested from him. The opportunity was missed and it was to the more formidable Jenkyns of Balliol that the Society had

B

to make its application in 1824. Jenkyns was unsympathetic. He complained that debating would interfere with the undergraduates' normal studies. It is true that under Jenkyns' rule the standards of scholarship at Balliol were greatly raised. Jenkyns transformed it from one of the most unlettered to the most learned College in the University, substituting, or at least acquiescing in the substitution of, open examination for scholarships for the old system by which a scholar was nominated by each of the Fellows in turn. Yet it could manifestly only be true of the very few who undertook the organising of the Society that their duties would be so onerous as seriously to interfere with their work, and it was not an argument of much sincerity since College authorities at that time took no steps to compel undergraduates to apply themselves to their books and there was no discipline applied to those who never opened a book. It was obvious that what Jenkyns really feared was free debate and perhaps the danger that such debates would be reported in the newspapers. When the Society was debating the question of acquiring accommodation at an 'extraordinary' meeting in February 1824 the Proctors sent word that they would interrupt the proceedings. The Society accepted their protest, cancelled the arrangement that had been made with the Masonic body, whose hall had been hired and, in spite of opposition led by Durnford, agreed to meet the next Sunday in a private room in New College. For the moment the authorities had won.

Their anxiety lest the activities of the Society should get undesirable publicity was, it must be confessed, not unreasonable. In May 1824, Samuel Wilberforce, afterwards Soapy Sam, the famous Bishop of Oxford, defended the dethronement of Charles I. The London paper, *John Bull*, got hold of an account of the debate and published a furious attack on the Society. The *John Bull* of that day was an anti-reform journal of a scurrilous type which specialised in discovering and exposing 'jacobinical' activities in places that ought to have been, according to its contention, devoted to the Establishment. It had been founded to write down the supporters of Queen Caroline, and had about it the marks of a Regency McCarthy. Its editor was one Theodore Hook, who had been for a short and dissipated time at Oxford, whence he was almost banished for the insolent flippancy of stating, when asked if he would sign the Thirty-nine Articles, that he was quite ready to sign forty if it would give anybody any pleasure. He had been for a time Treasurer of Mauritius but after a short term of office had to go to prison for deficiencies in the island's accounts. He had become interested in the doings of Oxford undergraduates because of a row between the authorities of Christ Church and an undergraduate, called Baillie. Baillie had been accused of drunkenness and rowdyism and his reply to the charge had been substantially that such vices were universal among Christ Church undergraduates and that it was unfair that he should be singled out for punishment. Theodore Hook, himself a man of loose life, had, improbably enough, a pious clerical brother, the Dean of Worcester. Walter Farquhar Hook, the Dean's son, afterwards to be the famous High Church Vicar of Leeds and then Dean of Chichester, was at that time a senior student at Christ Church. He persuaded his uncle to take up the cudgels for the College.

John Bull took the line that Baillie was a muck-raker, that his case was an isolated one and that it was intolerable that, in order to cover himself, he should cast aspersions on the general 'usages of the first College in the empire; perhaps in the universe'. It was thus that *John Bull* came to be in full fighting trim against the subversive activities of undergraduates. Walter Hook, seemed to be one of those who are found in every age who believe that the young have to an unique extent thrown over all the trammels of morality and are leading society to destruction—a tiresome belief in any man—doubly tiresome when one happens to be young oneself. He called his uncle's attention to the fact that while Baillie was getting drunk in Christ Church, even more heinous things were being done at Oriel. In that College Samuel Wilberforce and his brother were actually expressing before the United Debating Society the opinion that King Charles I was rightly deposed. *John Bull* went into action. 'The most active and virulent of disputants in favour of the deposition of Charles I,' it wrote, 'were the two sons of Mr. Wilberforce! And one of them—the more indiscreet perhaps than the other, or untutored in a higher quarter—let out secrets of the prison house at Clapham or Kensington by making a direct attack on the Established Church.'

What exactly Wilberforce said about the Established Church it is not now possible to discover, but the whole episode could not have been more unfortunate for the Society. It is difficult today to recapture the attitude of that time of persons of property towards the Church of England. It was not an age of great piety. Whether you saw fit to practise your religion either by regular attendance at church or by obedience to its moral code, was, so long as the offence was not too flagrant, to a large extent your own business. In the same way what you might believe in your secret heart was your own business so long as you were careful not publicly to proclaim your infidelity, but the Church of England was, even among the most irreligious, regarded as the most essential of the props of the Establishment—and nowhere more so than at Oxford. Any criticism of it, whether in favour of scepticism or of some other denomination, Papist or Nonconformist, could not fail to open the gates to 'red ruin and the breaking up of laws'. Dr. Jenkyns, the Vice-Chancellor, had been convinced that no good could ever come out of undergraduates debating—that with their innate folly they would inevitably get themselves into trouble and the University into the papers. It seemed that he was correct.

The objection of William Wilberforce, the philanthropist, to his son's frequentation of the Society was a very different one. It was that the Society was of its nature a worldly place and debating an activity all too likely to put the immortal soul into peril. 'Watch, my dear Samuel,' he wrote, 'with jealousy whether you find yourself unduly solicitous about acquitting yourself, whether you are too much chagrined when you fail, or are puffed up by your success. Undue solicitude about popular estimation is a weakness against which all real Christians must guard with the most jealous watchfulness. The more you can retain the impression of your being surrounded by a cloud of witnesses of the invisible world, to use the Scripture phrase, the more you will be armed against this besetting sin—for such it is—though styled the last infirmity of noble minds.' There was something in Wilberforce *père*'s point. As Jowett was to say of the later Samuel, 'Samuel of Oxford is not unpleasing if you will resign yourself to being semi-humbugged by a semi-humbug.'

Desperate diseases required desperate remedies. A special meeting of the Debating Society was at once summoned. Mr. Vane of Oriel, soon to be Duke of Cleveland and of birth so impeccable that it was absurd for a vulgar journalist to accuse a Society to which he belonged of 'jacobinism', made what the Americans would call 'the key-note' speech. Ignoring or transcending differences of rank, he was willing to vouch for his fellow Collegians, the Wilberforces, unconnected though they might be with any noble family. He demanded that the Society begin by passing a vote of 'regret and indignation' at the conduct of *John Bull*. This was done without opposition. He then announced that the Wilberforces had been misreported. Very likely they had. Anyway the Society accepted Vane's assertion. He then obtained a vote that *John Bull*'s sentiments were 'of such a nature as to prejudice the Society in the eyes of the authorities of this University'.

In one sense the Oxford of that day was more closely integrated into the national life than it is today. In so far as a main issue of controversy was the claim to privilege of the Church of England, Oxford and Cambridge—and Oxford far more than Cambridge—were the central homes of that privilege. Oxford and Cambridge had also explicit political privilege. The two Universities owned the only two nonterritorial constituencies, and the University Member, far from being regarded as an anomaly, enjoyed a special pres-

tige at Westminster. Oxford itself was of course a very
different place from the Oxford of today. There was 'town'
and 'gown' but there was no 'town' that was not in some way
connected with the University. The townsmen were, if not
directly University servants, shopkeepers or innkeepers who
ministered to its members. Physically the town hardly extended beyond the University precincts. We get a very good
notion of what it was like from Turner's picture of Oxford
from Headington Hill, whence the London coach descended
between open fields. The little township of St. Clement's,
where Newman for a time ministered, lay apart in the fore-
ground. Cowley Marsh was a common. There were no
houses on the Iffley Road. Only at Magdalen Bridge did the
town begin—a town of Colleges and beautiful gardens and
picturesque buildings in their winding lanes, here and there
disfigured by what the Georgians thought of as ugly modern-
isms but not substantially different from the Oxford which
Queen Elizabeth had visited and where Charles I had set up
his headquarters. The numbers of undergraduates was of
course very much less and all were easily accommodated for
all their careers in their Colleges. The main difference in
proportion from that of today was the exiguous dimension to
which New College had been reduced, owing to its obstinate
adherence to its privileges and refusal to submit its undergraduates to the ordinary University examinations. Hamilton, in his *Discussions on Philosophy and Literature*, gives the
numbers around 1840, as follows: Balliol, 84; Trinity, 83;
University, 63; St. John, 66; Christ Church, 186; Exeter,
134; Lincoln, 56; Worcester, 94; and New College, 20.

Before we abandon ourselves to sentimental phrases about
'dreaming spires' we must remind ourselves that there were
no slums worse than those of academic and university towns.
Employment was chronically casual and clerical Dons
notoriously the worst of employers. The days when arrangements would be made for College servants to obtain vacation
employment in holiday hotels was far distant. The days
when there would be talk of paying them a vacation wage

were further distant still. In the 1820s they were left to do as best as they could for themselves. Romantic Tories might contrast the beauties of Oxford with the dark Satanic mills of a Halifax or a Wigan, but the working class was only too anxious to get out of Oxford and get into Wigan and thought the exchange well worth while. Gradgrind might not be a very loveable man but at any rate he was better than the Dons.

Yet the undergraduates—even the Dons—did not by modern standards fare so very much better than the working men. There was plenty of distinction in class. The nobleman's gown marked him out from the commoner. In those pipeless days a gigantic College hall, warmed only by an open fire, was a very cold place in winter and baths were to remain almost unknown in Oxford for another three-quarters of a century. There was little in the way of playing fields or of organised games, though Brasenose and Christ Church had cricket grounds on the Bullingdon Green and Magdalen one at Cowley Marsh on which the University played. The main recreation of the respectable undergraduate consisted of gigantic walks. Gladstone records how he walked for fifteen miles along the road to Leamington until a thunderstorm drove him to an inn where he recreated himself and the innkeeper by reciting aloud the *Prometheus Vinctus* in the original Greek. Another day he walked to Banbury, breakfasted there, and then walked on twenty-two miles further to Leamington. Cards, Gladstone found, even after dining with a bishop, kept him awake at night and 'were too often accompanied by dissipated spirit'. But less high-minded undergraduates overcame this disadvantage and were willing to indulge in even coarser recreations!

Competitive games came in very much at the same time as the Society. Southey has given us reminiscences of boats on the Isis with students in caps and tassels at the oars at the time of Waterloo. When, after that, races were introduced the undergraduates rowed in high hats. The first boat race against Cambridge was organised in 1829 by Charles Wordsworth, a prominent light of the Society and afterwards

Bishop of St. Andrew's. It was not for another ten years that a regular University Boat Club was formed 'to defray the expenses of a contest with a foreign naval power'. Charles Wordsworth was also responsible for the first Oxford and Cambridge cricket match which was played in 1827.

Vane's intervention to save the Society had been successful. He was so manifestly the social superior both of the editor of *John Bull* and of the Master of Balliol that both were silenced. *John Bull* printed no more about the Society and the Vice-Chancellor took no action. The Society, though still without regular premises, continued on its tranquil way. There were slight constitutional changes. The office of vice-president was abolished and that of secretary substituted for it. Gradually the pretext that the Society was debating historical questions wore thinner and thinner. The topical came to be accepted, so long as the question was framed in general rather than in particular terms.

The mind of the Society, as is only natural, as indeed happens today, varied from term to term and indeed from debate to debate according to the accident of who happened to attend. What is interesting, if not in the least surprising, is the frank acceptance of class divisions as self-evidently necessary for the well-being of society. A member who at one debate as late as 1833 was rash enough to propose a motion deploring hereditary privilege did not find a single supporter. Nevertheless, within the limits of their frank acceptance of the class system the members of the Society were on the whole not ungenerous, even though they expressed their generosity in language which would today be thought either comical or unacceptable. They debated what education, if any, should be given to the lower orders and decided, on the whole the less the better. It must be remembered that at that time no provision at all was made for education out of public funds and that it was not until the next decade that Parliament was to pass its first vote for such a purpose. It was of course somewhat comical that young men who were enjoying the amenities of amply endowed Colleges which had been founded expressly to give education to the poor, should express such sentiments, but it would obviously be absurd to pick out these particular young undergraduates for a general censure which may have been deserved by the whole of society.

There was always at the least a progressive group in the Society, even when it did not constitute a majority. Wilber-force was its most prominent member. He argued, though without convincing his fellow members, against the motion that 'the system of borough patronage was perfectly con-sistent with the spirit of the constitution'. He also tried and failed to get a vote of the Society against the death penalty for forgery. Peel, it will be remembered, was Home Secre-tary at the time and bankers were petitioning him to remove forgery from the catalogue of capital crimes on the ground that, if the penalty were more reasonable, juries would con-vict in cases of guilt, which with a death penalty they were unwilling to do. Though the Society was not willing to abolish the death penalty for forgery, Parliament proved itself to be willing. Other speeches in another debate de-nounced the inhuman systems of discipline then in vogue for soldiers, sailors and slaves.

In the country the Government of Lord Liverpool still con-tinued in power but the direction of policy had passed from Castlereagh to Canning. Under Canning exceptional mea-sures of repression were abandoned and the country returned to its normal liberties. The Society seemed to have no objec-tion to such policies, but the great issues of the day that were coming up for decision were Catholic Emancipation and the Reform of Parliament. Oxford was of course, as we have said, a Church of England institution. When at the end of the decade Peel was to become a convert to Catholic Emanci-pation, it was to cost him his University seat. But notoriously, undergraduates, even when themselves the possessors of privileges, do not always follow the opinions of their seniors. Emancipation could not be kept out of the Society's debates. By its rules the Society was of course precluded from debating religious topics and such a debate as whether God exists, which the Union held in our own time, would not have been tolerated by the authorities, nor indeed desired by the members in the atmosphere of the 1820s. They would not have dreamed of debating whether the Roman Catholic religion was true, nor indeed had they done so would any member— least of all the Society's recent and most brilliant recruit, Mr. Manning of Balliol—have been found to argue in its favour. But whether Catholics should have votes was, they reasonably decided, not a religious but a political question. It was debatable.

The motion was therefore proposed: 'That religious differences are not a just ground for exclusion from political rights.' The Society was not prepared to accept the unqualified proposition. On the other hand some among them were not prepared to go on record as the friends of persecution. Therefore an amendment was proposed by Lord Mahon: 'That a difference in religion should not expose any individual to persecution or insults but may yet justly incapacitate him from possessing extended authority.' What 'extended' meant was not, as far as can be discovered, exactly explained. Not long afterwards the Society went on record as determined to uphold the Protestant ascendancy in Ireland. Had they been a little better acquainted with Irish affairs they might have been hard put to it to explain how that ascendancy as then exercised, if not a persecution, was not at the best an insult to Catholic Irishmen. Still it would again be absurd to blame this inconsistency on these young men in particular. It merely shows how they reflected, as one would expect them to reflect, the mind of the society in which they had grown up. But even such an amendment was not acceptable to some among the members who demanded an unequivocal assertion of Anglican privileges. The debate was fierce and noisy and at last, when C. E. Smith of Oriel was denouncing the Catholic claims, there was such uproar that the Society had to adjourn without having taken a vote either on the motion or on the amendment.

In order to escape such trouble, undesirable in itself and dangerous as likely to bring down on it the wrath of the authorities, the Society for some time after that was careful to discuss only trivial and flippant motions. But the policy was one of flight from the frying pan into the fire. As has sometimes been found in more recent years, the undergraduate who can make a witty speech is a much to be desired but very rare bird and, if an evening's debate is dedicated to a motion of mere flippancy, the result is apt to be one of excruciating boredom. The less serious the topics the more futile grew the debates and the smaller the audiences. In a fashion much more like that sometimes seen in modern times than may be generally imagined, interminable hours were wasted on pretendedly humorous interruptions and points of order. Yet it was not possible to muster a sufficient vote to revise the rules. It was Wrangham of Oriel who thought of a way out. On Saturday, December 3, 1825, he moved and carried a motion to dissolve the Society.

CHAPTER TWO

THE ERA OF GLADSTONE
AND MANNING

'ON SATURDAY LAST died of a deep decline the Oxford United Debating Society,' recorded the *Oxford Herald*. It misunderstood Wrangham's manoeuvre. On Monday, December 5, 1825, a new meeting established a new Oxford Union Society and annexed to itself—or to be more accurate, purchased from itself—the books and benches of the now defunct United Debating Society. To emphasise its continuity with the old Society it stamped the old Society's date of foundation, 1823, on its furniture. By constituting a new Society it was possible to draw up new rules which required the support only of a majority—not of the two-thirds majority which would have been required to change the rules of the old Society. It was possible to get this majority and thus to pass rules which gave the President ampler powers, by the imposition of fines, to maintain order. The only question was whether the authorities would accept this new Society. They had not been very favourably disposed towards the old one and perhaps had tolerated it only because they had thought that it was *in extremis* and would soon die of inanition. At one of the first meetings of the new Society when Samuel Wilberforce was speaking, the Proctors sent in a messenger commanding the Society to disperse and all Members to return to their Colleges. One William Patten, was in the chair. He replied in a manner worthy of a Caroline Speaker. 'Sir, this House has received the Proctors' message and will send an answer to the summons by an officer of its own.' Strangely enough the Proctors were not ready to meet this defiance and thenceforward the Society's existence was no longer menaced.

The Society had, if one may judge from its own private books, its own internal troubles in those early days. We find Wilberforce resigning. Odell, of Christ Church, the Treasurer, was censured for 'self sufficiency and general offensiveness'. Three lords—Ossory, Russell and Boyle—marched out in a huff. The motions do not seem to have been notably liberal. By a majority of one on a division of thirty-seven the House disapproved of 'Mechanics' Institutes as a means of educating the labouring classes.' By the President's casting vote it decided that 'the English Universities have sufficiently accommodated their system of education to the circumstances of the present generation.' Seventy-two members went to Christ Church to debate the character of Canning. The Society started spending money, by buying maps, lamps, books and other commodities, then found itself in debt. In 1828 a motion was passed that the Society be dissolved but was quickly repented of, and rescinded at a subsequent meeting.

By 1829 it felt strong enough in spite of previous opposition to acquire rooms of its own. The rooms that it acquired were at Wyatt's at 115 High Street. It also rented a Reading Room in another house nearby in the same street. The meetings of the Society in Wyatt's rooms do not seem to have differed much from the earlier meetings in members' private rooms except that the motions on the whole were more serious and at the same time reverted to what may be called the truly historical. The execution of Stafford was condemned by a large majority. The speakers seem also to have been more serious and to have consisted to a greater extent of those destined for Holy Orders. Samuel Wilberforce had gone off to be a curate and to matrimony. He had married the sister of the lady who was afterwards to marry Manning, but his brother, Henry, afterwards to be Newman's friend and reckoned Samuel's equal in eloquence, was still at Oxford. Future bishops—Durnford of Chichester—Baring of Durham

—Hamilton of Salisbury and Wordsworth of St. Andrew's—
were prominent in the Union of those days. The Union made
its large contribution to the Anglican clergy of the next
generation but it did not favour any special school of thought.
Its bishops were generally Low Church, if not latitudinar-
ian. Indeed, Charles Wordsworth owed his bishopric of St.
Andrew's to the fact that Scottish bishops are elected. There
were 17 electors of whom he was one. The other 16 were
equally divided, 8 for and 8 against. So he sensibly gave the
casting vote to himself.

A name that has played a more important part in religious
history than any of these was that of Henry Manning.
Manning, the son of a wealthy civil servant, had come up to
Balliol from Harrow in 1827. His main devotion at that time
was to cricket and he was an object of observation principally
for the magnificent topboots which he sported. A handsome,
indolent boy, he made it his first object to prove to his father
that the allowance of £250 a year was quite insufficient to
support the standard of life which he considered to be required by his Oxford ambitions. No very industrious scholar,
he yet turned off from time to time a copy of verses, but they
were not of high merit. Charles Wordsworth, who had encouraged his ambition at Harrow, was not much impressed
by his poetry, and Manning did not dispute his verdict. He
wrote to Wordsworth

> Dear Charles, I hope you'll make some small allowance,
>   Being a poet of the brightest rate,
> You would, I'm sure, be kind if you could know once
>   What pains I've taken to write verse of late.

One presumes that he must have pronounced 'allowance'
so that the second syllable rhymed with 'know', but even so
'rate' and 'once' are a little too obviously dragged in to make
their rhyme.

At Oxford Manning from the first showed himself more
industrious than he had at Harrow. He was, says Mozley of
Oriel in his *Letters*, 'a rather boyish freshman'. Yet Wickham

his fellow undergraduate, afterwards Dean of Lincoln, in a
letter, found him 'a very quiet and well conducted undergraduate unless you count boxing a reproach'. From the first
he both frequented and dominated the Society. Of his first
speech he recorded, 'I was half dead with fright and when I
got up, saw nothing but the President's head out of a white
mist. But I rattled on and got a majority. . . . I had always disliked the thought of being a clergyman and this political
aspiration finished.' (Of course for the time being.) Taking
his model from Fox, who during the years of his apprentice-
ship spoke every night in the House of Commons, Manning
spoke 'at every meeting, on all subjects, with unfailing fluency
and propriety of expression.' The Union, he decided, had
become 'very respectable'. It is not an altogether attractive
habit. It seems to indicate a desire both to dominate and to
succeed, indifferent to the comforts or ambitions of others,
and some critics may find in the Manning of the Union
some of the traits that were afterwards to show themselves
at the Vatican Council or in the controversies with Newman.

He spoke against excessive penalties for crime. He spoke
in Private Business in favour of taking in some American
papers such as the *Baltimore Democrat*. 'It was the order of
Providence we should be as one. If we could not be under
the same Government, yet we had a common blood, common
faith, common institutions. America was running a race
with us in literature, in science and in art, and if we ceased
to learn from her what she could teach us, we might find ourselves one day much behindhand.' At an earlier debate the
House had decided: 'That Government as conducted was
corrupt in practice and unpopular in theory'. But Manning
reversed this verdict. In opposition to the Reform Bill he told
the House that the unreformed constitution gave as much
weight to democratic opinion as was desirable and obtained
in his favour the heaviest vote of the House yet recorded. He
spoke in favour of free trade in wool. He was not above an
occasional joke or leg-pull. When Denison, of Christ Church,
George Denison's brother, asked him 'What was the barilla

duty?', barilla being in fact burnt seaweed on which duty
was charged, Manning without hesitation replied, 'At one
time you load your ship with a particular commodity such
as tea, wine or tobacco, and in the language of trade we
denominate this operation barilla.' There was of course at
that date no trace of his future religious opinions. Yet it is
amusing to note that his self-confident readiness to give an
unequivocal verdict on all subjects earned for him from his
contemporaries the nickname of the Pope.

In 1829 a wholly new experiment was tried. An invitation
was issued to the Cambridge Union to send over a team to
debate at Oxford. It was accepted. The Cambridge Union
at that time was a home of aesthetes where Oxford was dominated by Churchmen and politicians, and most of its prominent speakers were also members of the Apostles, those rare
aesthetic spirits whose habit it was to say of any philistine
bore, 'I found him very Oxford.' Cambridge debaters, unlike Oxford debaters, had scorn for success in the schools as a
plebeian achievement. Cambridge chose as its representatives Arthur Henry Hallam, Thomas Sunderland and
Monckton Milnes. Hallam was afterwards to earn immorta-
lity in death as the subject of Tennyson's *In Memoriam*;
Monckton Milnes—'he whom men called Baron Houghton
but the gods call Dicky Milnes'—was bibliophile and
politician, collector of pornographic books and friend of
Swinburne and was to be one of those curious figures who
prove to us that the Victorian age was not as universally
strait-laced as it is sometimes imagined to have been. But
of these Cambridge visitors the one who had at that time the
highest reputation was Thomas Sunderland. He was by all
admitted to be the greatest undergraduate speaker of his day,
'the greatest speaker I think I ever heard, a man with the
strongest oratorical gift'. He had an insolent way with him
and there were some who did not like him. Tennyson wrote
a satirical poem on him, the *Character*. When told of it
Sunderland commented, 'Which of the Tennysons did you
say wrote it? The slovenly one?' Yet, liked or disliked, all

ABOVE   The President's chair

OVERLEAF   Wyatt's rooms in the High Street in which the
Society met in the last century prior to the building of its
present premises

prophesied for him a great future. The reality was strangely different. A few years after going down he disappeared. His mind had given way while he was travelling abroad. He lived for another forty years—a strange Scholar Gypsy's existence. From time to time he would appear in public houses in quite unconnected parts of the country, talk meanderingly of Cambridge days to any that would listen and then disappear again. He died in 1867.

The three Cambridge orators travelled through the November snows to Oxford by the Pluck coach. On arrival they were welcomed by their Oxford hosts with Gladstone at their head, and suitably regaled. The print of the scene was reproduced in the *Graphic*'s Gladstone Memorial Number of May 1898.

The subject chosen for debate was that of the relative merits of Byron and Shelley—Byron being the most recent of Cambridge poets and Shelley of Oxford. In the eyes of the University authorities Byron was not an especially desirable character. Shelley, having twenty years before been sent down from Oxford for atheism, was wholly to be condemned. Monckton Milnes in asking leave to make the expedition had, as he confessed, to conceal from his Dean by a downright lie the topic of the debate.

A good crowd assembled. 'The Union benches,' it was recorded, 'instead of being scantily dotted with indifferent occupants, swarmed and murmured like a hive of bees.' Monckton Milnes was impressed by the appointments of the Oxford Union, which he found superior to those of Cambridge. 'The contrast,' he recorded, 'from our long, noisy, shuffling, scraping, talking vulgar ridiculous-looking kind of assembly, to a neat little square room, with eighty or ninety young gentlemen sprucely dressed, sitting on chairs or lounging about the fireplace was enough to unnerve a more confident person than myself.' Yet the debate as a debate was from the Oxford point of view a total fiasco. Out of courtesy Cambridge was to defend the Oxford poet and Oxford to defend the Cambridge. But it soon appeared that,

C

while both teams knew a little about Byron and the Cambridge men were well acquainted with Shelley, the Oxonians had not read a line of him. Their ignorance is extraordinary. One would have thought that the notoriety of Shelley's fate would have caused adventurous undergraduates to interest themselves in his work. It did, so it seems, at Cambridge. It did not do so at Oxford. It is an interesting example of how strong a horror at that date could be created by the tag of such a word as 'atheist'. It seems that they really almost believed that fire would come down from heaven and devour any who had any traffic with such a monster. As a result the debate was absurd. Sir Francis Doyle who had begun his debating in the Eton Society with Gladstone and who was afterwards to succeed Matthew Arnold as Professor of Poetry, opened but ineffectively. The Cambridge men developed their thesis in a high-flown but at any rate not totally irrelevant argument. On the other hand Manning, 'perhaps at that time the leader of our debates,' records Sir Francis Doyle, 'with great propriety rose. He felt that it would be a somewhat clownish and inhospitable proceeding if these bold guests went away unchallenged'. But he was reduced to basing his case on the absurd and question-begging contention that Byron must be a better poet than Shelley because they had all read Byron and had not read Shelley. He afterwards confessed to the absurdity. The vote, it is true, when it came to a vote, went to Byron by 78 to 45, but, as Manning admitted, 'we Oxford men were precise, orderly and morbidly afraid of excess in word or manner. The Cambridge oratory came in like a flood into a mill-pond. Both Milnes and Hallam took us aback by the boldness and freedom of their manner. But I remember the effect of Sunderland's declamation to this day. It had never been seen or heard before among us. We cowered like birds and ran like sheep. . . . I acknowledge that we were utterly routed.'

Manning's career at the Union was a curious one. He acquired there a dominating position as its leading speaker. His Oxford reputation, as Purcell, his biographer, records, rested mainly 'on his achievements as a ready and agreeable speaker'. He was in due course elected President and then, before his Presidential term began, a little unaccountably resigned and never went there again. It seems that he had decided to take his Schools more seriously than had been his first intention and discovered that the Presidency would take up more time than he was prepared to spare. Why he did not make this discovery before putting himself to the trouble of being elected is far from clear. He does not seem to have had any grievance against the Union and indeed in later life, while for religious reasons he fought, as Archbishop of Westminster, a battle against allowing Catholics to go to Oxford, whose atmosphere was, he thought, 'incurably Protestant' and therefore dangerous to faith, he never showed any hostility to the Union. In 1873 he attended as one of the guests of the Jubilee banquet and, though one Anglican clergyman stalked out in protest against his being given precedence over the Bishops of the Established Church, the general company received him with an ovation. He took the occasion to pay a generous tribute to some of those who had been his comrades in the Union forty-five years before— 'The Duke of Newcastle, whose measured eloquence was trained in the discussions of the Oxford Union' (Lord Selborne described the Duke as 'the worst speaker I ever remember in the Society')—'Lord Dalhousie and Lord Canning whose administrative powers were no doubt developed by the part they took in the debates of the Union'— and 'Lord Elgin, whose oratory, whose copious imagination and rapidity of speech when at the Union gave promise of the perfection he afterwards attained'—Sydney Herbert 'who to his last days continued to show the manly affection which was one of his greatest characteristics'—Samuel Wilberforce 'who recalled to him Homer's description of Ulysses with words flowing fast and soft as flakes of snow from his lips.' Yet he abandoned the Union before serving his Presidential term. Was it merely through a fear that the time demanded would militate against success in Schools?

That was a part of the truth. Half a century later we are to find such an undergraduate as Asquith reckoning success at the Union as one of the steps on the road to success all but as important as a First in the Final Schools. But such calculations were at that time for the future. In Manning's time people told one another that practice at debate might be useful for sharpening the intellect. But the barely tolerated Union with its still sketchy *cursus honorum* had not yet won for itself sufficient prestige to be considered as one of the stepping stones to success. It was therefore partly because it might rather prove a stumbling block to his way in the world that Manning abandoned it. But there was also another reason. From his earliest days Manning for all his cricket and his top-boots and his jokes about barilla, had, he himself told us, 'a lively fear of hell'. He did not pretend that his religious ideas in those years were other than crude. He had no full conception of the Christian scheme, but with him worldly ambitions were overshadowed by a real fear that hell might well be the reward of worldliness.

Among those who greeted the Cambridge debaters—though he took no part in the subsequent debate—was the young William Ewart Gladstone who had come up to Oxford from Eton in 1828. He had been, according to Sir Roderick Murchison, 'the prettiest little boy that ever went to Eton'—in some ways a dubious compliment. At Eton he had been virtuous and industrious but not portentously so. One of the members of each division was in turn praepostor. It was the duty of the praepostor to write down the names of any boys who were absent from the lesson. Gladstone was not above conniving with another boy of the name of Vowles who wished to play hookey and agreeing not to enter his name as absent. The master noticed and as a result both Vowles and Gladstone were duly birched. Gladstone had not wholly outgrown such harmless antinomianism even by the time that he reached Oxford. A year younger than Manning, he soon trod pressingly upon his senior's heels. Christ Church, with Dr. Samuel Smith as Dean, was a conservative College and Gladstone, the son of a well-to-do West Indian slave owner, shared the College's conservatism. Though Gladstone did not speak in the Cambridge debate, he impressed Monckton Milnes at their meeting. 'The man that took me most was the youngest Gladstone of Liverpool,' recorded Milnes. 'I am sure a very superior person.' Yet the word 'superior' does not seem deserved in any Curzonian or pejorative sense. The first notices of him seem to give evidence of a certain attractive lack of responsibility. 'Mr. Gladstone, after speaking at great length against the motion, voted for it,' record the minutes of the debate on the exclusion from the Union of a certain allegedly scurrilous paper, known as *The Age*. His first speech in general debate was on February 11, 1830, on a somewhat obscure motion whether Charles James Fox was a traitor. The speech that made his name a few months later was on the motion: 'That Mr. Canning's conduct as a Minister is deserving of the highest commendation.' The motion was topical. Canning had just died. Wellington and Peel, who had opposed Catholic Emancipation during Canning's lifetime, had turned round after his death and carried it. Canning was from Gladstone's home town of Liverpool. Gladstone worshipped his memory. In this Union debate he sprang to his defence, supported by his friend, Manning, who made what was to prove his last Union speech. As a result on May 13, 1830, Gladstone was elected to the Union secretaryship.

Gladstone was then, and for some years afterwards, to be what Macaulay described as 'the rising hope of the stern unbending Tories'. His speeches and votes during those years were almost consistently reactionary. Reform of Parliament was the issue of the day. He and the majority of the Union opposed the grant of any representation to Leeds, Manchester and Birmingham. (Liverpool, it must be noticed, was not mentioned in the motion.) He voted against the removal of the disabilities, which forebade Jews to vote for Parliament. On June 17, 1830, he opposed a motion that

'Colleges to be established in London for the education of the higher middle classes would be beneficial to the community'.

Gladstone was still secretary in the Michaelmas term. The secretaryship did not then, as it does today, change every term and it was this term which was the term of the great debates that raised the Union to a pinnacle at least of notoriety incomparably higher than it had ever previously occupied. In the earlier 1820s, while Canning was still in power, political issues were not clear-cut. Politicians, like Canning himself, who favoured Catholic Emancipation, agreed not to press it out of deference to George IV and Lord Liverpool. Peel's reform of the criminal code, immensely important as it was, did not easily divide the young into two debating sides of Aye and No. Power was in the hands of mildly reforming Conservatives—a situation that does not make for clear-cut issues. After Canning's death there were two great questions—Catholic Emancipation and Reform— on which it was necessary to take a definite stand.

Gladstone held in his youth, it will be remembered from Macaulay's Essay, a peculiar High Church doctrine that the Church was (or ought to be) the State and the State was (or ought to be) the Church, and that therefore those who would not accept the doctrines of the Established Church ought to be excluded from political rights and treated as second-class citizens. But, apart from that, he had a passionate loyalty to the memory of Canning. The Canningite interpretation of the events of that day was that his opponents within the Cabinet—Wellington and Peel—had hounded their hero into his grave by their obstinate opposition to his reforms and then, having formed a Government of their own, had rounded on their own principles and brought in that measure of Catholic Emancipation which they had been put in office to oppose. Wellington and Peel were in the position in which Conservative ministers have not infrequently found themselves in later years, of being denounced by intransigent Conservatives who accuse them of betraying the principles of their party and of governing by policies which they had been precisely elected to prevent. Then, as now, nowhere was this thesis that principle ought not to be sacrificed to expediency more eloquently upheld than by a certain type of undergraduate politician, for obviously it is a thesis which comes particularly easily to such a person since he does not have to submit the policies which he advocates to any immediate test of practicability. Incomparably the most eloquent of undergraduate politicians who upheld that thesis in the late 1820s was Gladstone.

He set himself to denounce the betrayal of Conservative principles by the Duke of Wellington's Conservative Government—what Newman called 'the dangerous liberalism of the Duke of Wellington'—with all the vigour with which so many Conservatives have in more recent times denounced the betrayal by Lloyd George's coalition, by Baldwin or by Mr. Macmillan. It is characteristic of such young enthusiasts that they very often do not stop to calculate exactly what they are likely to achieve nor ask themselves whether a Conservative revolt against a Conservative Government can have any result other than that of putting the opposite party into power. So now, when the Duke of Wellington fell, Lord Grey and the reforming Whigs took his place, as any practised politician must have foreseen would happen. Gladstone, thundering against the Duke of Wellington, does not seem to have looked as far ahead as that.

In October a debate was held on a motion which condemned the foreign policy of the Duke of Wellington, but it was rejected in spite of Gladstone by a vote of 48 to 24. Gladstone and his friends, determined on revenge, proposed another motion of general condemnation of the Government: 'That the administration of the Duke of Wellington is undeserving of the confidence of the country'. It provoked a tremendous debate. Gladstone prepared the ground for it by distributing pamphlets round the Union—*The Country Without a Government*—*The Duke of Wellington and the Whigs*—*Observations for and against Lord Brougham*, and the like. He attempted to exclude from the Union Reading Room the *Westminster Review*, the organ of the philosophic radicals.

When the debate was concluded it is recorded in the minutes by the hand of the Secretary, Gladstone himself, that 'the House then divided when the President announced that the motion was carried by a majority of one (tremendous cheering)'. After the word 'cheering' there is clearly an excision, and the inspection of E. C. Bentley nearly a century later showed that the words excised were beyond question 'from the majority of one'. Somebody had taken it on himself to excise Gladstone's improper and flippant comment. A few days afterwards Gladstone was elected President (elections then took place in the middle of the term) and he made it his first Presidential duty to condemn the practice 'which some honourable gentleman had adopted of defacing the records of the Society'. It is difficult to be sure of intentions but it looks as if Gladstone, while a strong fighter, did not yet think that undergraduate politics or his own antics ought to be taken too seriously.

When the Duke of Wellington's Government fell it was succeeded not by what a Tory diehard might have considered a real Conservative Government but by the far worse Whig Government of Lord Grey, pledged to a reform of Parliament. The country was in a ferment. The Tory University was generally opposed to reform. In a letter to the *Standard* of April 7, 1831, Gladstone denounced 'the unhappy multitude which was rushing along the path of revolution as an ox goeth to the slaughter or a fool to the correction of the stocks'. In the Union opinion was divided, but Gladstone's Presidential term had by then finished. Lyalls had succeeded him as President and Gladstone was once more free to agitate. He assumed the leadership of the opponents of reform. On May 16, 1831, Knatchbull of Trinity moved: 'That the present ministry is incompetent to carry on the government of the country', and opened a debate which ran on for three evenings. There sat listening to the debate what appeared to be an old gentleman with snow-white hair. A speaker denounced the Ministers as 'a vile crew of traitors'. The old gentleman jumped up and shouted, 'The honourable gentleman has called His Majesty's Ministers a crew. We accept that omen. A crew they are; and with Lord Grey for stroke and Lord Brougham for steerer and the whole people of England halloing on the banks, I can tell the honourable gentleman that they are pretty sure of winning the race.' There was loud applause from the friends of reform but no one knew who the interrupter was. It turned out that he was Robert Lowe, who was an albino, and who from this strange beginning was to make for himself a considerable career at the Union and to go on from that to lead the opposition to the extension of the franchise when the Liberals tried to take up reform again, and then to become Gladstone's Chancellor of the Exchequer, and as such a somewhat penurious enemy of the University which he considered a mere 'examining board'.

On the second day of the debate Gladstone spoke. He moved the amendment 'That the Ministry has unwisely introduced and most unscrupulously forwarded a measure which threatens not only to change the form of our government but ultimately to break up the very foundations of social order as well as materially to forward the views of those who are pursuing this object throughout the civilised world'. Thirty-odd years later at the time of the debates on the second reform bill of 1866, Disraeli was a little absurdly to bring up this speech against Gladstone in order to charge him with inconsistency. Gladstone sensibly and with dignity replied that of course he had changed his opinions over the years as everybody knew and that he had come with maturity to more sensible conclusions. He only wished that Disraeli had done likewise. Whatever may be thought of the opinions that Gladstone expressed at this earlier date, none disputed the power and effect of his oration.

Charles Wordsworth made lists and notes of all the speakers and marked off Lowe and Tait, the future Archbishop, and others who spoke in favour of reform as academically 'nobody'. While others looked to Gladstone, as indeed he looked to himself, as the champion who would preserve the nation from the evils of reform, George Denison with extraordinary acuteness argued that Gladstone would end up as a Liberal because he opposed reform 'on liberal grounds'.

Gladstone carried his amendment by 94 votes to 38 and, as a result of the reports which Lord Lincoln relayed to the Duke of Newcastle, the Duke offered Gladstone one of his pocket boroughs at Newark by which he made his way straight into Parliament. He spoke once more at the Union on June 2, 1831, on a motion calling for the emancipation of the West Indian slaves. Gladstone had, of course, a family interest in slavery and he therefore proposed an amendment calling as an alternative for a better guarding of personal and civic rights, for compulsory release from slavery and for Christian education, which would lead gradually to complete emancipation by following the earliest Christian procedure. The amendment had about it what a cynic might think to be one of the characteristic marks of a Gladstonian proposal—that no one was quite certain what it meant.

Gladstone's experience was a landmark in the history of the Union. It was only a few years before that that those who frequented the Union were still wondering whether their actions would be tolerated. Even when toleration was secured, it had never occurred to anyone—it had never for instance occurred to Manning—that pre-eminence at the Union could open a direct door to success in after life. Doubtless as with a hundred other activities, the Union debates, it was thought, played their indirect part in education—sharpened wits—taught young men how to get on with their fellows—but the Oxford career was, it was thought, judged success or failure by achievement in the Schools. All else was extraneous. Yet here was Gladstone, who had, it was true, on first coming up, taken life a little easily, who had surrounded himself with companions, who had been careful not to become like Pusey 'a reading automaton', but who had

nevertheless in the end buckled to and got his Double First.
As his diaries show, religion, that 'awful subject' as he
called it (using 'awful' of course in its proper meaning) had
even in these years before he put on a preternatural gravity,
been a dominating influence over his mind.   Friends complained that he was too much mixed up 'with the St. Mary's
Hall and Oriel set' who were 'only fit to live with maiden
aunts and keep tame rabbits' and there is much reason to
think that, as he wrote to his father, if he had only been left
free to choose his own profession, he would have taken Holy
Orders. Yet in the end it was neither Schools nor religion
which put his feet on the first rung of the ladder of success,
but the Union. The event gave the Union a new prestige.

CHAPTER THREE

THE 1830s

ANY MAN WHETHER at that or a later time would have been very foolish had he argued simpliciter 'The Union threw a political career open to Gladstone. Therefore it would throw open a political career to me'. Gladstone, tall, handsome, with coal black hair and resistless eloquence, proved himself at the Union able to dominate an assembly as probably no other member of it has ever done. The testimony of his contemporaries was that his dominance was extraordinary. He was unique. 'As far as mere elocution went,' wrote Lowe in 1876 concerning these earlier years, 'Mr. Gladstone spoke as well as he does now.' It is only the very exceptional under- graduate who can look at the Union as a stage on which he can prove to the world his immediate fitness for public life. Asquith, as we shall see, in his day, looking back to Glad- stone, treated his Union career as of equal importance with his Schools. Asquith had the right to do so. But who else had that right? To most undergraduates the Union is a place where they can learn—not a place where they can display themselves.

The issue of reform was to Oxford an issue of far greater moment than any other that had been raised since the foundation of the Society. Reform was demanded in the large towns with menace of violence. There were riots in Bristol and lives were lost. The opponents of reform thought that surrender would mean a total surrender to anarchy and the utter subversion of society. All property would be de- stroyed, the Church overthrown. Nowhere was this extreme opposition to reform more passionately held than in the Common Rooms of Oxford—more passionately even at

Oxford than at Cambridge. The whole position of the Oxford Fellows, as they then were, depended on the maintenance of privilege and the rejection of reform in any shape. Let the dyke but be breached at one place and the whole flood would come pouring through. Sir William Hamilton in 1831 had written two remarkable articles in the *Edinburgh Review* in which he said that Oxford was 'of all academical institutions at once the most imperfect and the most perfectible. . . . On the average,' he claimed, 'there is to be found among those to whom Oxford confides the business of education an infinitely smaller proportion of men of literary reputation than among the actual instructors of any other University in the world. . . . The causes of decay were the religious tests for entry and the disproportion by which the Colleges which ought to have been merely lodging houses had been allowed to grow at the expense of the University into self-governing schools.' Among undergraduates there were plenty who supported their Fellows—whether because they were aristocrats who wished to retain their political privileges or because they were aspirants to Holy Orders and a Fellowship, who were anxious for the privileges of the Church. There was a by-election in the Oxfordshire constituency and Lord Norreys was the anti-reform candidate. Two or three hundred undergraduates rode out to meet him, carrying with them a subscription of £800 towards his election expenses. Within Oxford there were battles between town and gown. In the Union itself there was bitter controversy. Palmer of Magdalen moved that since the demand for reform was manifestly an attack on the University and therefore an attack on the Union, the Union's funds ought to be devoted to repelling that attack. He moved that the entire funds of the Union be devoted to that purpose. He got considerable support but not a majority.

It is not the habit of undergraduates to allow themselves to become the mere mouthpieces of their seniors. There were undergraduates, such as Gladstone, who accepted the view of the Fellows that the reform movement was a subversion of all the foundations of society. But all did not take that view. Even in Gladstone's famous debate 38 out of a House of 132 had supported reform. Such a society, as the Union, is always much under the influence of a dominating personality. When Gladstone passed on, the friends of reform became more vociferous. But the times were very different from those of a few years before when the character of Oliver Cromwell or Julius Caesar could be dissected in friendly debate. At the Union, as elsewhere throughout England, both sides now felt that there was something desperately at issue. There was a bitterness, a violence and a lack of charity in the debates that had not been hitherto known. Meetings had to be abandoned owing to conditions of riot. It was moved that officers of regiments quartered in Oxford should become honorary members of the Union. The Liberals bitterly opposed the motion, arguing that to extend membership to those who had no connection with the University was to destroy the nature of the Society. There was bitter debate carried on until half past twelve on a Friday morning in defiance of the hour of return to College and, though the motion was not accepted, some officers over the next year or two seem to have found their way as guests into the Society's debates.

Gladstone and his friends from Christ Church in the midst of all this tumult withdrew into the tranquillity of a little private society which they called the W.E.G. after its founder and where they were able to discuss the affairs of life quietly and without interruption. In the Union it was a sign how times had changed when at the end of 1833 Massie of Wadham —a Liberal and reformer—was elected President. In order to show that it was not meanness which had caused the Liberals to object to the surrender of the Union's funds to the cause of anti-reform, they voted £30—the sum total at that time of the Society's possessions—to the relief of distress in Ireland.

Massie was not only a Liberal. He was a new phenomenon at the Union in that he came from Wadham—not until then one of the regular 'Union Colleges, Christ Church, Trinity and Balliol'—and in that he did not come from any of the major public schools. The Union in its early years had been generally under Etonian domination. After Gladstone it had passed from Etonians to Wykehamists. Palmer, afterwards Lord Selborne, Cardwell, afterwards as Secretary for War to reorganise the British army, Ward, soon to earn much greater fame in theological controversy, and Wickens were the Wykehamists who dominated the Society. They were all strong Conservatives and attempted to pack the Committees with their friends and in defiance of Massie. Massie and his fellow Wadhamite, Brancker from Shrewsbury, who had defeated Gladstone for the Ireland prize, and the albino Lowe who had made so notable a contribution to the reform debate, though Lowe was himself a Wykehamist, bitterly resented the attempted domination of the clique of Wykehamist Tories. They received some support from Etonians, who on a choice of evils inclined to prefer Wadham to Winchester. According to the constitution all the officers and the committee members were elected. In fact there had up till then been little in the way of elections and the President had usually been able to nominate both the members of the committee and his successor, and his nomination had been accepted without opposition. Modern and progressive opinion may condemn such a system. To supporters of the pre-reformed constitution it did not seem unnatural. It meant that, while there was a pretence of free election, in fact Etonian succeeded Etonian in office or Wykehamist succeeded Wykehamist by ritual co-option—a system not very different from that by which England was governed up till 1832.

In fact the revolt within the Union was very much in microcosm the revolt of the time of the new rising middle classes against the dominance of the aristocracy on the larger platform of British politics.

Massie of Wadham made himself the organiser of the reforming foes of the Establishment. The rules permitted proxy voting but, since elections were usually little more than a formality, few had up till then bothered to arrange them. Massie collected proxies secretly and on the day of election cast them against the Establishment's Wykehamist candidates and to their surprise defeated them. Massie himself was elected President. An able scholar who had beaten Charles Wordsworth for the Ireland prize, he was destined to devote his life to Wadham and to become, as one of its most successful tutors, involved a few years later in a curious row. In 1837 Arthur Stanley, afterwards the famous Dean of St. Paul's, had been coached by Massie for the Ireland prize of that year. His papers on the first day were so good that the examiners thought that he must somehow have obtained a preview of the questions. Since they had no evidence that this was so with which to meet Stanley's total denial, Massie was justified in resenting the accusation with 'preternatural fury'. Stanley refuted it by doing the later papers just as brilliantly, though why, if an excellent paper on the first day was reason for suspicion that he had seen the questions of the first day, an excellent paper on the second day was not reason for suspicion that he had seen the papers of the second day, it is not very easy to see.

The reply of the Conservatives to Massie's election was to break off and form a separate debating association of their own which they called the Ramblers. They did not resign from the Union and it is hard to see why they should not have formed this second society, if they wished. But the Liberals, as Liberals sometimes do, having denounced tyranny when in opposition, seemed a little inclined to turn tyrants in their turn when in government. They proposed a motion that all who were members of the Ramblers should be expelled from the Union. There was immense excitement. Wyatt's Rooms were not large enough to contain the crowd who wished to attend the debate. The meeting was transferred to the Star Chamber at the Clarendon Hotel. As Massie was to propose the motion, Lowe took the chair. There was uproar from the first. Massie's predecessor as President, Tait, afterwards Archbishop of Canterbury, took the leadership of the Conservative rowdies, angrily waved his battered trencher and refused to be silenced when called

RIGHT   Frescoes. The ceiling of the
present Library with Morris' 'vast
pattern work of grotesque creatures'
above two frescoes by Prinsep &
Pollen

BELOW   A general view of the Library

ABOVE King Arthur's wedding with the appearance of the White Hart, by Rivière. Part of the Union frescoes

BELOW The Education of King Arthur by Merlin, by Rivière. Part of the Union frescoes

to order by the chair. Lowe fined him a pound. When
Massie sat down, he resumed the chair and Lowe rose to
speak. His reception was equally hostile. On the Conservative side Cardwell, the real leader, though present at the
debate, preferred to remain silent. The case against ex-
pulsion was pleaded by Senior and Sinclair. Their speeches
were greeted with overwhelming enthusiasm and it must
soon have become evident to Massie as he ineffectively
banged his gavel that the sympathy of the House was against
him. To prudent persons it was increasingly obvious that
there was little reason to expel the Ramblers and that the
only consequence of expelling them must have been so fatally
to weaken the Union that its survival would be in jeopardy.
Charles Marriot, friend of Gladstone and Newman, Commoner of Exeter, then Scholar of Balliol, then Fellow of Oriel,
an inveterate peacemaker, tried to calm the troubled waters.

> Stung to the soul, he rose above the rest,
> Of Oriel's sons the dearest and the best.
> Cease then the war. Your dire divisions cease.
> And join the league of amity and peace.

Charles Marriot belonged to the school of peace through
breakfast parties. Dean Church in his *Oxford Movement* has
described his breakfast parties: 'a crowd of undergraduates,
finding their way with difficulty amid lanes and piles of
books, amid a scarcity of chairs and room, and their host,
perfectly unconscious of anything grotesque, sitting silent
during the whole of the meal, but perfectly happy, at the
head of the table'. But even in spite of Marriot, Massie
would not be appeased. He insisted on pressing his motion
to a division where it was defeated with, to quote the
minutes, 'tremendous cheering' by 107 to 63.

A debating society can only flourish if its members differ
in opinions but can do so with reasonable friendliness. It is
stultified alike by unanimity and by bitterness. Massie was
still President. Yet his policy had been rejected in anger.
The future of the Society did not look as if it would be happy.
That things did not turn out as badly as they might was

D

almost entirely due to a certain Thomas Jackson, at that time
an undergraduate of St. Mary's Hall, afterwards to be a
London Vicar. He had the happy notion of cooling the
tempers of the contestants by telling the story of their battle
in mock Homeric verse. He enlisted the help of Sinclair of
the same College, 'Skimmerian Sinclair' as he was called—
St. Marian Sinclair, that is—afterwards a Middlesex Archdeacon, who had played his part in the debate but who was
a man of peace, anxious that the conflict should not prove
a sundering one. Between them they concocted a work
known as the *Uniomachia*, which professed to tell in Homeric
Greek with a Latin translation and a version in English
heroic couplets 'after the manner of the ingenious Mr.
Alexander Pope' the story of the Union's battle. A generation that is not so easily familiar with Greek and Latin verse
as that of a hundred and thirty years ago can hardly be
expected to plough through these verses in detail, the more so
since, of course, as is only to be expected, many of the allusions
are personal allusions which today can hardly be recaptured
or can only be recaptured through elaborate footnotes that
are scarcely worth the conning. But those who shrink from
the enterprise of interpretation must take in that there was
a joke within the joke. In spite of first appearances the verses
were not really in Greek or Latin but in a peculiar dog-Latin
—'canino-Anglice-Graece et Latine'—the authors described
it. Thus the Greek version begins

    Ἡύτε τομκάττων κλαγγη περὶ γαρρετα σούνδει

and the Latin

      Sicut cattorum clangor circum attica sonat,

but, before the reader turns wearily to a long-disused lexicon
to discover the meaning of these words, he should look at the
English version which runs

      As, when some antiquated virgin's hand
      With baleful broom hath chased the feline band,
      Around the topmost garrets of the house,
      Each caterwauling Tom consoles his spouse,

and it is clear that the first Greek line means nothing more recondite than, 'as the clamour of tomcats sounds round the garrets'. The jest continues in this vein with equally outrageous verbal extravagances

῾Ρίτῳ ῾Ραῳβληροι σίττον λέφτῳτε Μασεῖχοι

we read, which means no more than that 'the Ramblers sat on the right and the Massieites on the left'. Tait, who, as we have recorded, had been fined by Lowe is greeted in the Greek as Φεινόμενος Ταεῖτος and in Latin as 'Fino mulctatus Taitus'. Tait's heckling was described in the Popean version in admirable mock heroic verse.

> The gen'rous hero ceased—with thund'ring sound
> Tait shook his tasseled cap and sprang to ground.
> (The tasseled cap by Juggins' hands was made,
> Or some keen brother of the London trade,
> Unconscious of the stern decrees of fate,
> What ruthless thumps the batter'd trencher wait.)

The squib fell into the hands of Dr. Scott, the lexicographer, one of the most erudite men in the University and he consented to adorn it with mock-learned notes, under the name of Slawkenberg, defending his readings against the '*Ineptam et stultissimam interpretationem*' of such rival commentators as Heavysternius and Dunderheadius. Another hand—it is not certain whose—added another version in the manner of Walter Scott. This perhaps a little spoiled the symmetry of the project, but, however that may be, the whole admirably served its purpose. Tables were dissolved in laughter, and it was not easy for any bitterness to survive such admirable fooling.

The *Uniomachia* very effectively took the sting out of the Ramblers' controversy. Those who had been protagonists in it were before long once again on speaking terms and a banquet was arranged at the Star Inn between them at which Browne, a clerical friend of Wilfred Ward, said grace and asked a blessing on their concord. To be honest, the blessing was a little needed. Hard things had been said, and even after the *Uniomachia* they were not wholly forgotten. But the controversy, in so far as it had an ideological basis, was to some extent confused by events. The extreme violence of the opponents of parliamentary reform had been caused by the fear that it would immediately usher in a period of revolution and ruin in which all property would be destroyed and the University be robbed of its privileges. Whatever the balance of merit or demerit in reform, such fears were at any rate proved unfounded. For the moment the members who were returned to the reformed Parliament were very much of a kind with those who been returned to the unreformed. The University apparently continued in its accustomed way. As Lord Melbourne and Sir Robert Peel took it turn and turn about to rule the country, there seemed for the moment no very drastic drama in the nation's political life and as a consequence party interest in the Union abated.

On the other hand Oxford of the 1830s was filled with a debate of another sort. Almost coincidentally with the Union's Battle of the Ramblers, Keble preached his famous sermon in which he denounced the Government's proposal to suppress a few Irish bishoprics as an act of national apostacy, and the Oxford Movement was launched. It would of course be a mistake to imagine that all Oxford—or all Oxford undergraduates—were passionately engaged in the controversy of the Tractarians. The majority quite certainly was indifferent to the issue and did not properly understand it, nor of course was the contention of the Tractarians that the Church of England was a branch of the Catholic Church one suited for debate in the Union or one which the rules of the Society would have allowed to be debated. The leaders of the Oxford Movement—Newman, Keble, Pusey—had at no stage of their lives anything to do with the Union and in a sense its life went on apart from Oxford's theological controversy. On the other hand there were great figures of the Oxford Movement who were also great figures of the Oxford Union—Wilfred Ward, for instance, and Faber.

Frederick Faber of Balliol was to become Secretary of the

Union in 1834, when he was wounded and almost killed by a glass bottle thrown through the window in the heat of the controversy whether the Union's rooms should be opened on Sunday. He was the special friend and companion of Roundell Palmer of New College, afterwards Lord Selborne. Roundell Palmer had in fact been one of the main actors in the Ramblers controversy, but when, owing to Jackson's happy intervention, the controversy was reduced to its proper proportions, Palmer was able to persuade himself that he had throughout viewed it all with a humorous detachment. This was not altogether true. Yet side by side with the political controversy between Liberals and Conservatives had run another controversy between the literate and the illiterate. In the early days of the Cambridge Union, as we have seen, the Union debaters had been to a large extent also the University's literary Apostles. But at Oxford then, as during long periods of the Union's history, while the Union's stars have been more ambitious than their Cambridge counterparts for success in the Schools and while many of them were of course in after life to give ample proof of their literary capacity, yet the young undergraduate writers of the day tended to shun the Union and the Union to be intolerant of writers. It was part of the ambition of Roundell Palmer to redress this balance and he started a politico-literary magazine which, though it only ran to six numbers, was to some extent a portent of Oxford history. In this magazine Faber, even then a poet though not yet a hymnologist, was one of Palmer's most notable collaborators. Palmer's brother was destined to make with Faber the journey into the Roman Church. Palmer himself was to remain a staunch Anglican, but I think that it is not fanciful to see a little of Faber's influence in the profound emotionalism which Palmer was afterwards to retain even in his days of greatest judicial eminence.

The main task which Faber set himself at the Union was to heal the wounds of the late controversies—a task in which he was not entirely successful. For the Union was, as Mowbray recorded, 'a great school for the combative element', and indeed if there is to be no disagreement a debating society could hardly have a reason for existence and, human nature being what it is and remembering that there are prizes of office in competition, it was hardly to be expected that the combative element would always be within itself entirely harmonious. It is only a little amusing to find Faber in the rôle of peacemaker, for, whatever may be said of his subsequent life, no one can call it entirely peaceable.

Ward was a more prominent figure in the Union than Faber. Ward was both then and throughout his life a man to whom argument was the supreme joy. He was later to exhaust the Balliol Senior Common Room with his un-flagging post-prandial dialectics and to make himself the centre of an Oxford controversy by his book on the *Ideal of a Christian Church*, in which he claimed the right to hold the whole cycle of Roman doctrine while still subscribing to the Thirty-nine Articles and remaining within the Church of England. When later he became a Catholic he preserved there his love of argument, of paradox and of extreme positions. At a time when Newman and others were anxious to keep within as strict bounds as possible the claims of Papal authority, Ward expressed his wish for a Papal bull on his breakfast table every morning. Corpulent, rolling of gait, untidy in person, the 'large, moon-faced man' as Arthur Stanley described him, argued with sincerity but with no pretence that he did not enjoy the argument for the fun of it. He was, said Tait, his colleague, friend and opponent, 'the prince of controversialists'. His Oxford career was wayward. He would have been elected a Fellow of All Souls had not the Warden taken a dislike to the shape of his boots. He kicked them off under the table during dinner, and an astute rival abstracted them and won the Fellowship. When he went in for the examination for his Balliol Fellowship, he stretched himself on the floor of the Master's dining room, went to sleep and was elected. He debated in true good humour. He had no difficulty in preserving friendliness with those from whom he differed. At his death Tennyson, his friend and neighbour in the Isle of Wight, wrote of him as 'the most unworldly of mankind' and the 'most generous of all Ultramontanes'.

He had been at school at Winchester and at a time when Winchester men were dominant at the Union, it was natural that he should join them. He prided himself on his indifference to what he considered the mere fashion of the time as much in political as in religious matters, and therefore was an extreme Conservative and an enemy of reform. He allied himself naturally to his fellow Wykehamists, Palmer, Cardwell and Wickens of Balliol. In Jackson's *Uniomachia* Ward appeared in the Greek version as τωρείιτος ὄαρδυς, which for those who might otherwise have found the meaning incomprehensible is explained in the Latin as 'Toryorum-praejudiciis-maxime-imbutus . . . Wardius'. He was one of the few people in the Union's history to serve two separate terms as President. He was first elected in the Michaelmas term of 1832 and then called back again to office in the Hilary term of 1835.

A result of the composition of the Ramblers controversy was that members of both factions had to serve together on the committee in, as it were, a coalition government, and such relics of feud as there had been between them were thus finally dissipated when they were compelled to stand shoulder to shoulder against an attack which was delivered most directly upon Cardwell, the Treasurer, but which incidentally involved the whole committee. In the absence of a Union Hansard it is not possible to discover the exact details of the controversy but the outlines are clear enough and throw a fascinating light both on the standards of the Union of that time and on the standards of Early Victorian society at large. A certain gentleman commoner of Magdalen Hall, named Trevor, accused Cardwell, the Treasurer, of having falsified the accounts and for a number of weeks Private Business was dominated by this controversy. Most vigorous in the defence of Cardwell was Lowe, later to be Cardwell's colleague in Gladstone's administration but, as will be remembered, recently his bitter critic in the Ramblers controversy. The young Benjamin Jowett records how immediately after being elected to a Balliol scholarship in 1835 he was hurried off to the Union to hear 'a great passage of arms between two heroes of debate, a gentleman commoner of Magdalen Hall, called Trevor, and Robert Lowe'. The Union, Jowett recorded, 'had much more than later, the character of a real House of Commons. . . . Those were the days of a political world before the flood, which has now passed out of remembrance. Never has there been so strong a party feeling as was manifested in England between the years 1829 and 1834'.

All this was true, but Jowett does not advert to the fact that he was writing of 1835 when a new spirit was coming in. To superficial observation at any rate the Reform Bill had made a much smaller difference to the constitution of the House of Commons than had been expected. Even the reformers were comfortably conscious that they had done their duty and thought that there was no need ever to pass another Reform Bill. A Whig Government had come back into power, but Lord Melbourne was at its head. A reformer less anxious that the principles of reform should unnecessarily triumph it would be difficult to imagine. Therefore in the nation at large controversy very gladly turned back again to personalities. The Ladies of the Bedchamber were more amusing than the reform of Parliament; whether Lady Hastings was pregnant more absorbing than whether Old Sarum should be disfranchised. It was much the same at Oxford.

'Trevor', continues Jowett, 'was supposed in some way or other to have compromised the dignity of the Union by his communications with an American bishop, which he had contrived to get posted on the notice board of the Colleges. This impertinence Bob Lowe, as we used familiarly to call him, undertook to chastise. There was an old score which he had to settle, for his opponent had a year or two before accused Lowe's friend and schoolfellow, Cardwell, of fabricating the accounts of the Union, a charge which with difficulty he was induced to retract.' Jowett does not seem to have known about the Ramblers controversy which occurred before he came up. The story of the American bishop it is unfortunately not now possible to recapture. The falsification of the accounts, though we do not know the exact details, is intelligible. The best authority on this, as indeed on most other Union matters of that date, is Lake, afterwards Dean of Durham, who was an undergraduate at that time and has much to say on Union controversies.

'When the Union was at its best it was most quarrelsome. Some of us who had been pupils of Ward or Tait early learned that a good speech on a personal matter was something not to be despised. I heard the last speech, and a very characteristic one, which Lowe delivered at the Union. This was at the end of the "Trevor row" and it may be worth while describing it shortly. As the row began before I came into residence I did not witness it myself, but the liveliest possible description was sent to me every week at Rugby by (Arthur) Stanley, who, though I do not think he ever spoke at the Union, took an intense interest in everything like a row. It was begun by a curious attack made by Trevor, a rather old, practised and fluent speaker, upon the Treasurer and some other member of the committee against whom he was supposed to have some grudge, for having—what I believe he called—"forged and fabricated" the accounts. This must have run off into an attack on the committee, or it is hard to see how it can have run into six or seven weeks of vehement discussion.

'In the end Trevor tried, I believe, to explain the phrase away, and in the last meeting made a general apology which was warmly applauded by Charles Marriot of Oriel, who acted as a sort of peacemaker and described Trevor's apology as "noble". This was however too much for his opponents and elicited one or two very sharp retorts, that of Tait, afterwards Archbishop of Canterbury, who was then as always unable to suppress an occasional outburst, being long remembered. It was very much in these words, "I, too, Mr.

Chairman, as an old and attached member of the Union, join my friend in congratulating the meeting—not indeed for anything 'noble' in the speech of the honourable member, but at the close of the most disgraceful scenes I ever witnessed." This, delivered with true Taitian vehemence, gave rise to a scene little less animated than one between the Archbishop and a well-known bishop in the House of Lords more than forty years afterwards. The "Trevor row" came to an end in June 1835, and I only witnessed an after-skirmish between himself and Lowe in October in which Lowe, who had often threatened to resign, certainly was worsted. Trevor reminding him with great effect how he had

> Oft fitted the halter, oft traversed the cart,
> And oft bid Goodbye but seemed loath to depart.'

The exchanges between Lowe and Trevor were, wrote Jowett, 'like pistol shots'.

Indeed Trevor's apology was, it seemed, a somewhat left-handed apology. He had only imputed fraud, he said, in what he called 'a mercanteel sense'. The truth is fairly clear. Trevor, who was in later life to become a Canon of York, was at this time twenty-five years old—considerably older than the other debaters of the Union. He had been for some years between leaving school and coming up to the University a clerk in the old East India House. Any accusation that Cardwell falsified the accounts in the vulgar and criminal sense that he had put the Society money into his own pocket was, of course, absurd. But the Union members were in Trevor's eyes financial amateurs whereas he, a little pompously perhaps with the pomposity of twenty-five, considered himself a professional. He was not satisfied with a slapdash assumption that anything would do in accounts so long as the sum came out right in the end. The conflict of temperaments is clear enough. But what throws an interesting light on the temper of the times is the strong prejudice of his fellow members that Trevor was a vulgar cad who by insisting that accounts be properly kept was betraying his plebeian origin. The fellow was in trade.

By no one was this line more strongly taken than by Ward, a large landed proprietor in the Isle of Wight. Ward took Trevor's attack as an attack on the integrity of the whole committee, which he insisted on calling 'the constitutional party'. He brushed aside Trevor's explanation that he only imputed fraud in a 'mercanteel sense'. He professed to be able to attach no meaning to it, though the meaning was in fact clear enough. It obviously meant that Trevor did not accuse Cardwell of personal speculation but that he did accuse him of presenting the accounts in so irregular a form that they had no right to receive an auditor's certificate. It was, thought Ward, so intolerable that gentlemen should be cross-questioned by a clerk on the way in which they accounted for money that he proposed that for the future Private Business should be abolished and the private members should no longer have any right to question officers on their performance of their official duties. Having elected them, they must lump them. It is not perhaps wholly fanciful to see displayed here in miniature some first evidence of the spirit that was afterwards to clamour for the most extreme exaltation and interpretation of the Papal claims. But anyway, if so, the Union was still incurably Protestant and even his fellow committee members were not willing to follow Ward in this extravagent demand. To his dismay he found himself left wholly unsupported.

The other great controversy of these years was that of the opening of the Society's rooms on Sundays. Sabbatarianism has ever since the Puritans' times been a stronger religious force in these islands than on the Continent—even than in the Protestant countries of the Continent, and religious young men, as, for instance, Mr. Gladstone, as Morley shows us, were horrified on their first visits to Europe to discover the wickedness of the Continental Sunday. That they who danced or played games on a Sunday should earlier in the day have attended a religious service or should have any sincere religious belief seemed to such persons impossible to believe. But the more worldly took a slightly different line. No one at that date would have dared to advocate any public amusement on a Sunday. No one must play a game or go to a place of entertainment. No one (except of course the servants) must do any work. One must go to church, but one could not be in church the whole day. What could one do with the rest of it? Enormous walks were permitted but little else. But there were those who argued that the Union's rooms were not a place of public entertainment. They had more of the nature of an extension of one's private home, and it could not be so grave an outrage in the eyes of Almighty God that members of the Union should go and sit in them on a Sunday. So far the friends of Sunday opening may seem, to some modern readers, to have had the better of the argument, but it is clear and interesting that the controversy was but a manifestation of a much deeper controversy. In spite of religious tests and formal conformity the age was far from being an age of universal piety. Among the young men who had signed the Thirty-nine Articles were clearly a number who not so much did not believe them as did not like them— that is to say, without perhaps explicitly rejecting Christian beliefs and labelling themselves what a few years later would have been called agnostics, they objected to the constant intrusion of religion, spoiling what they considered the fun of life. These were the years indeed of young enthusiasts of high idealism

> when each high morn
> England at one shall stand at the church gate
> And vesper bells o'er all the land be born
> And Newman mould the Church and Gladstone
> stamp the State.

But they were also the years when the undergraduates' betters, or at least their seniors, were bitterly at warfare with one another on the question whether Hampden should properly be allowed to be a Regius Professor. Some took one side and some took the other, but the methods of controversy were such that it was not altogether surprising if in some among their juniors such *odium theologicum* should have given birth to a general odium for all theology. The Evangelicals rejoiced that the Anglicans and the Prussian Lutherans were to share a bishop in Jerusalem. The Tractarians deplored. 'Jerusalem be damned,' muttered a clerical Fellow of St. John's over his port, wearied of the argument. 'Give us wine, women and horses.' In fact the point of view both of many of the Fellows and of many of the undergraduates was very much that of the Prime Minister of the day, Lord Melbourne, who thought that things had come to a pretty pass when we found religion intruding into our private lives. The 1830s were not a decade of unrelieved propriety in private conduct, nor was violence then a monopoly of the lower classes.

> Like many of the upper class
> He likes the sound of breaking glass.

The friends of the Sunday opening of the Union premises were by no means content merely to persuade a majority of the Members. Most of the most violent of them happened to come from Christ Church. Capes of Balliol, the President in the Trinity term of 1835, was reputed to be pious. The Christ Church men wrecked his rooms. Faber was even more pious and they threw a bottle through his window, which might well have killed him. Such tactics naturally defeated their own ends and left the regular members with little alternative, in self-respect, but for the time being at any rate to maintain their Sunday closing.

The result of this disreputable controversy was to damage the prestige of the Union. The rowdies disapproved of it as a sanctimonious meeting place. The studious, if they were not yet members, felt little temptation to join simply to have bottles thrown at them. The existing officers found themselves compelled out of pride to maintain a regime of restriction with which some of them perhaps did not greatly sympathise.

The main controversies of the time were in Private Business and turned on arguments as to what papers should be taken by the Society. Liberal sentiments of any sort were not tolerated. Indeed the division of the Society at that time seemed mainly to lie between bawdy Conservatives who wanted a rag and to beat the place up, and pious Conservatives who thought that the airing of progressive opinions would lead to the destruction of society. Membership varied from the hardly believing, barely conforming Anglican who, if he thought of the Church of England at all, thought of it as a bulwark of the propertied classes, to Frederick Robertson of Brasenose, Treasurer in 1839, afterwards the famous preacher of Brighton, who never spoke at the Union without first preparing himself with prayer. As Lake, himself a Liberal of a sort, recorded, 'such liberalism as Oxford possessed was very moderate, though the mere fact of being a Liberal had a very suspicious appearance'. Few, if any, of the members were radical enough to accept Cobbett's opinions, but there were some who thought that his *Register* ought to be taken, considering it a part of education to learn what such a man was saying. Others thought it no part of education to learn any such thing. On the other hand the bawdy Conservatives, who were against Cobbett, were all in favour of taking Bell's *Life in London* with its supposedly salacious accounts of the life of the metropolis, and here the pious were opposed. The debate in the Union aroused such heat that, when it was all concluded, the bawdy among Christ Church members went and broke the windows of their pious colleagues. 'It was,' recorded Lake, who was in the Chair at that time, 'about the noisiest time in the Union's history.' He professed to have enjoyed it all but everyone did not think that he came out of the controversy as well as he himself imagined. The nickname which he earned for himself of 'the Serpent' was not altogether complimentary.

The Union's debating in Public Business grew so tame and unsatisfactory, its time was so predominantly taken up by the rows of Private Business that Lake formed with his friends in Balliol a little private debating society known as the Decade. This society aroused none of the umbrage which had been aroused by the Rambler a few years before. Associated with him in this society were a number of very distinguished undergraduates, most of them, unlike Lake, perhaps a little too refined to bear the rough and tumble of the Union. There was Benjamin Brodie, afterwards to be Professor of Chemistry, Stanley, the future Dean of St. Paul's who liked to observe and comment on the Union's troubles but always shrank himself from becoming involved in them, and Goulburn who was afterwards to win the Headmastership of Rugby in competition against Lake. There was Coleridge, soon after to go over to the Union and to become President, and, in later life to be Lord Chief Justice.

> Fair-haired and tall, slim but of stately mien,
> Inheritor of a high poetic name.

Above all there were Balliol's two leading poets of the period —Matthew Arnold and Arthur Hugh Clough. The club was called the Decade but Lake's scout insisted on pronouncing it the Decayed. The mispronunciation was certainly not justified. At that time it was certainly the Union which was more decayed than its Balliol offshoot.

After a year Stanley moved from Balliol to accept a Fellowship at University, but worried there by religious doubts and 'the utter impossibility even of procuring toast for breakfast', he soon afterwards took Holy Orders and departed from Oxford. Our other authority on the Union for this period is Mozley of Oriel, who, in his *Letters*, kept a full record of the doings of the Society and of all else that was going on at the time in Oxford. Like Stanley, he was an observer rather than a contestant and an observer for a more humiliating reason. Stanley had chosen his rôle for himself. Mozley had come up to Oxford full of ambition to shine as a Union orator. He had gone there proposing to make a bold creation on the seizure of the Danish fleet. He rose from his place, but then a petrifying fear seized him. He collapsed without having said a word and never attempted to speak again. One might have expected that after such a humiliation he would have shunned the place but it was not so. He haunted it and delighted to record and comment on the future of those who were proving themselves less stage-frightened than himself.

The Union had one memorable experience during Lake's presidency in 1838. The motion of the evening was: 'That theatrical representations are on the whole highly beneficial to the nation'. It may seem a curious subject to debate in the land of Shakespeare. In the course of the debate a quite unknown undergraduate arose and set the House alight. 'We were electrified one evening by a singularly brilliant speech, more full of poetry than rhetoric, from a member quite unknown to us. This was Mr. Ruskin of Christ Church, and I was so impressed by it that I at once asked him to join the committee in its following term.' Ruskin spoke once more at the Union on a motion that 'poetry's true object was more realised by modern than by ancient writers', but naturally enough he did not proceed on the Union's regular *cursus honorum*.

The man who more than any other was responsible for re-introducing politics into the Union was Stafford Northcote, afterwards Earl of Iddesleigh, President of the Board of Trade, Chancellor of the Exchequer, First Lord of the Treasury and Foreign Secretary in the Conservative ministries of Disraeli and Salisbury. He rose to be Treasurer of the Union in the Hilary term of 1838 but never became President, Lake who had preceded him as Treasurer winning the Presidency. Politics under Northcote's introduction were of a very conservative hue. Oliver Cromwell was voted 'the greatest rascal that ever sat on the English throne'. Hereditary aristocracy was declared one of the most precious features of the constitution and the country. The principles of the French Revolution were condemned. The supreme purpose of the Government of Ireland was to uphold the authority of the Queen and the Protestant religion, and Northcote spoke on a motion which was carried without a division, declaring that 'the Ministry's neglect of the British navy, our first line of defence, reflected indelible disgrace upon it'.

CHAPTER FOUR

AN ABIDING HOME

THE 1840s—a stormy decade in Oxford history—came in with a curious double tempest, in one part of which the Union was involved. There was among the undergraduates of the first years of that decade a certain Paul Parnell, Scholar of St. John's. He was, according to Dean Burgon, afterwards Dean of Chichester and admittedly some few years Parnell's junior, a man of high ability, high principle, eloquence and self-confidence. Great things were prophesied of him. Whether the prophecies would have been fulfilled we can never know, for unfortunately soon after going down from Oxford he died at sea on the way to take up a position in West Australia. The Union at that date was still a club from which candidates could be excluded by black ball, and it tended to be dominated by the larger Colleges, particularly by Christ Church and Balliol. The Christ Church men in particular did not hesitate to use their black balls against those of whom they disapproved or whom they did not think to be quite gentlemen, and candidates from less fashionable schools or from less fashionable Colleges often found it difficult to get in. This exclusiveness also no doubt accounts for the fact that the Union's political opinions tended to be somewhat more conservative than those of the University at large.

This by no means suited Parnell, a member of St. John's, a College which, he claimed, suffered discrimination because so long as the Union's premises were in the High, it was of a suburban location. A Conservative in politics but a moderate and reforming Conservative, he was in favour of the revival of political activity in the Union. Of the form of its political activity under Stafford Northcote's leadership he was by no means in favour. He championed the cause of the emancipation of the Jews against Congreve of Wadham, afterwards the famous Positivist and leader of his private Positivist secession. Then, turning to the affairs of the Union, Parnell took up the cudgels which Trevor had laid down six years before and accused the Union officers of managing the Society's affairs in a very slovenly and slapdash fashion. The accusation was by and large almost certainly justified, but perhaps Parnell went on and on about it a little too much. Week after week, we read in the minutes, 'As there was sufficient Private Business to occupy the evening, no debate was held.' Yet at least the Johnians made sufficient impression on members to win a substantial success at the elections for the Trinity offices in 1841. Bellamy, afterwards to be for many years St. John's President, then one of its undergraduates, was elected Librarian in place of Congreve. Parnell himself was elected Secretary. Parnell's attacks had been particularly directed against a former Secretary, Blackett of Christ Church, afterwards Member of Parliament for Newcastle-on-Tyne, whom he assailed with violent sarcasm. The rule then was that one black ball excluded a candidate from membership. The Christ Church men, finding that they had not the majority to carry their candidates into office, reckoned that they had at any rate sufficient strength to exclude any aspirant from membership. They decided to use this veto of the black ball against all candidates from St. John's until Parnell might learn to mend his ways. Among them was Dr. Hayman, who was afterwards a very disastrous Headmaster of Rugby and who almost brought the school to an end by his mismanagement, until in punning reference to the story of Haman and Mordecai in the Book of Esdras,

> When Rugby, spite of priest and layman,
>   Pined visibly away,
> The Governors suspended Hayman
>   For fear of more decay.

At this time he was, as he himself records, an unknown, in-
offensive and undistinguished undergraduate of St. John's.
Yet he was excluded for three years from the Union simply
for being a fellow collegian of Parnell.

The conflict between St. John's and Christ Church continued with varying fortunes for a year and a half. The
controversy was engulfed into a larger controversy. One of
the Proctors for that year was a certain W. E. Jelf. He was
held to be the villain of the piece in procuring Pusey's
suspension for two years from preaching in Oxford because
of his sermon on the Eucharist, and was therefore unpopular
—the more so since he was an ill-tempered and irascible man.
Also he had the misfortune to come from Christ Church.
St. John's was a College, as Mark Pattison, the hostile Rector
of Lincoln put it in a characteristically acid phrase, 'corroded
by ecclesiasticism' and Parnell determined to organise an
undergraduate protest by hissing Jelf. It so happened that
at the same Convocation of 1843 it was proposed to confer an
honorary degree on the American Minister, Everett, and
it so happened that the American Minister was, or was said
to be, a Unitarian. The Tractarians chose to consider it an
insult to the Church of England that a degree should be conferred on such a man. Oxford was, of course, still a purely
Anglican preserve and a man of the American Minister's
belief could not have been admitted there as an undergraduate or a Fellow. Nevertheless no one could pretend
that a reception of an honorary fellowship on one single
afternoon would give him an opportunity to pervert the faith
of Dons or undergraduates, and the protest did not show the
Tractarians at their most attractive, even if they could argue
that they were only showing intolerance in reply to the
intolerance that had been shown to Pusey. If protest they
must, they should at least have done it in a constitutional
fashion and not through a display of hooliganism. Parnell
had no especial sympathy with Tractarians and was in no
way associated with their protest. But the two protests, by
chance as it were, coalesced. Proctors in his opinion ought to

be hissed whether they persecuted Dr. Pusey or not. The Convocation was reduced to utter uproar. The Vice-Chancellor had to dismiss it, having conferred the degree on Everett in the midst of the hubbub and ignoring the shouts of 'Non Placet' with which the Grace was greeted. The courtesy of the University was disgraced. There was a possibility of a diplomatic incident. 'The canonade of the angry youngsters drowned the odium of the theological malcontents.

> Another lion gave another roar
> And the first lion thought the last a bore.'

It so happened that the President of St. John's, Dr. Wynter, was the Vice-Chancellor of that year. He was furious at what had happened and still more furious that one of his own undergraduates should have been a ringleader of the disturbances. Parnell was incontinently sent down.

On the whole the Tractarians were not popular in the Union. They had of course introduced—their theology demanded that they should introduce—a habit of looking back into the past, into the days of the undivided Church, as to a golden age. Disraeli's Young Englanders indulged in similar nostalgia on a more secular plane. Whatever the real merits of such comparisons between age and age, it is certainly true that laudation of the past by a young sentimentalist who in the nature of things is not really competent to make the comparison is easily tiresome, and the majority of the undergraduates of the Union, their feet firmly fixed in the 1840s, grew easily tired of it. Spurious mediaevalism had no attractions for them. They voted on February 23, 1843: 'That undiscriminately to decry the times in which we live, upon comparison of them with any period in past history, is a dangerous and mistaken practise, but that it is our duty, while we acknowledge our own defects, to endeavour to amend them by imitation of the wisdom of our fathers'—a trifle smug, perhaps.

Hayman, when at last he managed to get into the Society,

made his name by an intervention in Private Business. A
motion had been moved that '*The Times* be excluded from the
Reading Room' on what seems to us the curious ground that
in considering the question of the Corn Laws it had published
two articles, one in favour of and one against their retention.
Such ambivalence, it was argued, showed unscrupulous lack
of principle. The whole episode is illuminating as showing
how recent is the notion, which most people would today take
for granted, that a University is a place for exploring all sides
to a question. It was still thought of as a place where the old
told the young what was right. But, whatever there may
be said for the more authoritative conception in general,
it seems a little odd to import it into a debating society. For
how can there be a debate if both sides are not fairly stated?
However, Plumptre, afterwards the Dean of Wells, who was,
though then an ex-President, that evening in the Presidential
chair was all for excluding *The Times*. It was, he said,
'a political Ishmael with its hand against every one and I, for
one, should be glad to see every man's hand against it'. The
next speaker, according to Hayman, was a bore and members, according to their custom, 'scraped him down', that is
to say, rasped the soles of their boots along the floor to make
a scraping noise—the common method at that time of
expressing disapproval. Later Hayman, then an unknown
undergraduate, rose and made according to his own account
a successful speech in favour of tolerance. Plumptre said at
the close of the debate in summing up. 'This motion has
been encountered by a new and unknown member from the
other end of the room in a very witty speech, and from the
nearer benches by a sample of folly beneath contempt,'
referring to the scraping. He at once had Hayman put on to
the committee.

The dominating figure at the Union in the years immediately after that was the future Lord Chief Justice Coleridge.
He was President in the Michaelmas term of 1843 when he
was still an undergraduate of Balliol, and then, when he
transferred to Exeter as a Fellow, stepped down and served

the Union as Librarian in the Trinity and Michaelmas terms of 1844—an unique progression. 'Pre-eminent among us Coleridge, afterwards Lord Chief Justice of England,' wrote Chase, later Principal of St. Mary's Hall, '. . . Tall, with really golden hair and the smile which was lifelong, though, I have heard, with a capacity for any expression, he seemed to be carrying all before him. . . . He had, as a speaker, every advantage; height without awkwardness; a beautiful voice; a grand manner; self-esteem *quantum suf*, of the best language an easy flow—like honey trickling down.' It was the age of the Chartists, and Coleridge, as his father's marshal, had seen a little of the nation's poor, and he made his maiden speech at the Union in championship of the Chartists. His father, who did not think as highly of him as his contemporaries, was alarmed. He thought his son 'surrounded by snares in his own conversational habits, general knowledge, desultory habits of reading'.

The printer Stockdale had sued Hansard for alleged libel in their official report on the Commission of Prisons. The Government passed an Act by which all proceedings in relation to a document printed by official command should be stayed. Coleridge attacked the Government, moving and carrying a motion that, 'the recent proceedings of the House of Commons were subversive of the Constitution'. The *Morning Post* reported that 'the Radicals were all for privilege, the Tories all concerned for the liberty of the subject'. He was, as successful barristers are, a little too inevitably successful—a quality which, when combined with virtue, is apt to make virtue appear somewhat unattractive. There was a certain barb in the comment of his friend, Matthew Arnold, that, if Coleridge went on rising, Arnold's place would be in the servant's hall.

Hayman was to be Treasurer in the Michaelmas term of 1847. His term of office was memorable. There was a general feeling, now that Parnell had departed and passions abated, that the black balling system and the St. John's–Christ Church feud could only lead to the disadvantage of the Society. If it was to claim for itself the title of the Oxford Union Society, then it should be open to all members of the University who were willing to comply with its rules and to pay its subscription. Therefore, to compose the quarrel a committee was formed, consisting of Hayman of St. John's, the Treasurer, Portal of Christ Church, the Secretary, with Bedford of Brasenose as an impartial third man to revise the rules. Out of the revision came the abolition of the black balling system, but—what was far more important—out of it came also the beginnings of the movement for giving to the Union a permanent home.

An incident during the Long Vacation of 1848 showed the extreme inconvenience of the existing arrangement. At Wyatt's the Society was the tenant of a book seller, called Vincent. The Society offered the hospitality of its rooms to the British Association which was to meet in Oxford that summer, but Vincent objected and refused to surrender the key. Hayman fetched a locksmith and, standing over him, watched him break down the door. Thus the learned scientists were able to go in and hold their meeting.

Dr. Philip Bliss, the Principal of St. Mary's Hall, was a venerable and much-loved figure of the Oxford of those days, who regretted perhaps a little uncritically the passing of the ancient ways and the wisdom of the ages which had been, at the time of the Royal Commission as, he thought, over-thrown by a revolutionary faction. Before he went to St. Mary's Dr. Bliss had been a Fellow of St. John's, and as such he had with his usual kindliness befriended and taken an interest in the career of the young Hayman. It was he together with Chase, afterwards to be Bliss' successor at St. Mary's, who was responsible for suggesting to Hayman and the other undergraduates the plan by which the Union was given the permanent home which would for the future safeguard it from such absurd embarrassments. He first found a suitable site for it in the centre of Oxford—its present home—and then, to meet the financial problem, devised a scheme by which graduates could become life-members on a payment of a single subscription of ten pounds. On top of that he made the Union a personal loan of £3,000 on very generous terms.

Dr. Bliss became the first of the Society's trustees. His action put the Union into a financial state to build its new home. Some time, however, was to elapse before the home was actually built, and for the moment the Society continued at Wyatt's. It was not a greatly distinguished period in its history. Politics in Oxford, as in all Britain, were largely dominated by Irish issues. No voice at the Union was, of course, ready to contemplate such enormities as the dis-establishment of the Irish Church, a radical reform of the land system or Home Rule. But motions were sometimes passed that did at least recognise that there were certain genuine Irish grievances. There were, for a time, names among the Union speakers which were later to occupy positions of political importance. In 1847 Ward Hunt, afterwards to be Disraeli's First Lord of the Admiralty, was first Treasurer and then President—'a tall, heavy-lipped man with a handsome face in which good sense and good nature often blended,' recorded Hayman.

By far the most distinguished political figure in the Union of those years was Lord Dufferin, afterwards to be Governor of Canada and Viceroy of India, who was President in 1847, when Ward Hunt was Treasurer. He was the first Lord to hold office at a time when Lords were still very important people. He was, said Jowett, 'a most excellent tuft'. He was the romantic aristocrat whom Victorian England so easily bred, who was moved by the sufferings of selected foreigners. 'Lord Dufferin's face was rather sad and thoughtful—a fateful visage, like Vandyck's King Charles,' recorded Bedford of Brasenose, who was Secretary in his Presidency. He made his maiden speech in May 1846 in favour of Polish nationalism. Then, after an excursus in criticism of 'modern theatricals' which he found 'detrimental to the morals of the age', moved by stories of the famine, he took up the cause of Ireland. He and his friend Boyle, afterwards Lord Glasgow, paid a visit during the vacation to Skibereen and on their return proposed that the Society make a grant towards the relief of Irish suffering. It will be recalled that a similar grant had been made in 1831, but, since then the rules had been revised and there was little doubt that under Rule 70 it was illegal to use the Society's funds for philanthropical donations nor, however great our sympathy with the starving Irish, can it seriously be denied that the rule was a sensible one. Dufferin himself in a memorandum written fifty years later from the British Embassy in Paris freely admitted as much.

The Society after a keen debate voted down Lord Dufferin's motion by a large majority. 'The attendance was so large that the doors which separated the part of the long room which usually sufficed for our meetings had to be taken away, and the whole space utilised,' wrote Dufferin in his Memoirs. He and his sympathisers then formed a private society in Oxford for the relief of Irish suffering—as they were most certainly entitled to do—and supported it with generous donations out of their own pockets.

When Dufferin was President and Ward Hunt Treasurer, the Librarian was Conington. In the years before the repeal of the Corn Laws, when Peel's ambivalence robbed politics of their clear-cut issues, the Union had often sought refuge in the literary motion. The future Dean Mansel of St. Paul's was prominent in such debates though he never stood for office. Conington, the great Virgilian, shared Mansel's taste. A demy of Magdalen, as that college calls its scholars, he was able, it was said, to repeat a thousand lines of Virgil at the age of eight. He held advanced views on 'the working classes', but those views, his friends maintained, were generalisations derived entirely from his scout, who was the only member of the working classes with whom he was actually acquainted. It was from his scout that he had acquired his trousers, 'based on a Christian Socialist pattern'. He had an odd halting manner of speech and other physical peculiarities which won for him the nickname of 'the sick vulture'. In general his political opinions did not greatly recommend him to the Union, which elected him to office in spite of them rather than because of them. They thought in a manner that was to their credit that they ought to pay tribute to intellectual and literary distinction.

Conington was succeeded as Librarian by Burgon, afterwards Dean of Chichester, but—what is perhaps of more moment—the author of the only line ever submitted in a Newdigate Prize Poem which has jostled for a place among the memorable lines of the world's poetry

A rose-red city half as old as time—

that 'dear old learned Professor of Billingsgate', as Dean Church called him.

Though a debating society ought to vary its fare and ring the changes between political motions and the literary or historical, though in a period where party lines are blurred, the party debate which inevitably compels speakers to paint their pictures as more purely black or more purely white than truth would allow becomes easily tedious, yet the political motion has one great advantage over the literary. Everyone knows that the Government of the day has both merits and demerits, that there are valid arguments both for and against a proposed bill, yet the legislator and the voter have to weigh the arguments, to take a decision which way on balance he will cast his vote. So it is not unreasonable to ask the audience of a debate to take a similar decision. But, if he be asked whether Keats is a greater poet than Shelley, music a more important art than architecture, Periclean Athens the superior of Elizabethan England, whether the invention of the steam engine has been for the benefit of mankind, the only sensible answer is that there is no cause for a decision at all. Such topics therefore make for good discussions but for bad debates. The House showed itself perhaps at its most realistic when, called on to debate: 'That eclecticism is the only sound system of philosophy,' it accepted with acclamation the amendment: 'That this House is unable to grasp the system of eclecticism', and adjourned.

An institution under sentence of death is, unlike a person so circumstanced, always at a disadvantage. The sentence does not necessarily, as with Dr. Dodd, concentrate its mind wonderfully, and by general agreement the latter half of the 1840s was a period of low water in the Union's history. The repeal of the Corn Laws by no means aroused the dramatic clashes that had been aroused by the Reform Bill fourteen years before. The reason was that the dominating name at the Union was still the name of Gladstone, and Gladstone had, of course, moved over with his leader, Peel, to support repeal. Had Gladstone stood in Disraeli's shoes and thundered against the treachery, the Union, and indeed by far the greater part of Oxford, would probably have supported him. As it was they knew that they were Conservatives but were not quite sure which was the Conservative cause. Gladstone in a few years was to become anathema to all good Oxford Conservatives, whether at the Union or elsewhere. In the last half of the 1840s it was not yet quite certain whether he and the other Peelites had left the Conservative party for good. In 1847 he stood as a candidate for the University seat which he desired, as he admitted, 'with passionate fondness'. The old Provost of Queen's growled that he 'would rather be represented by an old woman than a young man', but youth, it was objected, was, if a disease, a curable disease and it was a sign of the times that Gladstone was elected. His election was welcomed by the undergraduates not so much on his intrinsic political merits as because the election of a young man was calculated to annoy the Hebdomadal Board. He was given a rowdy ovation by the undergraduates of Christ Church in much the same spirit as that in which the undergraduates pelted the Vice-Chancellor with snowballs at the time of Ward's degradation before the Convocation. It was not so much that they liked Gladstone's politics or Ward's theology as that, like angry young men of every generation, they liked ragging the Dons.

> Old dreary dismal Dons, like oysters,
> Shut up in their Cimmerian cloisters,
> Who never yet have learnt the vanity
> Of churches, creeds and Christianity.

as Sewell, the founder of Radley College, wrote in his *University's Commission, or Lord John Russell's Postbag*. A lot of things were changing in the Oxford of the 1840s. The railway reached the city in 1844. The University authorities were able to keep it to the inconvenient neighbourhood of the Gas Works but not any longer wholly to banish it. Up till then those who wished to travel by train had had to go to Faringdon to catch it. In 1850 the Royal Commission was appointed and as a result of its report in 1854 the religious tests were abolished for undergraduates and Bachelors of Arts, though still kept for Masters, Fellows and for a vote in Convocation.

These changes seem to have had surprisingly little effect on the Union, which was during these years perhaps of all places at Oxford that which was least obnoxious to the winds of change. It escaped from the confusions of domestic politics and the boredom of constant historical or literary debates by suddenly developing a great interest in foreign politics. The age was not one of wide foreign travel. Since Napoleon had been defeated Englishmen had been glad enough to retire into a splendid isolation and the educated among them took little interest in any foreigners save those who lived in classical Greece and Rome. Therefore at the Union during the first years of its life motions on foreign affairs had been rare. This was changed now mainly owing to the influence of a few individuals. The change started when George Bowen, afterwards Governor of Hong Kong, was President. Bowen had two terms of office, first in 1843 when he was an undergraduate of Trinity and a second innings in 1844 when he was a Fellow of Brasenose. But the real change came a year or two later with Dufferin, with Grant Duff and Morier, '*le gros citoyen*' as he was called—one of Jowett's favourite pupils. They, unlike the average undergraduate, had all been brought up abroad. Grant Duff records in his diary, 'I see I made my maiden speech in Public Business in support of a motion by Morier, then like myself an undergraduate at Balliol, 'That the State of Europe is such as to require that England should have diplomatic relations with the court at Rome'—an opinion by the way I hold as firmly now (1897) as I did then.'

This debate was in February, 1848—in the early months of the year of revolution. Grant Duff also before this year was out had addressed the House on Austria–Hungary, championing the cause of the Hungarian revolutionaries. He spoke also on French affairs and moved a motion deploring the national indifference to India as a danger to the Empire.

The Union of the last half of the 1840s was certainly, as were many other people in Oxford in the disturbances of the Oxford Movement, more interested in religion than in politics. Yet its expression was hampered by the rule which forbade debate on theological topics. Therefore they skated round this prohibition by debating subjects which had a religious angle but could be debated in political terms. Representation at the Court of Rome was a good case in point. In fact the debate doubtless gave opportunity to speakers to indicate pretty closely—from the one side or the other—their opinion on the policies of Pio Nono. There was indeed a certain *odium theologicum*. There was on the committee in 1850 a certain Catholic called Wetherell. Since he was able to progress in course of time from committee man to Secretary and then to Treasurer it was clear that the Union was not dominated by bigoted prejudice. But, if not excluded from office by his faith, Wetherell had on account of it certain critics, and indeed it appears that he himself, as converts sometimes are, was at times a little guilty of trailing his coat. 'Not without literary grace and polish,' wrote his contemporary Plenderleath of him, 'but something of a copyist of Liddon, who spoke with great effect but was regarded beyond the measure of his hearers, in fact something of a Don.' Liddon did in fact abandon the Union in disgust at what he thought of as its triviality and superficiality, and Wetherell, quite apart from creed, seems to have given a certain impression of thinking himself the superior of his auditors. They ragged him. Hitting back, he threatened to impeach one, Bartlett, afterwards both a President of the Society and a Bampton lecturer. Bartlett went to Brodrick of Balliol, an Irish Protestant, for advice. 'Crush the viper,' said Brodrick.

It did not prove necessary. Wetherell himself brought his offensive to an untimely end by getting drunk, assaulting the College porter and getting sent down. Bartlett wrote in celebration,

> Why was his term at first so short,
>   Cut prematurely shorter?
> The reason was he floored the port
>   And then he floored the porter.

Some years before a motion of impeachment had been brought against Meyrick, the Secretary, for entering in his official report of the debate that there was a scene of great confusion. This was held to be an improper comment, but Meyrick was acquitted. He was a pious man—afterwards a Canon of Norwich—and was held fully to have redeemed himself when in the next term, when he was Treasurer, he insisted on visiting in prison a man who was serving a term there for stealing books from the Union library.

A few years before a committee had been formed, of which the Low Church Brooke Lambert was a prominent member for the suppression of Burgon, a High Churchman. It was not, it is true, for any directly denominational reason that Burgon was to be suppressed. Members of the Union at that time—and indeed up to the First World War—received as one of the privileges of membership free postage. Burgon, by then a Don, abused this privilege by sending out circulars and private notes to the extent of a hundred and twenty at a time. It was this excessive posting which Brooke Lambert succeeded in curbing.

Yet there was in a certain sense more to be said in Oxford for intolerance towards High Churchmen than for intolerance towards professed Roman Catholics. Whatever the assaults on liberty that the good Protestant might imagine that the Roman Catholics would deliver to England and to Oxford, if they ever found themselves in a majority, he had to confess that the chances of their being in such a majority in any foreseeable future in England were so remote that they could be neglected. In fact the Catholics were in no position to subvert Oxford's freedom whatever they might wish. But the Puseyite was in a different position. He was a member of the national Church—of Oxford's Church. He claimed also that that Church had a Catholic nature and that all Englishmen owed a duty to it in its Catholic nature, whether they were conscious of that duty or not. All Englishmen had a duty, according to the Puseyites, to support an ecclesiastical constitution which the majority of them in fact abhorred. From that it was an easy step—and a step which many Puseyites and Dr. Pusey himself did not shrink from taking— to say that those who failed to fulfil what was on Puseyite grounds their plain duty were wicked people. The Newmanites seceded from Oxford and no longer attempted to influence what happened there. The Puseyites remained in Oxford and fought every inch of the battle against its reform.

Wetherell had left Oxford before he could stand for the Union's Presidency. It elected in his place as President Henry Oxenham—a man, who, though he was not to prove capable of constancy in any faith, had an irresponsible love of shocking established prejudices. Not himself at that time a Roman Catholic, he found the Catholic stick a very convenient one with which to effect such purposes. His contention was that to a far greater extent than a secularly minded age allowed the great creative force in history had been religion and this he expounded without remorse in season and out of season in splendid language, delivered, so Plenderleath tells us, in a monotonous tone with his eyes fixed upon the floor demonstrating how the religious key was

the key to many of the problems of history which the superficial had attempted to explain by more worldly causes. He
had already fluttered the dovecotes a little by denouncing
King Henry VIII as 'the man of corrupt life; yet the so-
called Defender of the Faith'. It is a little curious that even
in the middle of the last century anyone should have been
surprised by such a judgement. In any event he brought
down on his head much more serious trouble when he
moved: 'That the Company of Jesus had deserved well of the
Church and of mankind.' To speak well of the Jesuits in
mid-Victorian England did a man no good and the phrasing
of the motion seemed to imply either that the Roman
Catholic Church was the Church or alternatively that the
Church of England was a branch of the Church, of which the
Roman Catholic body to which the Jesuits belonged was
another branch. However difficult to defend in history or
theology, common opinion in England at that day thought
that there were two Churches—the Roman and the Anglican. Oxenham lost his motion but beyond that his speech
dealt a fatal blow to his popularity and reputation. He was
driven out from a small essay society to which he belonged—
the Alfred Society. What was more important, although he
was almost pathetically devoted to Oxford and anxious for a
fellowship there, his speech proved an insurmountable ob-
stacle to his election. No less than ten Colleges, it is said,
turned him down and he was reduced pathetically to haunt-
ing the place with no occupation there and eking out the
time by writing little articles for the *Saturday Review*. His was,
I think, a unique example of a man who ruined himself by
his Union career. Later, as a master at the Oratory School
and as a biographer of Dollinger, he was to prove himself, as
Miss Meriol Trevor puts it, 'an inveterate trouble-maker'.
The indiscretions of youth are not generally so unsparingly
punished.

Up till the 1840s the Anglican point of view had been not
only the only legally tolerated point of view at Oxford. It
had also an intellectual monopoly. It was taken for granted.

RIGHT   The bust of Gladstone
by E. Onslow

BELOW   The old rooms from the garden

ABOVE   The Union building showing the extensions, built in 1911

BELOW   The outside of the present Debating Hall

It was the accepted key. The Oxford Movement—and Newman's conversion in particular—made people conscious of the Catholic challenge—more conscious indeed than they were to be some years later when the excitement had died down. Whether they liked or disliked it—the majority disliked it—Union-debaters had now come to understand that there was a Catholic point of view on these ultimate matters. But the controversy of the Movement had on some minds among the Oxford young men an effect quite different from merely causing them to set the Catholic and the Anglican claims against one another. If learned and holy men, obviously all in good faith, dispute with one another on ultimate truths, some taking the one side and some the other, it is natural that to some young and inquisitive minds there will occur the reflection, Does not all this disputing prove that we do not know nearly as much about these ultimate matters as any of the disputants pretend? Perhaps the main gainer out of all the controversy was the *tertium quid* of agnosticism—to use the word that was to be brought into fashion a few years later—and in the Union there appeared in those years for the first time quite a little knot of speakers who explicitly repudiated the supernatural claims of the Christian religion. They ranged themselves under the Positivist banner—followers of Auguste Comte—vowed, as they claimed, not to the service of the unknown God beyond the skies but to the religion of humanity. They came mostly from Wadham.

We have already come across Congreve back in 1841, debating against Parnell on the rights of Jews. He, like the Catholics, used to enjoy shocking the Establishment. 'Honourable members,' he said, 'seem as much excited as if I wished to upset the monarchy and remove the Queen from the throne; but I have no such design. The time has not come for it *yet*'. He was followed some years later by his pupils—Beesley, Bridges and, from Rugby, Frederick Harrison, who was to live on to see Clemenceau received in Oxford in 1921 and to describe the occasion in an article in *The*

F

Times. Once they had shown themselves able to battle down the preliminary shock aroused by their rejection of traditional Christian views, the Positivists were at a considerable advantage in such a place as the Union, for, whatever the truth about the ultimate mysteries, the Victorian world was certainly moving towards a pluralistic society, where it was coming increasingly to be recognised that the day for maintaining an established religion by test and privilege and police action was passing. The Positivists, though perhaps sometimes a little intellectually priggish in failing to conceal how superior they felt themselves to those around them, at any rate had no wish to invoke the law to prevent people from indulging in any religious practice that they might wish. All they demanded was the abolition of religious privilege and ever greater freedom. The tide of the times was therefore with them. Stanley, on his return to Oxford as Professor of Ecclesiastical History a few years later in 1856, after his period of residence in London, found the Union and Oxford sadly desiccated by the Positivists. He noted the undergraduates' stiffness and 'their marvellous lack of interest in theological study'. He deplored the 'dusty, secular, dried-up aspect of the place'. A new age with its new battles was coming to birth.

Frederick Lygon, afterwards Lord Beauchamp, became President in the Michaelmas term of 1851 and his term was notable for the final quarrel with Mr. Vincent, which led the Society to leave Wyatt's Rooms and to take up its present quarters. But it was also under his Presidency that the Union's fortunes saw their revival. As has been argued, interesting and important as may be the questions of religion or of literature, a debating society is much best suited for political motions, and the Union had suffered very much in the latter part of the 1840s because, owing to Gladstone's prestige and other reasons, it had not clearly divided itself on the issue of the day—the repeal of the Corn Laws—as it had divided itself fifteen years before over the Reform Bill. Wherever intrinsic wisdom and statesmanship might lie, the

Union for the liveliness of its debates badly needed some violent, courageous and eloquent diehard who would denounce Peel and Gladstone as traitors to Conservativism in the accents with which Gladstone had at that earlier date been willing to denounce the Duke of Wellington. During the 1840s it found no such Quixote. But in 1850, just incidentally as it was becoming clear that even Conservatives would not take up protection again, the Union found him in Frederick Lygon. To begin with Lygon, according to Plenderleath's reminiscences was not a ready speaker. 'At first Lygon had considerable difficulty in speaking. . . . When he first began to speak his humming and hawing were portentous. So much so that, after a little while his rising was a signal for a tempest of groans and a scraping of feet upon the boarded floor.' But he was a nice man. They liked him. He was a lord, and so in the end he won the members round to his side. They elected him, first, Secretary, then Treasurer, then President.

Union life had then as now its lighter moments. It is, to be frank, difficult to recapture the jokes of a debating society in a printed page. Whether they happened yesterday or a hundred years ago, whether they happened in Parliament or at the Oxford Union, humour so much depends on atmosphere that it is idle to pretend that the mere record of what happened moves us easily to laughter. Thus there was a scholar of Wadham in that year who had been gated. He was in the middle of an oration when Tom started to strike nine. The strokes reminded him, and leaving his oration unfinished, his notes scattered on the floor, he fled helterskelter from the Chamber in a vain hope of reaching his College before the strike was finished. That, at a distance of time, we can see, was funny enough to the spectators. Like the jokes of Rabelais, we see that such incidents are funny rather than are ourselves moved by them to laughter. The Union had, as in every generation it has had, its licensed jester—a certain Higgin of St. Mary's Hall. When the debate flagged a cry would go up of 'Higgin, Higgin' and Mr.

Higgin, arrayed in faultless evening dress with monocle and buttonhole, would arise and, whatever the subject, pour out his stream of inconsequent nonsense. It would be idle to pretend that the unconnected samples of his oratory which have been preserved are sufficient to enable us to enjoy the joke, but we have no reason to doubt that it was a good one and the story is mainly valuable to remind us that undergraduate nature has not changed so much over the generations as is sometimes thought.

Yet for all that the Union in the last years of the 1840s was dying, and it was dying because of Mr. Gladstone. Gladstone's name hung with such oppressive prestige over the Union that its present members could not fully breathe. The issue of protection was, as has been said, the case in point. When Peel proposed to repeal the Corn Laws, his action was, as it should have been, challenged at the Union. Hardinge Gifford, afterwards as Lord Halsbury to be the veteran of Tory Lord Chancellors, challenged Peel's action in a debate that ran for three nights. But Gifford was not the man to dethrone a Gladstone. The issue was allowed to lapse. The undergraduates turned out to support Gladstone's candidature for the University, indifferent whether he was a protectionist or a free trader. Such was not the atmosphere in which controversy would thrive. What the Union needed was a speaker who, if not perhaps quite Gladstone's equal, would at any rate have the brashness to challenge him and the ability to offer a challenge that was not contemptible. Such a challenge was forthcoming in the new decade in the man who, after Disraeli, was destined throughout life to be Gladstone's greatest rival.

CHAPTER FIVE

THE AGE OF CECIL

———

LORD ROBERT CECIL was the second son of the then Lord Salisbury. He did not seem likely to succeed to wealth or title and he came up to Oxford, imagining that he would have to make his way in the world. From the first he had planned for himself a political career and took more seriously and more definitely than most of his colleagues the Union as a first step in a political career. He went through its *cursus honorum*—served first as Secretary, then afterwards for a whole year as Librarian and as Treasurer, though never as President—and took his duties very seriously.

The Robert Cecil of those days was unqualified in his opposition to change and his support of existing privilege. Oxford was and ought to be thought of as the University of the Church of England. If tests were abolished, the University would be abolished. Sir Robert Peel, even after his death, was in Cecil's opinion lying in 'the grave of infamy'. Here was then a man made to challenge the Gladstonian tradition.

The great debate which by general agreement put the Union back on its feet and made it once more the central political arena of Oxford life was the debate on Protection which was opened on February 14, 1850. No reports of Union debates had up till that time been permitted, and this is the first debate of which we have a full record. It was kept by Knatchbull-Hugessen of Magdalen. Knatchbull-Hugessen and Bedford of Brasenose had formed a small society for the propagation of protectionist principles, which, organising itself on the lines of a political party or pressure group, had succeeded in packing the committee with protectionist members and now, under Knatchbull-Hugessen's Presidency, bringing on this debate. Knatchbull-Hugessen, who had a young man's fanaticism on the subject, was a good-looking Etonian, who had constituted himself the champion of the landed interest. He had already published a small volume of satirical verse in criticism of Cobden and Peel. The arguments used, as indeed was only to be expected, were the common arguments of the controversy. The free traders argued that it was to the advantage of the working class if they could get cheap corn from abroad rather than the more expensively produced home-grown corn. The Protectionists argued that it was a national interest to assure the prosperity of domestic agriculture and that cheap corn would not benefit the working man because the capitalist, determined to pay no more than a subsistence wage, would reply to cheap bread by reducing wages. No doubt the debate was a good debate, as undergraduate debates go, but there is little purpose at this distance of time in reproducing its arguments. The motion in favour was moved by Lygon and the ball of argument was thrown to and fro in conventional fashion. Robert Cecil spoke towards the end of the first evening's debate. It was a speech of aggressive defence. He spoke for the agricultural and landed interests whom he depicted as ruined by free trade but proudly refusing to surrender. The picture of the Cecils of a hundred years ago as already reduced to beggary may strike modern taste as vaguely comic, and free trade speakers even then naturally did not fail to make some fun of it. The best speech by general agreement on the free trade side came from Lomer of Oriel who gave a hard-hitting statistical analysis of the state of the country under free trade, designed to demonstrate that all classes were in fact better off than they had previously been. The prophets of that day all confidently predicted a great political future for Robert Cecil. 'Lord Robert Cecil showed a considerable power of speech,' recorded Prebendary Mayrick. 'Not at all of the gibes and flouts character but of deadly earnestness,' but they predicted as confidently a brilliant future on the Liberal side for Lomer. It was thought that they would go forward together in rivalry much as F. E. Smith and John Simon were to go forward together in rivalry forty years later. It might well have been so, but unfortunately Lomer died young.

In its early years the Union had been mainly an Eton Society. Then, as we have seen, there came a Wykehamist period. Now it was on the whole Rugbeians—Lomer was for instance a Rugbeian—who predominated there. There was Lomer. There was Henry Smith. There was Shirley of Wadham, 'a crawling and servile Whig', as he described himself in mock derision, afterwards a Doctor of Divinity, Regius Professor of Ecclesiastical History, a pupil of Arnold who took some pains to dissociate himself from Arnold's opinions. There was Pearson, Christian Socialist, enthusiast for education, who thought his fellow Rugbeians 'too self-consciously moral', later to go to Australia and become there Director of Education in Victoria. There was Bartlett, Wetherell's antagonist, President in 1855. There was Bridges, one of the Wadham Positivists, afterwards to be General Inspector of the Local Government Board. There was Fitzgerald of University who, unlike most Rugbeians, was a Conservative, but who was solemnly rebuked by Goschen and his other schoolfellows on the ground that he too often 'played the fool'. There was Charles Bowen, 'beloved by all' according to Burne-Jones—'the only person I ever knew,' as his brother said of him, 'to jump a cow as it stood.' Destined for peerage and judgeship, he was at Oxford more closely associated than any other undergraduate with the pre-Raphaelite decorations at the Union. He was later to leave the staff of the *Saturday Review* because of its attacks on *Essays and Reviews*. Above all there was Goschen.

In our foreshortened view of history we are apt to think of all the early nineteenth century Rugbeians as products of Doctor Arnold and of Arnold as the essentially Christian tutor. In truth it is a very open question whether Newman was not right in doubting whether Arnold was a Christian at all, so broad were his views, and in fact, though doubtless not in Arnold's intention, the boys who came from Rugby in those years were by and large less likely to be Christians than the boys from any other public school. They were fuller, doubtless, than the average of moral earnestness but Arnold's non-dogmatic ethical religion was much more easily accommodated to Positivism than to any traditional form of Christianity. Those of them like Shirley and Pearson who retained some traditional Christian pattern tended to be somewhat in reaction against Arnold and, in so far as they looked back with gratitude to their schooldays, focused that gratitude on Arnold's successor, Goulburn, rather than on Arnold himself. Among them all, Christian or non-Christian, there tended to be a certain parade of moral earnestness. Of course they were consciously provoking and doing it to annoy. Yet there was something a little typical of their origins when Pearson and Goschen insisted on collecting into a little private essay society those members of the Union whose opinions they thought really worth listening to and calling it the Wise and the Good.

By far the most distinguished of the Union Rugbeians of this period—the man who after Robert Cecil had the largest part in placing the Society back again on to those paths of politics from which it had strayed in the years after Gladstone was George Goschen—Goschen whom so many years afterwards Robert Cecil was to remember when Randolph Churchill had forgotten him and thus to change the face of history. Would he have remembered him if it had not been for the Oxford Union?

There was from the first an earnest careerism about Goschen. It was imposed upon him by his father who brought up his son to be a success in life. There were no doubts in the Goschen household about the importance of success—no hesitations about the desirability of offering incense to the bitch goddess. 'George,' said his father, 'must be ambitious. He must become a great merchant—a little one is a poor beast.' One of the first rungs in the ladder of success was the Oxford Union. It was as such that he approached it. Not for him any light-hearted indulgence in debating for the fun of it. He prepared his speeches 'for telling delivery' much more carefully than other members. From the first he made his mark, 'Goschen made a brilliant speech the other night on the papal aggression, and on the right side, too. He is far the most eloquent person I have heard anywhere,' recorded Jex Blake, later the Headmaster of Rugby and Dean of Wells. He spoke on a wide variety of subjects—on Tennyson and on Shelley as poets—on the Maynooth grant, on the admission of Jews to Parliament, to which in spite of his own origins he was opposed. He refused to follow his schoolfellow Pearson into flirtations with Socialism and opposed Pearson's motion, condemning concentration of capital in too few hands and equally opposing a motion: 'That the increasing power of great towns is opposed to the idea of the English constitution and inconsistent with the national prosperity.' In November of 1851 he proposed: 'That the French Revolution of 1789 was justifiable and has conferred the greatest blessings on mankind.' His friend, Arthur Butler, afterwards Headmaster of Haileybury, proposed an amendment: 'That it is premature to pronounce definitely concerning the good effects resulting rom it in consequence of the excesses in which the Revolution terminated.' But Goschen was a Liberal and the Union still Conservative. Both motion and amendment were lost.

On the great issue of Gladstone—great issue at any rate to the Union—Goschen was a defender. Gladstone's party position was of course, then still indeterminate. The Conservative party had split over the repeal of the Corn Laws, but there were many who thought that—particularly after the Protectionists had abandoned protection—the Peelites and the Protectionists both ought to and would come together again. To such students Gladstone must return to the Conservative party, if only because there was no place else for him to go. The notion that he would go over to the

Liberals was to them unthinkable. He was, they thought, a Conservative, but a Conservative to be somewhat censured because he was not a good party man. It was as such that it was proposed to censure him in a motion that was debated by the Union on three evenings of February, 1853. Goschen, speaking in favour of Gladstone, defended his mugwumpery. 'He who has fettered his actions by joining a party, not by conscientiously subscribing to a creed, has committed a crime against his country and done himself an injury of which he must reap the fruits,' argued Goschen. Gladstone, since there was no party which stood for the principles in which he believed, was right to continue in independence. But this was by no means the general opinion of the Society. Benjamin Bickley Rogers of Wadham, afterwards a scholarly barrister who was compelled to abandon practice by increasing deafness and who occupied his enforced leisure by making an excellent verse translation of Aristophanes, moved an amendment: 'That we view with regret and disappointment the position assumed by Mr. Gladstone towards Lord Derby's Government and his subsequent coalition with the Whigs, as uncalled for by political exigencies, inconsistent with his past career and tending to render permanent the disruption of the Conservative party.' Gladstone had indeed come to the parting of the ways and was soon to join the Liberal Government of Lord Aberdeen and thereafter of course definitely and finally to cast in his lot with the Liberals. It was natural that members of the Union should have to make their choice between Conservative principles and personal loyalty and affection for the Union's most distinguished member. Beesley, one of the Wadham Positivists, criticised Gladstone from the Liberal point of view, girding at him for not having the courage to declare himself an out-and-out Liberal. Pearson made what seems to have been an amusing and clever speech, sketching the character of a turncoat and opportunist politician which all the Conservatives imagined to apply to Gladstone and then turning and saying, 'This, sir, is the character of an inconsistent

statesman, and this has been the career of Lord Derby.'
(For Derby had himself of course been a Whig on his first
entry into public life.) But in general the House divided,
Liberals for Gladstone and Conservatives against him. After
immense excitement Gladstone was condemned by 110 votes
to 104, and Rogers was carried shoulder high to Wadham by
his cheering supporters.

His triumph won Rogers the Presidency at the next election, and with him the Union entered into new life. Whether
Gladstone was or was not a good man, whether little Liberals
were to be preferred to little Conservatives was as it might be,
but certainly it was for the health of the Union that it should
not relapse into merely servile hero-worship of Gladstone.
Left to itself, it would have been a Conservative body. The
influence of Gladstone, while not sufficient to switch it over
to Liberalism, was sufficient to make the Liberal and Conservative votes more nearly equal than would otherwise
have been the case. As long as Palmerston was nominally the
Liberal leader Liberalism in national politics was not a very
easily recognisable creed and the period not a very thrilling
one.

On the whole the Union's politics were perhaps more lively
than those of Westminster. Since there was little to excite
enthusiasm at home, undergraduates' enthusiasm tended to
be aroused by the movements for national freedom on the
Continent—more particularly, of course, by that of Italy.
The religious controversy which in the 1840s had revolved
round the intrinsic merits of Newman's argument about the
nature of the Church, now diverted itself into the political
form. There was little chance of England becoming the
slave of a Catholic clerical reaction. There was, or was
thought to be, considerable chance of such a reaction
barring the way to freedom on the Continent. The Italian
issue, as Oxford undergraduates saw it, was an issue between
the Italian people rightly struggling to be free and a clerical
tyranny seeking to deny them their freedom. The Jesuits
were taken up again and debated in a very different spirit

from the philosophical spirit in which Oxenham had sought to estimate their achievement a few years before. They were now denounced as the arch-enemies of national freedom in Italy, and thirty-five speakers in a crowded and turbulent debate jostled one another to make the point that they would be an enemy of national freedom in any other country, too, if they got the chance, and to vote them 'a menace to the safety of any kingdom'.

As one looks through the lists, one finds a number of respectable and honourable names from these years. There is little purpose perhaps in recording them, unless their possessors were connected with some extraordinary event during their Union career or unless their subsequent careers were such as to make them memorable. The long list of worthy Deans and Professors, back-bench Members of Parliament, judges and civil servants bears witness to the part that the Union was still playing in the training of worthy citizens, and it is interesting to note that, in spite of prophecies of atheism, red ruin or Catholic perversion, which were at that, as at all times, so common on some lips, future clergymen still seemed to manage to obtain for themselves as many offices as ever. As Lowell was soon to write in the *Biglow Papers* on the other side of the Atlantic,

> It seems just like the fulfilment of prophecies
> When all the best people get all the best offices.

But what was interesting was, side by side with the clerics who maintained their strength, went the steady growth of the Positivists. Doubtless it was only a small minority of members who were willing to call themselves Positivists, but this age differed from its predecessor in that these young men were now willing openly to proclaim themselves as unbelievers and were not shunned by their fellows for doing so. Congreve, their first master, had gone down, but Frederick Harrison was still there and the Positivism of Wadham was reinforced by two formidable recruits from Lincoln, Cotter Morison and John Morley. Cotter Morison who combined his Positivism with a love of horsemanship and boxing, was to win for himself a minor reputation as biographer of characters as incongruous as St. Bernard of Clairvaux and Lord Macaulay. John Morley was, of course, to win for himself a major reputation both in literature and in politics and to leave behind the record of having offered his resignation more frequently than any other figure in political history. But, whatever the eminence to which they were destined, these Positivists, while they added a certain tone to the Union, were not prepared to take it very seriously or to think a career there important. They considered its tone insufficiently earnest. Yet the consequence of their influence was that the Society now began to debate a new sort of social problem which it could hardly have touched in previous years. Two generations were indeed to elapse before debates on such intimate personal matters as birth control and another generation before the general issue of chastity could be explored, but it was a sign of the times when John Morley in the 1850s was able to move a motion in favour of divorce. That would hardly have been possible a few years before. It was not, of course, merely the Positivists who were responsible for this new adventurousness. The times were changing, and the Union was merely changing with the times. The Crimean War had a curious left-handed effect on Oxford life. Previous to that undergraduates had been forbidden to wear whiskers and in the early 1850s an undergraduate had been sent down from St. John's for not shaving. The beards and Dundrearies which came into fashion with the Crimean campaign made it impossible any longer to enforce such a rule. The 1850s saw a general growth in undergraduate freedom—a wider recognition that a place of education should be a place where students can freely exchange opinions, and the subject of divorce became a subject on which debate could be tolerated because, of course, in those years for the first time a regular divorce law was put on the Statute Book. Divorce was indeed then and throughout the whole of the nineteenth century discussed in a comically different fashion from that in which it is discussed today. Today at Oxford or in any other debating society a reasonable proportion of the participants, it is to be presumed, will be themselves the children of divorced parents. Whatever their own matrimonial intentions, they must be conscious from the law of averages that a reasonable proportion of them will in due course appear in the divorce courts. In the 1850s things were very different. Divorce was discussed very much as such a problem as capital punishment was discussed. It was asked whether facilities should be provided for the wholly abnormal people whose marriage was a failure. It was not envisaged then, in the one case any more than in the other, that anyone present would dream of taking advantage of such facilities.

The Union's new buildings had been begun in 1853. The Society's income at that time was about £500 a year and this was just about sufficient to meet its current expenses. The debating hall—where the present Library now stands—did not come into use until 1857. In the previous term the President had been Oakley of Brasenose. He was one of the ecclesiastically minded members and was in later life to be Dean of Manchester. But he was an ecclesiastic of both an erratic and an original nature. A High Churchman, in his undergraduate days he insisted on acting as a server at Communion—a functionary not common in those days even in High Anglican Churches—and in order to fit himself for the part equipped himself with a cassock adorned with thirty-nine buttons, each one in honour of one of the Thirty-nine Articles. On account of the colour of his hair he was known as 'the Red saint'. In spite of, or it may be because of his religious fervour, he did not at all approve of Brasenose Chapel and objected to compulsory chapel not because he objected to obligatory church going, of which on the contrary he strongly approved, but because he did not recognise the services that took place in Brasenose Chapel as in any proper sense of the word Christian services at all. As a consequence during his presidential term he was sent down for cutting chapel.

He returned the next term in time to see Eliot of Trinity, afterwards the Dean of Windsor, installed in the presidential chair and presiding in the new debating hall. He celebrated the occasion by a witty mock examination paper, supposedly to be set for candidates for the presidency. It begins with '1. When were the claims of incompetence first recognised? Apply your answer to the present contest between Tallcombe and Howle.' The two presidential candidates of the moment were Halcomb and Fowle. It continues in this vein through twelve questions on pseudo-history and ten questions on pseudo-law. Such jests, of course, predominantly depend on topical allusions, which are at once familiar and funny to the immediate reader but which are hardly worth disinterring in footnotes a hundred years later. But one can easily trace the hand of a competent parodist in such a History question as 'Describe the Battle of Coffee, the Battle of Composition and the Battle of the Casino. In which engagement were Dons first used?' or in such a Law question as 'What steps would you take to get back Stolen Books by Common Recovery? How was this statute suppressed in a recent instance? (Candidates from Christ Church need not attempt this question.)'

There had been a lot of controversy about the provision of refreshments to members. That was the Battle of Coffee. The Battle of Composition was the controversy already referred to, whether Burgon should be allowed to take advantage of the Society's free postage to send out his circulars, and the Battle of the Casino refers to a controversy about what games should be allowed on the Union premises and to the objection of the anti-gamblers that the place should not be turned into a casino. The query about the Dons refers to the fact that Burgon was by this time a Don. It was thought an addition of insult to injury that it should be a Don, in receipt of a salary, who should abuse the postal privileges which had primarily been conceded in order to make the Union more attractive for impecunious undergraduates. The question about the theft of books refers, as one might guess, to a recent incident, and, as one might also guess, the culprit in that incident was from Christ Church. The other questions are in similar style but it would exhaust patience to go through them and expound them all in detail.

Oakley was one of the new religious aesthetes. He spoke in favour of the pre-Raphaelite Movement. The philistine Positivists rallied against him and Frederick Harrison moved and carried an amendment of almost unendurably priggish pomposity, 'That, though the pre-Raphaelite School gives hope of a revival of Art, it does seem to be affected with some deplorable delusions.' This proved important. The Positivists were, to the members' credit, more than the Union could stand.

The new Union buildings were soon faced with much more serious issues. The architect of them had been Benjamin Woodward. His great work before that had been the Museum in the Parks. It had aroused a very great deal of controversy, both from old Dons who saw no reason why the University should teach Science or why it should have a Museum at all and from those who thought that Oxford must keep pace with the new learning. Ruskin's influence was then strong in Oxford, his interest more in the architecture of the new building than in the science that was to be taught in it. He persuaded the authorities to bring over Benjamin Woodward from Dublin, a charming, quiet, modest man, 'the silliest creature that ever breathed out of an oyster,' Rossetti called him. Ruskin encouraged Woodward to erect a building of Gothic design—not, as he put it, one of those 'commonplace and contemptible imitations of the Italian masters'. This Woodward did, ornamenting with an exuberance of decoration that will perhaps seem excessive to most modern tastes—stone birds and beasts, wrought iron ornaments representing branches of lime and chestnut, sycamore and walnut, a laboratory for chemical students modelled on the Abbot's Kitchen at Glastonbury. 'Parrhots and Owwls,' exclaimed in disgust James O'Shea, the Irish workman, who had the task of blocking out the ornaments,

THE GRAPHIC

AN ILLUSTRATED WEEKLY NEWSPAPER

VOL. VII. No. 184
Reg^d at General Post Office as a Newspaper

SATURDAY, MAY 31, 1873

PRICE SIXPENCE
[Daily Post Sixpence Half-penny]

THE CHURCH DISESTABLISHMENT DEBATE AT THE OXFORD UNION SOCIETY

Debating Hall in the Old Library. At the time of the Union
Jubilee on May 8, 1873, a debate was held on the Motion
'That the Church of England ought to be disestablished and
disendowed'. The Motion was lost by 88 to 40

LEFT   The bust of Asquith
by Clare Sheridan

BELOW   A notice put up in the Billiard Room by F. E. Smith
(afterwards Lord Birkenhead) when Junior Treasurer

OXFORD UNION SOCIETY

BILLIARD ROOM.

Players are requested to enter
their names, with the amount
paid to the Marker, in a book
provided for the purpose.

13th October 1893.   F. E. Smith

Junior Treasurer

'Members of Convocation.' In the Ruskinian fashion enthusiastic young undergraduates went and lent an aesthetic
hand at the building for nothing and the love of art. Ruskin
wrote to Acland, 'Your Museum is literally the first building
raised in England since the close of the fifteenth century,
which has fearlessly put to new trial this old faith in nature
and in the genius of the unassisted workman who gathered
out of nature the materials he needed.'

As with so many Ruskinian sentences it is not quite certain
on analysis what it means and most modern opinion would
say that the Ruskins and the Pugins, in so far as they attempted merely to impose on one age the architecture of another
whose social and economic circumstances were totally
different, were in error. However that may be, the importance to the story of the Union is that Woodward's work at
the Museum resulted in his being awarded the contract for
building the new debating hall—the present library—for the
Union.

In 1857 two young undergraduates, William Morris from
Marlborough and Edward Jones from King Edward's
School, Birmingham, made one another's acquaintance at
Exeter College. Morris was at that time a romantic full of
tales of 'knights and lorn damsels' but without any very
specific achievement to his credit. Jones, or as he afterwards
came to call himself Burne-Jones, had already begun his
career as an artist, drawing 'delicious devils', when still at
school. They became inseparable friends. Both were then
destined, as they imagined, for Holy Orders. They went
about together railing at the stuffiness of Oxford. They
admired Gothic architecture and subscribed money which
they could ill afford to the hideous defacement of their own
College. For nowhere was the influence of Gothic more disastrous than at Exeter, where during those years the old
seventeenth-century chapel, the old eighteenth-century
library, Prideaux' Buildings and the Rector's Lodgings were
swept away and the present undistinguished work of Gilbert
Scott substituted for it. They read widely and wildly and

G

without discipline. Their closest friend among other undergraduates was Cormell Price, 'the dearest Crom' of Morris's
letters, who was destined of all improbable fates to become
the hero-headmaster, an almost godlike figure, of Kipling's
Stalky and Co.

Morris fell for a time under Newman's influence and
almost joined the Roman Church. Then Tennyson came to
supplant Newman. The two friends went with others to the
Sheldonian in 1855 to give Tennyson a 'tremendous ovation'
when he came to take his degree. Dreadful as the Dons
might be, Oxford had at any rate its architecture. George
Street was then living in Oxford as diocesan architect and
restoring the city's churches. They fell under his influence
and, when Street moved to London, he took Morris with
him.

Morris and Burne-Jones conceived the notion of forming a
Brotherhood of men dedicated to the creation of beauty. In
1856 they started a paper called the *Oxford and Cambridge
Magazine*. Tennyson and Ruskin gave them their blessing,
but it had no financial basis and after twelve numbers it
failed. It was mainly memorable because it brought Morris,
who had up till then never met a painter, into contact with
Rossetti. He visited Rossetti one day at his Working Men's
College in Great Ormond Street and had with him his 'first
fearful talk'. As a result a friendship was formed and in the
summer of 1857, during the Long Vacation, Morris took
Rossetti to Oxford. They ran into Woodward, who took
them to see his new Debating Hall at the Union. Rossetti
looked round the hall and saw that the walls were bare.
Then, as he records, 'Without taking into consideration the
purpose it was intended for (indeed hardly knowing of the
latter) I offered to paint figures of some kind on the blank
spaces of one of the gallery window bays; and another friend
who was with us, William Morris, offered to do the same for
the second bay. Woodward was greatly delighted with the
idea.'

Bowen of Balliol, was the President-elect. He was enthusiastic for the scheme. 'A courteous and delightful fellow, and always regarded in the University as a man of exceptional promise, whom Rossetti loved at once,' Burne-Jones recorded of him. He obtained an authorisation from the Building Committee and, before the Long Vacation was through, they had already started on their work. Rossetti's plan was to collect half a dozen of his friends. He and they were to cover the wall with pictures of scenes out of the *Morte d'Arthur*. The pictures were to be painted 'on a large scale in distemper'. Rossetti set to work on a picture of Sir Lancelot's Vision of the Holy Grail. Morris started and completed his Tristram and Iseult and, that done, turned to decorating the ceiling with a 'vast pattern-work of grotesque creatures'. Oxford friends came in to look, to criticise and to admire—most notable among them a young undergraduate from Balliol, Algernon Charles Swinburne, who had already taken a certain minor part in the Union's debates, speaking on the Liberal side in favour of the extension of the franchise and of penal reform. A somewhat older man, John Hungerford Pollen, a Fellow of Merton, who had already decorated the roof of his College chapel, came in to paint King Arthur receiving Excalibur. Burne-Jones undertook the Death of Merlin.

Val Prinsep, then a youth of nineteen but already weighing fifteen stone, was brought down from London to share in the fun. He arrived at the railway station and, hailing a cab, told it to drive to the Union. The cabman took him to the workhouse, but that mistake was soon rectified. He sought out Rossetti and dined with him that evening to meet Morris and Burne-Jones. He returned to the Mitre at midnight, his head awhirl with wine and Morris's poetry. 'What fun we had at the Union,' he recorded. 'What jokes! What roars of laughter!' A few days later he was to be seen carrying Burne-Jones under his arm up the steps of a ladder to the roof. Val Prinsep's painting was of Sir Pelleas and Etarde. Morris, his Tristram and Iseult finished, was in the meanwhile busy at a smithy near the Castle designing mediaeval armour, and appeared one day in a well-fitted coat of mail, with basinet attached, designed by himself. Then he and Rossetti set forth on a tour of Oxford churches to find a Guinevere. Rodham Stanhope from Christ Church was brought in to do Sir Gawain and the Three Damsels at the Fountain—if not the best, at least the best preserved of the pictures. Arthur Hughes did the Death of Arthur. Over what was the entrance door—now a little side door in the Union forecourt —Alexander Monro carved the King and his Knights. The stone has today outlived the distemper and is still to be seen.

The work went forward in a curious, high-spirited amateur way. The Union had voted unanimously £500 for the 'executive expenses' of the enterprise. That and free soda water for the artists was the extent of its original commitment, and it was hoped that the work would be begun and ended in the Long Vacation of 1857. On Ruskinian principles the artists did their work as nearly as possible for nothing. The hope of getting all completed in a couple of months proved impossible of fulfilment. It was not until the next spring that the work was done and the cost came to something more than the originally estimated £500, but not very much more and most of the extra expense was covered by a private donation. The financial problem, though not managed in a very business-like manner, was yet more or less solved. It was other troubles which led to catastrophe. Some of the work done, if we may judge from photographs and sketches now at Birmingham and from Ruskin's judgement, was very fine. He thought Rossetti's picture, unfinished though it was, 'the finest piece of colour in the world'. Burne-Jones' Death of Merlin was in his opinion almost of equal merit. But the whole scheme was, as Morris afterwards confessed, 'too piecemeal and unorganised'. For a few months the colours survived, 'so brilliant as to make the walls look like the margin of an illuminated manuscript,' as Coventry Patmore, who saw them, recorded. But in their enthusiasm the artists had not taken the trouble to give a proper preparation for distemper painting to damp, newly-built walls. 'The fact is,' wrote Ruskin, 'they're all the least bit crazy and it is difficult to manage them.' Very early in 1858 it became obvious that the pictures were rapidly fading and would soon all but disappear. The temperamental Rossetti began to lose interest where he had at first been so enthusiastic. He could not be bothered even to finish his painting. He picked a quarrel when William Rivière, a teacher of painting on Oxford at that time but not strictly a pre-Raphaelite, was commissioned to fill the three unpre-empted bays with pictures of Arthur's Education under Merlin, Arthur's First Victory and the Wedding of Arthur and Guinevere. He refused to interest himself in any of the suggested plans for the rescue of the paintings—indeed almost took the line that, if Rivière's paintings were to be rescued, he would prefer the whole to perish. 'The one remedy for all is now whitewash,' he wrote, 'and I shall be happy to hear of its application.'

In the end as is known, the paintings were neither washed out nor restored but left to do as they might do and to leave their faded traces on the present Library walls. Professor Tristram restored them in 1930, but, though now it is possible to make out something of their outline, no restoration has been able to give us again the blaze of colour at which Ruskin marvelled. Modern taste has reacted from the bowdlerisation of Malory which Tennyson favoured, and the writers of today, still fascinated by the Arthurian legend, prefer to recreate it in a coarser and more primitive framework. Nor is the picture that tells a story now very much in fashion. Yet for all that the pre-Raphaelites with their sensuous calligraphy of form and line have sufficiently withstood the years. Nothing fails like failure and it was perhaps inevitable that with fiasco the Union authorities should have come under a certain amount of mockery and criticism. Even before this Francis Jeune of Balliol, soon to be President of the Union, later a distinguished Judge and Lord St. Helier, had condemned them as 'disastrous'. Yet C. J. Holmes in his introduction to Holman Hunt's booklet on them published in 1906 said that Oxford at that time was 'the focus of artistic life and energy in England' and described the Union frescoes as 'the most important corporate effort of the pre-Raphaelites'. Whether the room remained a debating hall or whether it was turned into a library, it would have transformed the nature of that not very exciting building had the colours of Rossetti's work continued to blaze forth from its walls. As it is, the Union, over a large part of its history, has been for all its distinction a distressingly philistine place. The churchmen and the lawyers and the politicians of the future have competed against one another in its debates. The poets and the artists have paid it less attention. It was perhaps uncharacteristic, but therefore the more welcome, that on this occasion at any rate the Union should have been the patron of the most vigorous and artistic movement of the times.

The Victorian age, if not an age of progress, was at any rate most certainly an age of change. Nineteenth-century Oxford can indeed be most neatly bisected, for the Commission of 1850 exactly divides the old Oxford from the new. But in Oxford, as at Westminster and elsewhere, the full effect of the changes took a little time to show itself. Just as at Westminster the Reform Bill brought to power a new type of politician but did not do so immediately, so at Oxford the old pre-reform Fellows were not expelled. They were allowed to run down, and it was not until about 1860 that the new shape of things was apparent. Old hoary traditions— the annual sermons, for instance, on the anniversary of the Gunpowder Plot, the execution of Charles I, and the Restoration of Charles II—were abolished. Perhaps the new order showed itself best at the Union in the election to the Presidency in the Trinity term of 1861 of T. H. Green. Up till then Presidents of the Union had tended to be either men destined for Holy Orders or men destined for a political career. The few Positivists had not gone forward to academic posts. Indeed it was not possible for them to do so so long as an assent to the Thirty-nine Articles was required

for a Master's degree and for a Fellowship. Green was the
first of what one may call the secular priests in which late
Victorian England abounded—those to whom earnest young
men looked for a spiritual direction and to whom they gave
an authority which they were no longer willing to give to
orthodox creeds.

We first come across Green as the leader of the *claque* of
undergraduates who cheered for Professor Huxley in his
famous encounter with Bishop Wilberforce in the new
Museum in 1860 on the subject of the descent of man. In
the Trinity term of the next year he was elected President of
the Union. He went on from there to become a Fellow and
Tutor of Balliol and one of the founders of the Workers'
Educational Association. He was one of the first of those who
looked to find almost a new religion in education and to
think that the spread of it throughout all classes of society
would bring a great liberation of the human spirit. It was
the early days of the American Civil War and Oxford
opinion was predominantly for the South. Green took
strongly the Northern side—perhaps in a slightly extravagant
form. 'It is not a republic which is responsible for this war,'
he argued, 'but a slave-holding, slave-breeding and slave-
hunting oligarchy, on which the curse of humanity rests.'
The problems of philosophy were to him not mere exercises
in logic chopping. He thought to find in philosophy a key to
truth similar to that which the Early Fathers expected from
the Gospel texts.

Green's term of presidency marks the time of a great
change in the Union's conception of its place in Oxford life.
The Oxford undergraduate of the first half of the century
had been very literally *in statu pupillari*. At Brasenose undergraduates still submitted to impositions. At Christ Church
Charles Dodgson—better known as Lewis Carroll—used to
set lines to those of his pupils who missed his lectures in
mathematics. In 1865 Matthew Arnold in his *Essays in
Criticism* spoke of Oxford as 'the beautiful city, so venerable,
so lovely, so unravaged by the fierce intellectual life' of the

time. In the early days of the Union, as we have seen, the question was whether the authorities would tolerate its existence at all. There was no question of the undergraduates being invited, through the Union or anywhere else, to express their own opinions on how the University was to be run. By the 1860s things were beginning to change. Even then there was not, indeed, any more than there is now, any question of the undergraduates being given in any way responsible government. They did not at all demand it. When they expressed their opinions on Oxford customs, those opinions were usually conservative and opposed to change. Thus they debated classical education, married Fellows, women at the University, the management of Colleges, the awarding of scholarships. They were opposed to all change—at least to all rapid change. They had no wish to see the Classics deposed from their primacy in the educational system, no wish to see married Fellows nor women at Oxford nor to see closed scholarships abolished, no sympathy with the demand that the University be made more important and the College less important. But it is a mark of the times that they claimed the right to debate these questions. The first step to reform is to get a problem talked about, to transfer it from the realm of the taken-for-granted to the realm of the debatable. It is then after it has been tossed to and fro for a little time that the pattern of the solution emerges. 'The country is becoming more and more democratic,' old Bishop Durnford told the Union Jubilee banquet in 1873. The remark was not received with general approval—so much so that the Bishop, in protest against the jeers, decided to resume his seat without properly concluding his speech, but before doing so he insisted on obstinately repeating his prophecy.

When the Union was first formed there was, of course, no intention that it should speak for all undergraduates. It was by definition a small, exclusive club which used the black ball to keep itself exclusive and which was interested only in the exercise of debating. With the virtual abolition of the black ball its doors were thrown open and by the 1860s the policy was to keep the subscriptions as low as possible so that as few undergraduates as possible were excluded by finance. Yet some were excluded. There were plenty of modest incomes—plenty of undergraduates whose parents could only afford to send their sons to Oxford by rigid economy—in that Victorian world, where grants and scholarships were very much fewer than today. There were others who did not join the Union because they were not interested in its activities— aristocrats who thought it a vulgar, plebean place—bookworms who grudged time lost from their textbooks—hearty philistines who thought it a highbrow place. It could not therefore claim, and was indeed careful not to claim, any right to speak for the undergraduates on Oxford matters. On the other hand, if it had no right, it had at least a less imperfect right than anybody else. There were no Student Councils in those days. The Union was the only undergraduate Oxford Society of any sort.

1859 brought a great, if somewhat adventitious and somewhat ludicrous, addition, to the Union's prestige. In that year the Prince of Wales came up as an undergraduate to Christ Church. By modern standards his life there was as absurd as it could be. The modern view is that it is important that young princes, if they go to a place of education, should be treated exactly like their fellow pupils. Such was not, of course, at all the Prince Consort's view. The Prince, although nominally an undergraduate, lived in a private house, Frewin Hall, next door to the Union. On his arrival Dean Liddel went to the station to meet him. He conducted him back to Christ Church where he was greeted with ringing bells and the cheers of his fellow undergraduates, drawn up to greet him in the quadrangle. 'The Prince himself,' wrote the Dean, 'is the nicest little fellow possible, so simple, naif, ingenuous and modest, and moreover with extremely good wits, possessing also the royal faculty of never forgetting a face.' 'The only use of Oxford,' said the Prince Consort, 'is that it is a place for *study*, a refuge from the world and its claims.' Consequently the Prince had a private tutor, Colonel Bruce. He was not allowed freely to mix with the other undergraduates. He attended his own special course of lectures, to which, to make a company, one or two sheltered fellow undergraduates were admitted. Smoking was forbidden. Invitations were, in all but exceptional circumstances, declined. Dinner parties were occassionally permitted provided that they contained an element of instruction. He wore a nobleman's gold tassel.

The general result of course was that the Prince, who loathed nothing more than reading books, was bored stiff and derived about as little profit as was possible from his Oxford career. Compared with the rest of his life there, going to the Union was a positively thrilling excitement. He went every Thursday. On his first appearance the whole House rose to its feet and cheered. The President, Beaumont of St. John's, had some difficulty in restoring order. After that a custom was established that no notice should be taken of his presence. He sat on the right of the President with Colonel Bruce by his side. Naturally enough perhaps he never took any part in a debate. A division in those days was taken by each member according to his choice ranging himself, when the division was called, to the right or the left of the chair. Those who did not wish to vote stood up and were not counted. At his first division the President asked whether His Royal Highness wished to vote and, before the Prince had an opportunity to answer, Colonel Bruce replied, 'Certainly not.' The Prince, not permitted to express his opinion, at least offered to stand up along with the other abstainers, but he was not permitted to do so.

When the Prince of Wales left Oxford he presented the Union with £100 to spend on the purchase of books. It is safe to say that he would sooner that other people read them than read them himself. But the fact that he made his thank offering in this form is proof that the Union had a little changed its nature with its new premises. To many members now the Library was more important than the Debating Hall, and by consequence the officers tended for a time to be

more literary and scholarly than they have ever been before
or since. After T. H. Green, the next President was Ma-
grath, destined to reign for more than a quarter of a century
as Provost of Queen's; after him the eccentric and attractive
Auberon Herbert, who was to astonish his constituents of
Nottingham by his individualistic conduct and Tolstoyan
opinions and who was even in the Union's Presidency to give
evidence of waywardness by getting bored with the office
after five weeks of term and incontinently resigning. Then
in the Trinity term of 1862 Bryce was President. With him
came in a new tradition—what might be called the positively
nonconformist tradition. Bryce refused to sign the Thirty-
nine Articles and Trinity very sensibly let him in without
them. After two hundred years the Nonconformists were
back in Oxford—the Nonconformists who, as Fairbairn,
the first President of Mansfield College put it, in the six-
teenth century 'went out sadly and with many a backward
look, as men who loved not Oxford less but conscience
more'.

Bryce was, of course, to hold both political and diplomatic office, but he was not what is ordinarily meant by a
politician or a diplomat. He was primarily a scholar and a
man of letters, whose *Holy Roman Empire* grew up out of an
Oxford Prize Essay. He was a scholar and a man of letters
who had the capacity to play temporarily and without much
personal ambition a part in public life—'that awful Scotch
fellow who outwrote everybody', an unsuccessful competitor
said of him in an examination. It is not fanciful perhaps to
believe that his career at the Union was one of the factors
that enabled him to play this double rôle. He took his
Presidency very seriously—some might say, too seriously—
insisted on worthy and dignified motions for debate and also,
first as Librarian and afterwards as President, took great
interest in building up the Library. The Union in its new
premises had, of course, the chance to build up a far more
extensive Library than in the High Street days. It soon made
itself the best lending library in Oxford generally available to

undergraduates. The literary enriched it by their gifts. Robert Browning presented to it an autographed set of his poems and plays 'with respectful regards'.

The Union about now was also enriched by the series of cartoons, drawn by Sydney Hall, of Pembroke, afterwards to win a national reputation as an artist on the *Graphic* and elsewhere. The cartoons, all now hung in the Union's smoking room, are an interesting commentary on Oxford life of those days. Hall's main interest was perhaps in the professional literary, rather than the passing political, figures of Oxford. Goldwin Smith and Thorold Rogers were the two figures most constantly recurring in his sketches. Goldwin Smith, Professor of History and History Tutor to the Prince of Wales—the 'Oxford Professor' of Disraeli's *Lothair*—was a keen and liberal critic of all that was going on in the Oxford of his day. He criticised matters that to others might not have appeared central to Oxford life—launched a violent attack on the architecture of the Randolph Hotel which he considered 'out of scale'—in this respect comparing it to Exeter College Chapel, and attacked Jackson's elaborate decorations of the new Examinations School in the High as 'like chasing and gilding a treadmill'. He had always taken an interest in the Union's debates and had been one of the first to recognise John Coleridge's eloquence, but he had never himself been prominent there. He was, as he said, essentially 'unrhetorical'. Thorold Rogers was also an interesting and important figure in the Oxford and the England of that day. At a time when the general progressive assumption was that material conditions of life, bad as they might still be in some respects, had at any rate over the generations been steadily improving, Thorold Rogers by his statistical collection and collation of agricultural wages and prices at the various dates argued that the standard of the agricultural worker had been in steady decline from the Black Death to the repeal of the Corn Laws. He was a strong critic of the Oxford educational system of the day, saying that there had been no research in Oxford since the time of William III and the Professors and

University teaching ought to be strengthened at the expense of the Colleges. He was a ripe subject for an undergraduate satirist not so much for any of his careful statistical conclusions as because he was one of the first, in an age in which such a contention was still considered ridiculous, to argue that women should be admitted to sit in the University examinations. Another favourite figure for caricature was the then Bishop of Oxford, Soapy Sam Wilberforce, who had, of course, impinged on undergraduate life more than Bishops of Oxford usually do because of his famous duel with Huxley in the Museum. These Oxford figures jostled one another in Hall's drawings with the familiar figures of the day in the national public life—Derby, Disraeli, John Bright and the like. There was one man who predominantly belonged both to Oxford and to public life—and also to the Union— and that was Gladstone. In 1865 Gladstone was defeated for the University seat by Gathorne-Hardy and naturally the whole story of his rise and fall was matter for Hall's satire.

In 1866 certain Oxford men planned a magazine called the *Harlequin*. Hall with his illustrations and comments prophesied, all too justly, its difficulties, for it lasted only eight numbers. He decorated the cover with a somewhat confused 'Sketch by a young and ambitious draftsman to the Editors (unknown) of the Harlequin', with the severed head of Gladstone in the centre of the stage. In one of the numbers appeared a cartoon entitled the Spirit of the Age, showing Dr. Lightfoot, the Vice-Chancellor, armed with a cane entering a room in which 'some young gentlemen are amusing themselves in rather a significant manner'—that is, in writing a magazine with their backs invitingly presented to Dr. Lightfoot's cane. He was more interested perhaps in the poets. There was a cartoon, pretendedly drawn by Rossetti, of Swinburne. There is nothing of caricature about the actual figure of Swinburne, but the attached verses of parody are savage, not very witty and not very poetical.

Your beautiful Lady of Pain, o Swinburne, the love you adore is
A *leper*, a stench and a stain; for dead is the leper, Dolores,
The hut where you kiss her decay is the *Flesh* that shutteth
    out Heaven
Where foul things may be rotting away and the dead leaves
    of *Passion* are driven
Oh, kiss her cold corpus no more. Turn to *Nature* as drawn
    by Rossetti
And vote not old Wordsworth a bore, and own that the Sky-
    lark is pretty.

There was another controversy of poets which attracted
Hall's satire. In 1867 Matthew Arnold's term as Professor of
Poetry came to an end. It was suggested that Robert Browning should succeed him, but Browning, though he was a
little later in 1870 to be made an honorary Fellow of Balliol,
at the time lacked the statutory qualification of an Oxford
degree. The appointment therefore went to Sir Francis
Doyle, a man worthy enough but by all standards less truly
qualified and less distinguished than Browning. Hall's
cartoon shows Oxford, the Alma Mater, fussing over her
recognised sons, among whom Doyle and also Ruskin are
prominent, while Browning as an orphan lies outside un-
recognised. Another cartoon, in parody of the famous contest between Aeschylus and Euripides in Aristophanes'
Frogs, shows Burgon as Aeschylus and Ruskin as Euripides
pleading before Dionysus as Convocation for a Professor of
Poetry. It is not very clear from the cartoon which side Hall
is himself on. Aristophanes, it will be remembered greatly
preferred Aeschylus to Euripides and so far one would sur-
mise that by casting Burgon as Aeschylus Hall was intending
to imply that his claim was a good one. On the other hand,
though of the scales of the two contestants that of Burgon is
heavily down and that of Ruskin up, nevertheless in Ruskin's
scales there is a mountain of books and in Burgon's only a
piece of paper. I suppose that the moral is meant to be that
Ruskin had written a lot but that it was all rubbish while
Burgon had not written anything substantial.

Yet, as I say, the Oxford figure and the Union figure of
this period who dominated all was Gladstone, and it is
naturally to Gladstone's electoral defeat for the University
that Hall turns his main attention. There is one cartoon from
the election period, entitled Iconoclasm, and showing
Gathorne-Hardy, the rival candidate, attempting to fight
his way up the pedestal on which is the statue of Gladstone,
with the intention of casting it down. The other drawing
after Gladstone's defeat is the Gladstone Memorial—a bust
of Gladstone with Thorold Rogers and Dean Mansel as
symbolical mourners from Church and State joining hands
beneath it 'in memory of a man not dead except to Oxford'.

CHAPTER SIX

JUBILEE DAYS

TWO YEARS AFTER Bryce, in the Trinity term of 1864 Jeune
was President. He, if not intrinsically one of the most interesting of the Society's Presidents, is at least a witness in
the case as he has left a full account of his reminiscences and
opinions of his Union days. He was a dry man who was a
little fond of his dryness. It was he, as already recorded,
who dismissed the pre-Raphaelite frescoes as hideous. He
did not look on his time at the Union as a golden age. He
thought that the level of debate was higher both before and
after it. The Union in his day was, he said, dominated by
what he called 'liberals of the Goldwin Smith type'. To
annoy them and to make the running he declared himself a
Tory, but the most lively debates were those of Private
Business—in particular the controversy whether the Union
premises should be open on Sundays. Before becoming
President he was Treasurer, and the Treasurer according to
the rules as they then were—they were soon afterwards to
be amended—had a very free hand in carrying out structural
alterations in the Union premises. He took out the floor
between the two rooms so as to make the old reading room
an enormously lofty chamber. Critics said—and on the whole
justly—that by doing so he had spoiled the proportions of
the room. He was also the subject of a vote of censure for
having erected a vestibule of curtains at the entrance to the
debating hall, though it is not easy to see where in this case
he had been at fault, and the Society's grievance against
him cannot have been very deep as it afterwards elected
him President. Among the Presidents of the next years there

are a number of interesting names—Courtenay Ilbert, afterwards Clerk of the House of Commons, Sanday, later Lady Margaret Professor of Divinity and Strachan-Davidson who became Master of Balliol. Then in 1868 the Union suffered a curious hat trick. Its three Presidents were all destined to be distinguished Bishops. Copleston of Calcutta, Talbot of Winchester and Creighton of London.

Talbot served two terms as President—the one in 1866 and the second in 1868. He was succeeded after his second term by Mandell Creighton, and Creighton too has left us his reminiscences of his term of office. They are particularly interesting as throwing an unexpected light on what the Presidency then was. For, as Creighton tells us, he took no interest at all in the Union's debating and had never spoken in a debate. His interest was only in the Library. He had served on the Library Committee and then for a year as Librarian, where he had worked hard at making a new catalogue. When Talbot came and asked him to take on the Presidency he agreed somewhat reluctantly—and said that, if he were to become President, it was only decent that he should make one qualifying speech in a debate. This he did with even greater reluctance for he was one, as he himself put it who 'never felt any good came of talking for talking's sake'. He was, as he candidly confessed, a very bad President, as he only sat through Private Business and could not be bothered to remain for the public debate, handing over the chair to a deputy.

He was succeeded by an Irishman called Redington, afterwards Commissioner of National Education in Ireland. He, too, has left us his reminiscences. He recalls as one of the debates that had stuck most vividly in his mind that on the restoration of monasticism. The speeches of that debate that he especially recalled were those of Addis of Balliol and of Shee, the Treasurer from Ireland, but the most lively debates to him were those in Private Business on the pre-Raphaelite frescoes. He was, as he records, an exception in that his election was contested.

H

In spite of the growing secularisation of the national life and in spite of the rule against theological motions the keenest and most exciting debates were usually about the disestablishment of the Church of England. Today the subject of disestablishment arouses only very torpid interest whether among its advocates or its opponents, but in the last half of the last century it was the first item in most radical programmes and the cry of 'the Church in danger' was the rallying call of all good Conservatives.

The fullest picture of the Union, as it then was, was given by Herbert James, the President of St. John's, in a paper to the St. John's Essay Society in 1923. James was President in the Trinity term of 1871. 'The Union buildings,' he records 'were far more primitive than now; there was no such thing as afternoon tea to be had on the premises, for indeed afternoon tea did not exist as an institution.' But, if we are to judge from a satirical poem by Germaine Lavis, written as long before as 1857, Bennet, the Treasurer, had introduced 'Coffee and Conversation' into the Lower Writing Room. The debates, James tells us, were held in what is now the Library, the President's chair being at the east end of the room. There was then only one speaker on what would today be called 'the paper', who was the member who had suggested the debate. The suggestion was made in writing in a suggestion box. He who suggested a motion had to move it himself. Only those who remained to the close of a debate could vote—which means incidentally that the division figures give a very imperfect notion of the attendance. As has been said, contest for either the Committee or the offices was rare.

The majority of members, James recorded, were Conservative, but the majority of prominent speakers were Liberals. Officers were not elected on any party basis. Indeed, James records that when an unworthy Conservative put up for President he was defeated. Campbell McKinnon of Queens, the defeated candidate, appears to have been something of a P. G. Wodehouse character and Dr. Merry, afterwards the Rector of Lincoln, in reporting on a debate at which he spoke wrote, 'Then there arose an eyeglass with a man at a convenient distance behind it.' James gave Lyulph Stanley the prize for 'absolute eloquence' in his day. Lyulph Stanley, a Balliol freshman of 1857, afterwards Lord Stanley of Alderley, made his name with a great speech in favour of the North—the unpopular side at the Union—in the American Civil War and also delivered a speech that was much praised against the curious motion: 'That the use of euphemisms, in as much as they tend to conceal the depravity of vice, is prejudicial to morality.'

As to the debates in general James records that, contrary to the custom of 1923 and still more of recent years, they never invited distinguished strangers. The greater number of motions were political but other topics were discussed perhaps in a greater variety than in more recent years. There were debates on the public school system—on classical education—on the proctorial system in the University—on the poetry of Tennyson and the novels of George Eliot. Capital punishment was debated three times between 1863 and 1873. All these motions might well be found today, but there was at that time a question whether the Great Western Railway should set up at Oxford the works which it did in fact set up at Swindon. To this proposal the Union was opposed by eighty-five votes to nine. There were other motions which one would hardly expect to find today. 'That the habitual use of strong terms is unworthy of an Englishman.' 'That the disadvantages of novel reading on the whole over-balance its advantages.' There were debates on spirit rapping and clairvoyance—on the abolition of oaths in courts of law. (Bradlaugh's claim to affirm rather than take an oath was to come up before many years had passed.) James records some of the Union jokes of his time. Most of them, though pleasant enough, are perhaps hardly worth recalling, but one should be rescued. The debate was on the perennial topic of the pre-Raphaelite frescoes. One of the Union's 'funny men' caught the President's eye. 'When I saw,' he said, 'the subject announced for debate, as I knew nothing whatever about it, I searched all the dictionaries in the Library for some notice of the great Pre-Raphael himself, but would you believe it, sir? without success. However I was informed that if I went to a certain gallery in London, I should see a specimen of this form of art. Sir, I went; I edged my way through a reeking crowd and found myself face to face with a most disreputable looking goat.' The picture was of course Holman Hunt's 'Scapegoat'. I recall this anecdote from oblivion not because it is exceptionally witty but because the speech is exactly the sort of speech that a funny man would have made at the Union in my day or that he would have made today. If I have heard it once I have heard it a dozen times. It shows that undergraduate humour does not change so much over a hundred years.

In those days there was no bar to graduates—even those who had graduated some years before—becoming officers at the Union and indeed several held office not only, as they often do today, a term or two after they have taken their degrees, but when they were already Fellows of Colleges and some held the Presidency twice—sometimes at an interval of some years. We have given the example of Bishop Talbot. James himself had come up to Oxford from a country grammar school and with an inadequate grounding in Classics. He was ambitious and therefore all through his first years at Oxford stuck very close to his books and did not allow himself time to go to the Union. He only made his maiden speech after he had taken his degree. Grose of Queen's, afterwards the Registrar of the University, was President in the Hilary term of 1871. Much to James's surprise Grose asked if he might nominate him as his successor, and he was elected without opposition for the next term.

The Union, as has been recorded, claimed continuity from the United Debating Society, and thus advertised 1823 as the year of its birth, 1873 was therefore its Jubilee and it was natural that it should be celebrated. There was then as the rising star at the Union, young Asquith from the City of London School and Balliol. He had been Treasurer for a year in 1872 and it might have seemed natural that when that term was completed, he should succeed to the Presidency. However, he was a little too aggressively Liberal, a little too aggressively Balliol for the Union's tastes, and Ashmead-Bartlett of Christ Church, a good safe Conservative, stood against him and defeated him at his first contest. There were at that time no definite rules against canvassing and Ashmead-Bartlett gave lavish breakfast parties, which the impecunious Asquith could not rival and which were designed to influence, and probably did influence, votes. So Asquith had to wait another year for his Presidency. But, unrepentant in his contempt for the Establishment, he took during Ashmead-Bartlett's Presidency a very prominent part in a debate on the disestablishment of the Church of England in which he spoke in favour of disestablishment. Yet, though not President, Asquith was secretary of the Special Committee for the Jubilee celebrations and had probably a larger part in those arrangements than anybody. By the time that the Jubilee banquet took place in October 1873 the President was Robert Mowbray, afterwards a Lancashire Member of Parliament, the son of a President of 1836, who was at the time of the Jubilee one of the Members for the University.

The Jubilee banquet, for all the advertisement of it, was not an unmixed success. In 1873 Gladstone was still in the fifth year of his first premiership but the popularity of his Government was low. It was in the next year to be dismissed from office and political life was bitter both at Oxford and elsewhere. Whether because he was afraid of the reception that he would get, whether he was offended because both the Conservative Members for the University, Mowbray and Gathorne-Hardy, who had unseated him, were invited to speak was not apparent, but Gladstone, the Union's most distinguished member, did not come to the banquet. Nor did the Prince of Wales, nor did Prince Leopold, who was

also a member. Yet even without them there was a formidable high table and formidable toast list, but the trouble
was that there were too many speeches and some of them
went on far too long. The result was that the company did
not rise from the table till half past one in the morning.
This would have been bad enough in any event. What made
it worse was that, while the orators showed no signs of breaking down, the caterers broke down completely. Poor Dr.
Hayman wished that it had been the other way round and,
when he got back to St. John's where he was staying at
around two o'clock in the morning, was compelled to beg a
biscuit with which to fill his stomach.

The list of speakers was impressive. If Gladstone did not
come, no more did Lowe, then his Chancellor of the Exchequer, but Lord Selborne, the Lord Chancellor, who had
been Roundell Palmer at the time of the Rambler controversy thirty years before was there. So was Cardwell, who
had been Lowe's opponent in that controversy and was now
his colleague as Secretary for War. Goschen, First Lord of
the Admiralty was there. So was Sir John Coleridge, the
Attorney General. The Opposition was represented by
Lord Salisbury, then Chancellor of the University. The
Church of England was represented by Tait, the Archbishop
of Canterbury, and Durnford the Bishop of Chichester, the
Roman Catholic Church by Cardinal Manning, who received
in general an enthusiastic welcome, marred only by the
vociferous protest of one angry cleric, Professor Heurtley,
who objected that a Roman Catholic bishop should be seated
at the table above two bishops of the Church of England.
Matthew Arnold spoke for poetry and Acland for medicine.

The speeches have been published and they make interesting but not very entertaining reading. The Victorians off
parade were not perhaps so very different from ourselves.
On parade they were totally different. On parade they
thought it necessary to preserve their dignity to an extent
that is not today in fashion, and at the Union Jubilee banquet
they were emphatically on parade. The speeches read to us

as portentous, pompous, platitudinous, the humour laboured and elephantine. There hangs about them a kind of feeling that it would be almost indecent to say anything interesting. Truth as such in a formal oration is in bad taste. One wonders how even a Victorian audience could have borne to sit through an evening of Victorian oratory. It is only in the speech of the Lord Chancellor, Lord Selborne, that the evening at all came to life. Lord Selborne spoke of the foolish motions that were proposed in his day. He spoke of a motion: 'That the whole funds of the Society at present in the hands of the Treasurer, be subscribed to promote the election of anti-reform Members of Parliament and that any deficiency that may accrue in consequence be made up by extraordinary subscriptions from the members generally.' Lord Selborne, of course then a Liberal, spoke of the 'outrageous motion' which was indeed proposed by a member called Palmer— his own name—but not, he assured the company by himself but by 'a namesake of mine—a near relation—belonging to a different College—who, I am sorry to say, was not always sensible of the duty of seriousness in the speeches and motions which he made in this Society.' It was tolerable after-dinner stuff, but in his reminiscences Lord Selborne trod on dangerous ground. 'In those days to which many of my generation look back,' he said, 'there was one pre-eminent above all—a man who even then seemed to promise to be equal to the greatest men who ever adorned the senate with their eloquence—a man not behind Pitt or Canning—and that man was Mr. Gladstone.' This was too much for some Tory hearers and there were groans, ironical cheers and expressions of disgust. Lord Selborne covered himself. 'If there are any to whom my remarks are not acceptable, I hope they will remember,' he said, 'I am speaking not of Mr. Gladstone's opinions but of his elo-quence,' and they let that go.

The debate the next night to which Mowbray, the Presi-dent, had invited all the banqueters, was on the somewhat curious motion, 'That the restoration of the Empire would

form the best guarantee for the future prosperity of France.'
Mowbray's father took the chair. The Empire had fallen
at Sedan three years before. Napoleon III was dead. It
was still a very open question whether France would turn
to a republic or to a monarchy, and, if to a monarchy, to
which monarch. The chances of a Napoleonic restoration
under the Prince Imperial were not great. Still it has always
been the métier of the Union to debate subjects of pure
theory without considering whether what they advocated
as desirable had any great chance of happening.

Asquith in the Trinity term of 1874 avenged his first defeat
and held the Presidency. He was of course the third of the
Union's Prime Ministers. Asquith was a Balliol man, almost
the ideal of Jowett's pupils, a young man obviously pre-
destined to success and determined to succeed. He came to
Oxford in order to obtain the qualifications for success.
He was a brilliant classical scholar and his primary task at
Oxford as he saw it, was to obtain Firsts in his Schools.
Next to success in Schools the most important prize which
Oxford had to offer was the Presidency of the Union. He
was not interested in games. His only recreation was an
occasional walk. The social pleasures which in later life
came to mean so much to him had little appeal to the impecunious undergraduate. It was enough for him as President of the Union that he introduced afternoon tea and
lifted the ban on smoking in the Society's premises. He had
little sense of the Union as a place of knockabout fun. He
planned his career there as a campaign. He was careful
not to speak very often. When he did speak, he spoke with
meticulous preparation. His maiden speech was in favour
of the removal of bishops from the House of Lords. He
followed it up, less characteristically, with a speech in favour
of conscription. He was of course of Liberal and Nonconformist origins and of an ambience very different from
that of the average Union member. He understood very
well that this was an immediate handicap to him and indeed
he paid a certain penalty for it in defeat at his first candidacy.

Oxford often does not take very kindly to 'effortless superiority'—particularly when it is on the other side—or to scholarship used too obviously for a purpose. Yet undergraduates are on the whole fair-minded and they gave Asquith his due in the end.

In the next year, 1875, one of the Presidents was Sloman, interesting in the Union's history because as Canon Sloman he was afterwards to be Headmaster of Birkenhead School, where he presided over the first oratorical escapades of the young F. E. Smith. In the year after that the Presidency came to another Balliol man, only less famous than Asquith—to the future Lord Milner. Milner, ex-President, went out to be private secretary to ex-President Goschen, just as some years later ex-President Buchan was to become one of Milner's young men in South Africa.

As has been said, the debating hall in those days was the present Library. In the centre of that room, as frequenters of the Union know, are two fireplaces back to back. They are covered by a slab of marble and the fireplaces by an ingenious arrangement of flues beneath the floor consume their own smoke. Members used to gather round these fireplaces when the debates were popular. It was a homely and animated scene, but the trouble was that the room with the fireplaces taking up all the centre of it was not nearly big enough for its purpose, and, as the Library grew under the rule of energetic Librarians who according to the custom of those years held office for a year—Courtenay Ilbert, to be Clerk of the House of Commons, Caird and Strachan-Davidson, to be successive Masters of Balliol—Mandell Creighton and others—more room was needed for books. The fading of the Rossetti frescoes made the old debating hall a somewhat depressing place. So, what with one thing and another it was obvious by the 1870s that there was nothing for it but to turn the old hall into the Library and to build a new debating hall. This was done. Waterhouse, who had designed the new Hall at Balliol in a style which Jowett thought 'really beautiful' but which Ruskin, expressing a more general opinion, described as 'a dull sort of a church' was employed as architect. There were plenty of undergraduates from other Colleges at that time, as indeed at other times, who complained that Balliol had altogether too dominating an influence at the Union. It was bad enough, it was argued, that Balliol should to so inordinate an extent provide the Union with its Presidents. It was the last straw if it was going to provide it with its architecture, and indeed the new debating hall—the present hall—did and does have a look somewhat depressingly like something out of Balliol. Its foundation stone was laid on May 8, 1878, by Stafford Northcote, at that time Chancellor of the Exchequer. Germaine of Brasenose, who was a strong Tory, was then the President and, just as at the time of the Jubilee in 1873 when the Liberals were in power there had been some criticism of Lord Selborne's praise of Gladstone as unseasonable Liberal propaganda, so now, the year of the Congress of Berlin and 'peace with honour' there were those who complained that Tory politicians were unduly prominent at the ceremony. There was not much force in the complaint. By the time that the hall was opened a year later the President was Edward Cook, a good Liberal, afterwards to be for many years editor of the *Westminster Gazette* and the *Daily News* and to be the collator of the works of Ruskin.

Yet it is true that politics were in these years growing more bitter and more intolerantly Conservative. Ireland was the cause. Irishmen who came to Oxford were predominantly of landlord and Unionist origins. They were naturally bitter against Gladstone for what they thought of as his surrender of landlords' rights to the demands of murder and were to become more bitter still when a few years later he was to make what to their minds was the yet more abject surrender of espousing Home Rule. Home Rule was to cause a large proportion of the Liberals of means to change their party— among them several of the most distinguished of the past members of the Union such as Selborne and Goschen—and to leave the Liberals at the Union a small minority, by no means regarded with the kindly tolerance of eccentricity, with which they had been regarded when party divisions were less keen, but sometimes looked on and treated as little better than traitors.

In the Michaelmas term of 1880 the Union elected another remarkable President, the 'superior purzon' of Oxford days, destined to fill almost all the high positions of state save only the highest—and among them that of Chancellor of the University, to which he brought the conscientious energy that he brought to all his tasks. It was Curzon's misfortune that with all his great qualities and in spite indeed of a considerable verbal wit, yet his lack of humour caused him always to be a slightly comic figure. He was laughed at by others because he never learnt to laugh at himself. He had an insensitiveness to the feelings of others—particularly of those of a different social origin to himself. Thus it was characteristic of him that as Chancellor he should prepare a most able and conscientious Memorandum on the Principles and Methods of University Reform, taking over it a great deal more trouble than most Chancellors would have taken and showing himself sympathetically alive to the need to make a University education available to a wider section of the population. It was also characteristic of him that he should have thought it a satisfactory solution to the problem to provide a special College devoted exclusively to poor undergraduates. The formality of Curzon's demeanour was not, of course, as remarkable then as it would be today. It was a more pompous age. Charles Oman, who was Librarian in 1883 and who was responsible for the Union's first subject catalogue, has given us in his *Memoirs of Victorian Oxford* a good portrait of undergraduates as they were at that date—with their black coats, top hats, fancy waistcoats, brilliant neckties and mutton-chop whiskers. One could see, he records, as many as seventy top hats outside on the pegs when a debate was going on at the Union.

Though the Society in the early 1880s was predominantly Conservative, it was not so unfair as to refuse to elect a

Liberal—or at least a man of liberal mind—when he was the obviously deserving candidate. Michael Sadler was President in the Michaelmas term of 1882. Young ex-officers at that time were prominent in giving lectures up and down the country on behalf of the new University Extension movement. Sadler was its secretary. Shaw and Mackinder who succeeded him as Presidents of the Union became also Extension lecturers. Asquith had shown them the way some years before as Lecturer for the London Society. Gordon Lang was among those who lectured a few years later and he was elected President in the Michaelmas term of 1884.

Gordon Lang, the future Archbishop of Canterbury, then a young Glaswegian on the make with mind bent on a legal and a political rather than on an ecclesiastical career made the most mark of any at that time. His maiden speech was against the disestablishment of the Church of Scotland, to which he then belonged. 'It seems probable,' recorded the *Oxford Magazine*, 'that at last the Union Society may congratulate itself upon the possession of an orator who is something more than a mere debater. The young gentleman who opposed the motion last Thursday in favour of the disestablishment of the Scottish Church spoke with such fire and intensity of conviction that the House was fairly carried away and accorded him a hearty ovation which was thoroughly deserved. It is the general opinion that no more eloquent speech has been heard in the Union during the last three years.' Other speeches followed. Lang was the Conservative leader against Anthony Hope Hawkins for the Liberals. 'I can see him now,' wrote his friend, Tupper-Carey, at one time Secretary of the Union, 'standing at the table with his chest thrown out, his head thrown back, pouring out a torrent of words to the assembled undergraduates. I was enthralled. I had never heard anything like it in my life.' Such was his dominance that, when his time came, he was elected to the Presidency unopposed, even though by that time a general habit of opposing elections had grown up.

F. H. Coller of Christ Church, afterwards Chief Justice of

St. Lucia, was President in the Trinity term of 1890 and it is
his reminiscences, given to Herbert Morrah, which are the
best authority for the Union of that time. The Oxford of
the eighties was, he says, a strongly Conservative place—so
much so that it was difficult to get good speeches to sustain
the Liberal side in debates. On the other hand political
interest was not strong. The two Conservative clubs were,
as he puts it, 'affected with sleeping sickness'. Therefore in
order to revive political interests, a new more strongly
Conservative club, the Strafford, was formed. It took its
politics more seriously than the other two. Its name was
symptomatic. Lord Salisbury was soon to offer 'twenty years
of resolute Government' as the alternative to Gladstone's
Irish policy of Home Rule, and it was the Irish issue which in
the 1880s roused the passions of English politics.

The Strafford Club brought a new and not very healthy
element into Union politics. Up till then the Union had
prided itself—and on the whole with justification—on electing its officers on their merits rather than on their politics.
The majority of members might be Conservative and vote
Conservative in debates, but they did not think that the
Union was the place for political organisation. The Strafford changed all that. They frankly organised themselves to
carry elections at the Union. Of the six Union Presidents between Michaelmas, 1888, and Trinity, 1890, Coller records
that four were members of the Strafford Club, elected largely
by their fellow members. Relying on their majority, they
tended to harry and ridicule the few Liberals. Doubtless
some of the jokes that they made against them were mediocre.
At least one good crack in a typical Union style has survived.
Mortimer, afterwards Recorder of Rotherham, was Librarian for two terms and then President in the Michaelmas
term of 1889. He was attacking the Liberals for their opposition to the House of Lords and ridiculing them for their
internal divisions. 'The Liberals,' he said, 'might blow their
trumpets, but the walls of the House of Lords would not
fall down. For that purpose there should be more accord

in the playing and each man should not blow his own trumpet.'

This was the decade when in national politics Chamberlain on the radical side and Gorst on the Conservative were importing American ideas and giving their parties much more definite organisational machines than had prevously been thought necessary or desirable. It was also a decade in which there was more contact between undergraduates and the general life of the nation than heretofore. The railway made travel between London and Oxford a great deal more rapid than it had ever been before or was ever to be again, and politicians who could easily pop down from London began to court the bright young undergraduates. In such a situation it was natural enough that the undergraduates anxious to ape their elders and to play at being grown up politicians, should give themselves formal organisations on the adult model, and natural enough too that the masters of the machine in London should encourage the formation of a machine in Oxford. Whether it was a good thing is another matter. There is a great deal to be said for undergraduates being taught and encouraged to air their political opinions but doing so irresponsibly. The time for commitment, the time when it is reasonable to allow oneself to be captured by a machine or to sign on a dotted line, comes later in life. Yet so important did the Conservative machine think the Strafford Club that, when owing to the collapse of the case of *The Times* against Parnell over the Pigott forgery, Sir Richard Webster, the Attorney General, wished to make a vindicating speech in defence of the part that the Government had played in that affair, it was a dinner of the Strafford Club that he chose as the platform for his exculpation.

On February 22 and February 29, 1888, what was then an entirely new experiment in the Union's history was tried. McGregor of Oriel, afterwards a South African judge, was President. He invited two politicians from London— Lord Randolph Churchill and John Morley—to come down and take part in a debate on Home Rule for Ireland. The two speakers did not confront one another. They spoke on different nights. Morley, as has been said, had, when an undergraduate, played a modest part, though he had never held office, in the Union debates. Randolph Churchill had been for a short time a member of the Union but had been expelled for not paying his subscription. This was discovered by the undergraduates and gave an opportunity for a certain amount of good humoured ribaldry in Private Business. The debate in itself passed off without great incident. The young Gilbert Murray was one of the undergraduate speakers who supported Home Rule. But there were many who argued that the whole point of the Union was to provide a forum where undergraduates could learn to speak and could exercise their wits at one another's expense. Its very *raison d'être* would be destroyed if it was to become a platform for London orators. As *The Times* wrote in a leading article, 'Both these statesmen were once members of the Union, but their coming down to make set speeches is a novelty in the history of the Society. The only fear is lest the Society should be tempted to repeat the indulgence too often; which, it need hardly be said, would be unfortunate from every point of view.'

Oxford politics certainly suffered from this improper use of it as a kind of prologue to national politics. English people in general were well alive to the horrors of student politicians, so familiar in many other countries, marching in procession through the streets and bringing pressure to bear on Governments. They did not wish such a phenomenon imported into English life, and the result of the courting of Oxford by the Conservative party machine was indeed that the Strafford Club became very largely the master of the Union but that the Union itself declined disastrously in prestige. In June, 1886, when a new Lord Robert Cecil, Lord Cecil of Chelwood was President, Gordon Lang, the President of the year before, brought forward a motion that the position of the Society was unsatisfactory and carried it by 154 votes to 32.

Professor Freeman, returning to Oxford after an absence of forty years, complained bitterly in the *Contemporary Review* in 1887, of the time that modern undergraduates wasted on pursuits extraneous to their main task of reading for their Schools, 'the direct glorification of idleness, the amazing importance attached to mere amusements'. The only thing to his mind worse than the Union was the O.U.D.S. 'the portentous rage for play acting', encouraged, it seemed, to Freeman's horror and amazement by the Vice-Chancellor, Dr. Jowett himself. Even among the most conservative and most politically minded of undergraduates a number, though they attended regularly at the Union, refused to stand for office. Lord Hugh Cecil is a case in point. He refused on the somewhat quixotic ground that, since he was a Cecil and since both his father and his brother had been Presidents, he, if elected, would have been elected on the merits of his family rather than of himself. We can be sure that, had he really wished to have been elected, he would hardly have been deterred by such a scruple.

Even though Oxford had repudiated him and though a great majority of members were strongly opposed to his politics, the Union in a day of great bitterness had still the grace to remember that Gladstone was incomparably its most distinguished member. The new precedent of visiting speakers had set the Society a difficult problem. If anyone was to be invited to come down from London, Gladstone had certainly the first claim on such an invitation. On the other hand, if he came and spoke to a political motion, the House would certainly have voted against him. Therefore the happy notion was formed of inviting him to come, not to take part in a debate, but to deliver a non-political address. He chose Homer as his subject, as indeed he not infrequently did, and came down, escorted by Mrs. Gladstone in February 1890. Peel, afterwards M.P. for Spalding, was President and introduced him in an appropriate speech. Gladstone addressed his audience as 'gentlemen and friends!' He delivered an erudite lecture on the thesis that Homer was acquainted with the Babylonian religion, on which, it is safe to say, that the greater part of his audience did not know whether he was or whether he was not. Yet at least young men on the threshold of their careers and tempted to dismiss academic learning as a waste of time, must have been impressed by the intense survival of the passion for it in one who had attained the summit of practical success. At the end Archdeacon Palmer, the Archdeacon of Oxford and one of the Trustees of the Union, in a vote of thanks, referred to Gladstone as 'a characteristic Oxford man'. It is not very clear what the phrase can have been meant to mean, if indeed it was designed to have any meaning at all. The Archdeacon can hardly have thought that most Oxford men were like Gladstone. In reply Gladstone said, 'To call a man a characteristic Oxford man is to pay him the highest compliment that can be paid to a human being'—again an extravagance that can hardly have pretended to any serious meaning. Gladstone could not accept this, but, he said, 'there is not a man who has passed through this great and famous University that can say with more truth than I can say that I love her, I love her, I love her from the bottom of my heart.' He commented afterwards with disapproval on the informality of dress of the young men in contrast to the top hats of his own day. There was not, he said, one member there present who 'could not have been dressed for ten pounds'.

By the Hilary term of 1890 the Society had so sunk in general estimation that its financial situation was truly serious. Grose, the Registrar of the University, who had been President immediately before James of St. John's in 1871, was persuaded in 1888 to take on the newly created post of Senior Treasurer, It was thought desirable to supplement the ephemeral undergraduate Junior Treasurer by a mature Senior Treasurer, a man of financial experience, who would remain in office for a term of years. In 1890 William Gill, whom many still remember well, was appointed Steward. Grose made it his first business to go over to Cambridge and see how the more nearly solvent Union there was conducting

I

its business. It was Grose's belief that money could only be raised if money was spent. The rooms had been allowed to get shabby. Grose got leave to spend £1,000 on a new smoking room and to issue an appeal by the Oxford Union Decoration Fund to raise the money. The appeal was successful. The Queen, the Prince of Wales, Lord Salisbury, who was not only a past officer but also at the time both Chancellor of the University and Prime Minister, and many other notable people subscribed. The subscription substantially exceeded the cost of the smoking room and the balance was spent on various other works of redecoration. The occasion was taken to get articles on, and pictures of, the Union into most of the leading London papers.

As far as undergraduates went, most of the work on the appeal had been done by two Trinity men, Knaus and Ripley, and they were rewarded for their hard work by being elected President and Junior Treasurer for the Michaelmas term of 1890. But they were also both Conservatives and members of the Strafford Club, and there were those who thought that the Union was now in as grave a danger from a domination by Trinity as it had been some years before from a domination by Balliol. The Liberals decided that, if the Conservatives organised themselves in the Strafford Club, the Liberals must organise themselves through the Russell. By tremendous efforts they succeeded in electing a New College President, Cozens-Hardy, a Liberal.

When Cozens-Hardy's term was up, the Conservatives put up Magee of Merton as their candidate. Magee, the son of the turbulent Archbishop who would sooner see England free than England sober, 'the bijou Boanerges' as he was called, was an uncompromising Unionist in politics, who lived for the Union. He had a long Union career which extended from 1887 up till 1892 and devoted it to a fanatical defence of the Church of England and the Union of Great Britain and Ireland. His first speech was made in 1887 under the Presidency of Godfrey of Exeter in opposition to the lawfulness of suicide. He defended capitalism against the

criticisms of Gilbert Murray, but his main efforts were de-
voted to the defence of the Established Church, whether of
England or Wales, Ireland having by then to his regret lost
her establishment. In this he had the support of a doughty
Church-and-State phalanx, consisting of Arthur Griffith
Boscawen, of Lord Hugh Cecil, and a little more surprisingly
in view of his later Socialist development, of A. J. Carlyle
of Exeter. New College ran against Magee not another
Liberal but Lord Ampthill, a very popular President of the
Oxford University Boat Club, and succeeded in carrying
him to victory. Then after Ampthill, Ripley, having served
his year as Senior Treasurer, determined to stand for the
Presidency and break the New College dynasty. It was the
most bitter and hard-fought election in the Union's history.
Canvassing was rife and unashamed and after the declara-
tion a formal inquiry under the chairmanship of Charles
(afterwards Sir Charles) Oman, who had been Librarian
in 1883 and was now a young Don, was set up. It found the
accusations against the New College men proved and
awarded the Presidency to Ripley. Magee who had been
Ampthill's opponent had his turn after Ripley.

CHAPTER SEVEN

YEARS BEFORE WAR

WHEREAS A SENIOR TREASURER was appointed in 1888 there was no definitive office of Senior Librarian until 1907. However, senior members of the University interested themselves in the Society's library and York Powell, who succeeded Froude as Professor of History in 1894, in fact performed for the Society many of the functions of a Senior Librarian. He was much assisted by that improbable Fellow of Brasenose, Walter Pater, who can hardly have found in the Union an atmosphere sufficiently exquisite for his needs but was attracted to its Library by the twin facts that it was adorned by pre-Raphaelite paintings and that the paintings had deliciously perished.

As a result, many of the Union's most lively controversies of those days turned on what books should and should not be admitted into the Library. The Library's taste in earlier years had been staid. Ouida and Rhoda Broughton had been rejected, but by the '90s more daring views were being aired. There was a great fight whether the works of Zola should be purchased. The motion was defeated on the somewhat disingenuous plea that it was not the business of the Library to keep up to date with French literature, and then by a typically Oxford compromise, while the proposal to buy the works *en bloc* was rejected, they were afterwards purchased one by one over the weeks without exciting remark or debate. The incident was of interest because it brought a characteristic intervention from Hilaire Belloc, who was always ready to show himself an Englishman before Frenchmen and a Frenchman before Englishmen and to

lecture the English on their appalling insularity and ignorance of the culture of Europe.

If the Union, which at the beginning of the decade of the
1890s was in a sad way, revived during the decade so that
some consider the next years to be its golden age, it was
undoubtedly due to some extent to Grose's competent financial management, to some extent to a revision of the rules
which definitely forebade and, for the moment at any rate,
put a stop to, canvassing and thus made less scandalous the
conduct of elections. But these after all were but reforms of
the infrastructure. What the Union needed for its revival
was the infusion of some remarkable personalities, and the
Union of the first half of the 1890s was undoubtedly above
all the creature of three very remarkable personalities—
F. E. Smith, Hilaire Belloc and John Simon. Nothing in
such a Society as the Union succeeds like success. When
its reputation is low, able men shun its debates. When its
reputation is high, even the second-class go to it, looking to
shine in the reflected glory of the first-class. As late as
October 1892 the Union was still discussing Morrah's
motion, 'That the Society views its present position with
regret and its future with apprehension,' and in 1893 party
bitterness had grown so strong that a Conservative member
was unmannerly enough to call Gladstone 'that garrulous
old mountebank'. There were other men at the Union in
those years who played both at the Union and in after years
parts of distinction. Lord Beauchamp, to be a Liberal
Minister up till his resignation at the outbreak of the
First World War, was President in the Trinity term of 1893.
Lord Crawford, then Lord Balcarres, was President in the
Hilary term of 1894. Phillimore, afterwards to be the famous
wit and Professor of Humanity and Greek at Glasgow, was
President in the Michaelmas term of 1895. Phillimore pre-
ceded Simon in the chair. Simon was succeeded by Boyd-
Carpenter, son of the Bishop of Ripon, father of the present
Conservative statesman and himself to hold office in Con-
servative administrations. Boyd-Carpenter was succeeded

by F. W. Hirst, the well-known Liberal and pacifist economist.

There were others who played their parts in the Union and were little heard of afterwards. There was von Zedlitz of Trinity, a German and a Protestant, who assumed the rôle of a licensed jester and was something of a foil to the French Catholic Belloc. Von Zedlitz declaimed against the suggested erection of a statue in Oxford to Cardinal Newman. He obtained a ruling that questions could be put to the officers in relation to the discharge of their official duties from any part of the debating hall and then catechised the President from a position in the gallery behind the clock. Morrah in his *History of the Union* strangely speaks of von Zedlitz' subsequent career as a mystery and speculates facetiously about him as driving a taxi or counting paper marks in his native Germany. He in fact went to New Zealand and there enjoyed a long and respectable career as a University professor. There was Claude Eliot, President in 1892 and to be known in later years throughout North London as 'the smiling parson'. But the Union of the early 1890s was predominantly the Union of Smith, Belloc and Simon.

First of the trio in time was F. E. Smith, later to become the famous Lord Birkenhead. A young man from Birkenhead with no advantage of family, the son of an army sergeant, he came up with a scholarship to Wadham. It was a time when those who accepted the position in life into which they were born were often Conservatives, but when the unprivileged, who wished to make a stir in the world, tended to resent the monopolisation of the posts of power by those with advantages of birth and to take the radical side. Smith was an exception to this general rule. In the atmosphere of Liverpool people tended to take their political side from their religion. Smith was hardly an ecclesiastical politician of the type of Magee or Boyd-Carpenter or Lord Hugh Cecil, and indeed his plea that he was shocked by the Welsh Disestablishment Bill was in later years to call forth G. K.

Chesterton's most famous satirical poem of *Chuck it, Smith*. Yet he was a Protestant who later was to throw himself with vigour into the Orange cause and only towards the end of his career to be convinced by circumstances of the necessity of Irish freedom. At the Union he was a strong Conservative, the superior in talent as he was the inferior in rank of the other Conservative undergraduates of his time. His maiden speech which was a brilliant success was against Local Option—the scheme by which the inhabitants of each locality should be allowed to decide by poll whether they wished to have licensed premises within their locality. Local Option was supported by Sir Wilfrid Lawson, the famous teetotal orator of those days. In a scintillating peroration Smith rebuked Sir Wilfrid, who in teetotal fanaticism had recently poured away the whole contents of a magnificent cellar, and announced that, on account of this barbarity, when in a future life he, Smith, was 'lolling in Abraham's bosom', he would not grant Sir Wilfrid the drop of cold water for which he would doubtless beg. The *Isis* said of this speech, 'The speech of the evening, with all respect to our guest, was the amazingly vivacious and brilliant performance of F. E. Smith, the Wadham freshman.'

He played hard, lived hard, worked hard and prided himself on defying rules and conventions with a certain carefree insolence. There was a rule against taking dogs onto the Union premises, but Smith, who was fond of dogs, took pains to defy it. To his extraordinary readiness of wit and vigour of oratory and what Garvin in an obituary notice was to call his 'Sheridanesque quality of concocted impromptu', he added, if we can trust the records, a certain indifference whether his arguments had a real validity or not. Simon has given a full account of the debate which won Smith the Presidency. Simon, a slightly younger man and not at that time a member, listened to it from the gallery. The debate was on the motion that the House 'would welcome any scheme for associating undergraduates with the government of the University'. It is interesting that such a motion should have

been debated and should indeed have been thought worthy
of a place as the motion of the presidential debate. The
notion that it is only in recent years that the Union has
interested itself in Oxford politics and in undergraduate
claims to self-government is quite false. Such ideas, little
as may have come of them, have been in the air for a century.

In this debate Smith was opposed by Belloc. Belloc spoke
first and argued that undergraduates at Oxford should be
given the freedom of undergraduates at Continental universities, about which Belloc knew or professed to know more
than the ordinary Oxford undergraduate. He was always
ready to twit English complacency by maintaining, contrary
to the general English opinion of that day, that things were
very much better done on the Continent—and particularly in
France. Smith in reply took the strict wording of the motion,
pointed out to the House that, if they passed the motion,
they were committed to the support of any scheme of University reform, produced an absurd scheme of his own and tore
it to pieces. Simon reports that the performance was both
very brilliant and very amusing and doubtless so it was, but
it was, I think, characteristic of Smith as an undergraduate
that he should have preferred to slide off on this verbal point
rather than address himself to the more serious issue whether
a scheme of undergraduate self-government was desirable.
Anyway, the speech attained the purpose which Smith
had then in mind. 'I think I've pricked the Belloc bubble,'
he said as amid applause he made his way back to his
place, and he won the Presidency.

Smith's finest hour at the Union was beyond question on
the day of Gladstone's death. It so happened that Gladstone
died on the day of what was to have been the traditionally
light-hearted Eights' Week debate. It was of course in
1898—a few years after Smith's Presidency—he then still
resided in Oxford as a Don and he had been invited to speak
on the paper. Garbett, afterwards the Archbishop of York,
was the President. It was properly decided that the House

should adjourn and the debate be cancelled, and Smith was invited to move the motion of adjournment. He did so in a speech which, even if it bears some of the marks of period, was of an extraordinary felicity.

He said, 'Nearly seventy years have passed since Mr. Gladstone sat in the chair you fill tonight. He enjoyed in the discharge of your office a wealth of contemporary reputation to which I conceive that none of his successors has even approximately attained, and during these seventy years all parties in this House have admitted him with ready assent the most illustrious ornament in the annals of the Society. Other great statesmen, sir, have sat since Mr. Gladstone in your chair; there have debated within the walls of this Society poets like Swinburne, known wherever the English language is known; men of letters like Ruskin and a long roll of prelates and judges, the mere recital of whose names would exhaust the patience of this House—yet I think it was said of none of them, as it was said of Gladstone, the undergraduate, "A man is risen in Israel this day."

'In public some of us have exercised from time to time our wit and rhetoric against him, but in private, when we would give a high impression of this Society to those unfamiliar with its history, it was the name of Gladstone which rose first to our lips. There are times, and I think this is one, when we who have busied ourselves in however inconsiderable a degree in party politics, are glad to say with Mercutio "A plague on both your houses" when the desire is strong within us to express sorrow with more than the perfunctory courtesy of political opponents. We remember that the last seventy years have been pregnant with changes in our national life—social changes—political changes—economic changes. Of these Mr. Gladstone *pars magna fuit*, and the part he played was always distinguished, always strenuous, always single-hearted. When we think that after the stress of these anxious years the tired body and the busy brain are still, we can think of no better epitaph for him than, "After life's fitful fever he sleeps well".'

Two terms after his debate with Smith, Belloc was elected President. During his presidency he arranged for a delegation from the Union to visit Brussels University. His Librarian, Bradbury, whose name as Secretary to the Treasury was afterwards for very many years to appear upon our banknotes, but who was at that time a young Socialist defiantly disporting a red tie, was a member of it. They took with them a banner, and this incident got into the London papers and excited some ridicule. Bradbury wrote to the *Pall Mall Gazette,* in a spirit worthy of Belloc and, one cannot but suspect, to some extent under his inspiration, 'As the invited guests of a foreign university, we were bound to adapt ourselves to the customs prevailing there. If a settled conviction prevails that good taste does not exist outside England, it would be better to remain at home wrapped up in our own insularity.'

Basil Matthews in the *Young Man* gives us a vivid picture of a debate on the behaviour of the Turks in Thessaly when according to the account Smith and Simon made brilliant speeches and then an unknown orator, Belloc, rose and held the House breathless with his eloquence. As can be seen from the previous quotation, Matthews' memories were more vivid than accurate. Belloc was President of the Union before Simon was heard of in it.

In the 1890s boys from Catholic schools at Oxford were few and far between and, such as they were, played for the most part an undistinguished rôle. Belloc, who had been as a boy at Cardinal Newman's Oratory School at Birmingham, was an unique exception. His father was a French barrister. Born in 1870, he was only born in England through the accident that his mother took refuge in England to escape the siege of Paris. He was until his later naturalisation still a French subject, and therefore after leaving school went to France to do his military service. As a result he was twenty-five before he became President of the Union— older than most undergraduates who had come straight from school—and whereas most of the few Catholics at

Oxford were more unsophisticated and ignorant of the world than their fellow undergraduates, Belloc had seen more of it than those with whom he crossed swords.

Belloc carried in his mind's eye a picture of the sweep and pageant of history such as neither Simon nor Smith possessed. He had little sense of political tactics or manoeuvre. It was easy for Smith to put him in a false position by getting him to speak first, but none who heard him at that time have ever denied his unrivalled oratorical power. To Smith success was to an unbalanced extent competitive and political success, and because Belloc did not take kindly to the House of Commons or achieve political office, Smith a little absurdly wrote him off as a failure, blind to the much deeper influence that he was able to exercise over the mind of England than is wielded by the ephemeral politician. 'A brilliant man doomed to sterility, who sought consolation in the art of letters,' was Smith's verdict on Belloc, but of Belloc as a Union orator he wrote in his *Points of View*, 'Mr. Belloc was undoubtedly a great orator. At Oxford he spoke out of the sincerity of his heart in noble English and out of a fund of natural genius. . . . At the Union he was an immense and unparalleled success. I can bear testimony to this because I opposed Mr. Belloc on nearly all his great occasions.'

Belloc spoke frequently throughout 1894—on republicanism, on democracy, against temperance, in denunciation of Prussia. The debate when he was candidate for the Presidency was on the London School Board Election. The *Isis* said of his performance that he displayed 'a consistent view of almost every subject, based on intelligent and broad principles; an elaboration of forcible and easily comprehended argument; an appropriateness of phraseology adorned by appositeness of analogy and delivered with an irresistible vehemence of utterance—each of these Mr. Belloc has in greater abundance than any other member of the Society. And they were never more effectively displayed than on Thursday.' He was elected by 327 votes against 196 for Bruce of Worcester.

After his election the *Isis* wrote of him, 'From Mr. Belloc you get a speech different from anything else you will hear in the Union. He dares to be serious and to show it; the ordinary speaker is too much afraid of being taken to mean what he says. He loves general principles; has a perfect lust of deduction; and it is the unity in which he comprises all departments of politics, the consistent measure to which he reduced them all, which gave colour to the taunt that he had one speech of all work. Of course that kind of oratory is a prey to the scoffer, but its effect outlasts the laugh; Mr. Belloc, alone almost of Union speakers, makes converts.'

John Simon, like Smith, was a Wadham man. Those two, along with C. B. Fry and F. W. Hirst, gave to that generally inconspicuous College a brief period of enormous glory. Fry never took part at the Union. Hirst, a man of high honour, of great ability and charm, was President two terms after Simon. He continued the Wadham tradition but he was never a national figure of the order of his two predecessors. Simon was the son of a Nonconformist minister. He had been at school at Fettes, though he was of English, or it may be of Welsh, origin. The days of National Government were then far ahead and he was in his undergraduate days as for many years after the most doctrinaire and uncompromising of Liberals. He advocated the granting of degrees to women. He attacked Church establishment. He criticised the House of Lords. Some said that he had a sense of humour. Others said that he saw that Smith made jokes and was a success. He therefore thought it necessary for success that he too, should make jokes and he studied how to make them. When he was President he allowed a motion: 'That this House would view with horror the prospects of a teetotal England.'

The experiment of having visitors to the Union had been repeated. John Dillon and Colonel Sanderson had followed in the footsteps of Morley and Randolph Churchill to debate all over again the question of Home Rule for Ireland. Simon was then, and indeed remained until the end of his life, one of the sternest critics of this new custom which he thought had greatly damaged the Union. The visitor, he thought, should be rare, 'a statesman of first rate eminence. The occasions should be limited and the individual carefully chosen from a very small list. Otherwise the Union throws away its opportunities of paying a real compliment to a distinguished man, and the result is that really distinguished men will not regard it as a compliment to be asked'. He was greatly disturbed when after the First World War the custom grew of sometimes inviting visitors to more than one debate in a term. I tremble to think what he would have said of the present custom of having them every Thursday. He thought that leading politicians could not be expected to come if they had another visitor to oppose them and therefore inaugurated the custom, which persisted for a quarter of a century or more, of having only one visitor for the Presidential debate. The visitor whom he invited was Asquith, recently Home Secretary in Gladstone's Government. Asquith had not been back to the Union since his Presidency twenty-two years before. He spoke against the granting of public money to the voluntary schools.

Simon's Presidency was also notable for a revival of the old custom of receiving visitors for a debate from the Cambridge Union. Three Cambridge orators came to debate the admission of women to University degrees. Among them was Pethwick Lawrence, afterwards to be the most persistent of all male supporters of women's suffrage. The women were heavily defeated. At another debate F. W. Hirst moved and Belloc opposed a motion for the substitution of arbitration for war. That too was heavily defeated.

It is often said that the period of Belloc, Smith and Simon was the golden age of the Union. It may well be so. Each member has his own Union period, and who can easily compare the orators of one generation with those of another? It is certain that in the twenty years between their time and the outbreak of the First World War the Union had memorable officers and memorable debates. On April 28, 1905, there was a debate on the Anglo-French agreement, notable for its aftermath rather than for itself, for it ended up with all the officers of the Society being arrested. 'Four weary officers and the movers of the motion,' records the *Oxford Magazine*, 'wending their way to a haven of rest, were encircled by the arm of the law in one fell swoop. An attempt was made to institute an immediate *al fresco* Union debate in due form, but realising its disadvantages, the Law insisted on an adjournment in order to prepare a speech. Fortunately mild counsels prevailed in the morning and it is said that no further indignity was put upon the Society's officers than a journey to Christ Church at the uncomfortably early hour of 9.0 a.m.' I suppose that this somewhat arch account means that they were progged—probably for being without gowns.

The custom of inviting guest speakers was gradually growing more and more firmly established. The arrangement of the programme rested with the President, and both then and indeed until quite recent times he arranged the motions week by week. They were not settled for the whole term in advance as they are today. No President invited a guest for any but the one gala Presidential debate, and there was never more than one guest at one time with the sole exception of a first visit of F. E. Smith and Winston Churchill to debate the merits of the Liberal Government of 1906, when first it came to power. It was thought that a distinguished guest could not be expected to submit himself to the quips of a rival guest in order to provide an entertainment for ribald undergraduates. It was the general custom for the majority to support the guest in the voting—whether as an act of courtesy or because his oration was more convincing than that of the undergraduates. Some Presidents—Ronald Knox was one—preferred to have no visitor during their term of office. It excited no remark if such was their choice. The paucity of guests naturally meant that only persons of the highest distinction—as a general rule only leaders of political parties—could hope for an invitation. Sir Henry

Campbell Bannerman spoke and was a great success. Lord Roberts spoke in favour of conscription, T. P. O'Connor in favour of Irish Home Rule, Austen Chamberlain—of all the Presidents of the Cambridge Union the one who up till the present has come nearest to being Prime Minister—received a warm welcome, Lloyd George a noisy one, Bonar Law, then the new leader of the Unionist cause, was, said the *Isis,* 'not a success'. He 'does not treat the Union as if it were an adult body'.

The two most memorable visits of those years were the visit of John Redmond and that of Lloyd George. Redmond came on June 6, 1907, to speak, of course, in favour of Home Rule for Ireland. It will be remembered that the Liberals, having been returned at the 1906 election with a majority that made them independent of the Irish vote, were in no mind to do anything for Ireland. Therefore Redmond had to face not only hostile Conservatives but also indifferent Liberals with a bad conscience. Yet he won a tremendous success and carried the day by 359 votes to 226. The usually Conservative reporter in the *Oxford Magazine* recorded, 'Mr. Redmond's speech was thrilling and the result of the division sensational. We had prophecied that Mr. Redmond would win but we had thought of a majority nearer thirty three than a hundred and thirty three. Such a majority is the highest compliment that could possibly be paid to Mr. Redmond. It is doubtful if the Union has ever heard or will ever hear again a speech that will have such influence on its hearers.'

Lloyd George came in 1913 during the Presidency of Gilbert Talbot, when hostility to him among the Establishment was at its height. He was in real physical danger. He dined with the Dean in Christ Church and, to assure his safety, decoy cars drove straight to the Union after dinner, while Lloyd George was taken there by a roundabout route. But he was spotted in St. Michael Street, and mangel-wurzels were thrown at him, one breaking the windscreen of his car and wounding his chauffeur. When he reached the Union Sir Ernest Roberts, then an undergraduate, who was

to open the debate against Lloyd George, apologised to him
for the mob's behaviour. 'Oh don't worry about that, my
boy,' said Lloyd George. 'It's what you Tories call the sweets
of office.' Lloyd George carried the day in an immense
house of 1,234 voters by 654 to 580. 'Those who have been
wont to read the spiteful passages selected by a hostile press
will, when next they see the most glaring headlines in their
morning papers, remember the speech they heard on Friday
night,' said the *Isis*, 'and recall the eloquence, the humour,
the courtesy by which it was so happily characterised.'

Hilaire Belloc came on February 28, 1912, to denounce the
party system, and the *Oxford Magazine* reported, 'We do not
remember any visitor in the last four years who seemed to
grip his audience so thoroughly from the first word to the
last. It was not a long speech but in the course of it Mr.
Belloc succeeded in convincing everyone of his complete
sincerity, delighting the House with his eloquence and persuading a large majority to vote for the motion which was
carried by 130 votes.

F. E. Smith, a frequent visitor, denounced Welsh Disestablishment. 'In this House and in the University,' he
claimed, 'which, whether it had belonged to the Church or
not, had always revered it, an appeal should not be made in
vain which asks only this—that money originally consecrated
to the service of God, should be maintained for that service
and should not be diverted in a Christian community to
purposes which were admitted to be secular in character!'
'F. E. Smith,' reported the *Oxford Magazine*, 'has the perfection of the Union manner at its best—witty, logical and
convincing.' It was a different comment from that of
Chesterton.

There were also occasions when, following the precedent
of Gladstone, the Union hall was thrown open to distinguished persons to address the Society other than in debate. Old Archbishop Temple, when over eighty, addressed
the Society on 'Things Indifferent' in 1904. His son, the
future Archbishop, was the President. The father confessed

Portrait of Hilaire Belloc by James Gunn

A WOMAN SPEAKING AT THE OXFORD UNION FOR THE FIRST TIME.

DRAWN BY OUR SPECIAL ARTIST, S. BEGG.

Mr. E. P. Swain, Junior Librarian.   Mr. Richmond, President.

Mr. R. A. Knox, Exclusive Librarian.

**AN INNOVATION AFTER EIGHTY-THREE YEARS: MRS. MILLICENT GARRETT FAWCETT, LL.D.
ADDRESSING THE OXFORD UNION SOCIETY.**

For the first time since its inauguration eighty-three years ago, the Oxford Union has been addressed by a woman. The event took place last week, and the question for debate was "That in the opinion of this House the time has come when the Government should be urged to remove the electoral disabilities of Women." Mrs. Millicent Garrett Fawcett was the first speaker, and was, of course, a supporter of the motion. She was received with great enthusiasm and courtesy; but the side to which she gave her adherence lost by thirty-one votes. The debating-hall was so crowded that permission was given members to sit on the floor and in the gangways.

The first woman speaking at the Union on November 20, 1908

that, though he had been a member of the Union since undergraduate days this was his maiden speech. Lord Rosebery, who like later Oxford Prime Ministers, Lord Avon, Lord Attlee and Sir Alec Douglas Home, had, when an undergraduate, taken no part at the Union, came down in the same year to unveil the bust of Lord Salisbury. Although the day was still far distant when women would be allowed to become members of the Society, although such a suggestion would at that time have been considered as no more than a joke, two ladies—Mrs. Henry Fawcett, the Suffragette leader, and Mrs. Humphrey Ward—took part in debates as guests. The rhythm of Oxford and the Union was not much disturbed by the Boer War—not disturbed at all, naturally enough, in comparison with the two World Wars. The Union only marked it by sending an address of congratulation to Sir George White on the relief of Ladysmith.

In the list of officers of those years there are as many names of those who afterwards rose to distinction of various sorts as in any period of the Society's history. The list would undoubtedly have been yet longer had not the war of 1914 brought untimely death to so many who were so certainly destined to higher things. Six ex-Presidents and numerous ex-officers were killed in action. Of these most, or all, might well have played great parts in the nation's life. Of two at any rate—Raymond Asquith and Gilbert Talbot—we can say almost with certainty that they would have done so.

For a time after Smith and Simon the Union did not number among its officers any destined for quite the first rank among politicians. Boyd-Carpenter was Simon's contemporary. Sir Arthur Steel Maitland, then known as Steel, was President in the Trinity term of 1899. Auberon Herbert was Treasurer in the Easter term of 1901, following E. T. Nelson, of St. John's, a negro. Lord Selborn, then Lord Wolmer, was Librarian in the Hilary term of 1908, Lord Monckton President just before the war in the Hilary term of 1913. Had it not been for the war the Union would in all probability have had yet another Prime Minister among its

K

ex-Presidents, for in the Hilary term of 1914 Harold Macmillan was its Secretary, Treasurer in the Trinity term and
had been elected Librarian for the Michaelmas term.

There were plenty of officers during these years who were
to be distinguished in other fields than the political. Among
academics was Ensor of Balliol, President in the Hilary term
of 1900, A. D. Lindsay, afterwards Master of Balliol,
President in the Hilary term of 1902 and Nathaniel Micklem,
President in the Hilary term of 1911. G. B. Allen, to be
Principal of St. Edmund Hall, was Secretary in the Michaelmas term of 1906. Lord du Parcq, as he was afterwards to
become, who was President in the Michaelmas term of
1902, showed the Union as the training ground for future
judges, Sir Victor Mallet, Secretary in the Trinity term of
1914 for future Ambassadors, Alexander Paterson, the famous
Prison Commissioner and penal reformer, was Librarian
in the Hilary term of 1906.

There is no point in trying to make the list inclusive, but
it is interesting to note how many writers in this period held
office at the Union. There were journalists like F. W. Hirst,
to be the editor of the *Economist*, or Barrington Ward, to
be editor of *The Times*, or W. A. Moore, editor of the *Calcutta Statesman*. There is also a long list of book writers who
combined their books with journalism. Sir Anthony Hope
Hawkins—Anthony Hope—is of an earlier period, but from
these years come John Buchan, E. C. Bentley, Algernon
Cecil, Herbert Asquith, Sir Arnold Lunn, Philip Guedalla,
Sir Alan Herbert, Douglas Jerrold. They make a formidable
list, to which other names could be added. The name of
Bonnerjee of Balliol as Treasurer in the Michaelmas term of
1905 shows, along with that of Nelson, a superiority to racial
prejudices at a date when such a superiority was not as common as it is today.

But what is most interesting is the number of clerical names
in the list. In the early years of the Union, as we have seen,
Oxford was still a clerical training-ground more than it was
anything else, and almost half of the Union's officers in its

first fifty years went forward to clerical careers. Since the First World War there have been very few clerics. But in the years before the First World War the number of Union officers destined for Holy Orders, while, of course, far less than in the Union's early years, was still considerable. The contrast in that respect between the habits of 1823 and the habits of 1914 was far less than the contrast between the habits of 1914 and those of 1939. Thus in these last twenty years before the First World War we find among the Union's officers two future Archbishops. Garbett, later to be Archbishop of York, was President in the Trinity term of 1898 and Archbishop Temple was President in the Hilary term of 1904. Neville Talbot, the son of the Bishop of Winchester, who was twice President in 1866 and again in 1868, was himself President in the Hilary term of 1907 and afterwards Bishop of Pretoria. His brother, Godfrey Talbot, one of those lost in the war for whom a brilliant future was most confidently prophesied, was President just before the war in 1913. Allen of Wadham, Secretary in 1906, was afterwards to be Principal of St. Edmund Hall and then Bishop of Dorchester. Swain of St. John's, the President of the Trinity term of 1909, was to be Bishop of Burnley. Maynard Smith of Trinity, Secretary in the Hilary term of 1890 though he was never to be either President or Bishop, was as a Canon of Gloucester for twenty-five years to be one of the best known ecclesiastics of his day. Swain's Presidency was sandwiched in between that of Ronald Knox and Robin Laffan. Both of these ex-Presidents were for a time in Anglican orders, but both abandoned them to enter the Catholic Church. Laffan was married and therefore had to revert to lay status, becoming Bursar of Queen's College, Cambridge. Ronald Knox, who had already shown himself to be one of the most notable of the Society's Presidents, was destined as Monsignor Knox to be the translator of the Bible, for many years the Catholic chaplain at Oxford and one of the most notable of the Society's ex-Presidents both on account of his general fame and because for many years both before and after the

Second World War he used every year to take part in the Eights' Week debate.

Morrah in his *History of the Union* says of Ronald Knox that his 'reputation was such that it may be said that he kept the Union going, intellectually speaking, till the Great War broke out.' If this verdict is true—as most contemporaries allow that it is—it throws an interesting light on the Union of those years. Nothing could be more false than the notion that the years before 1914 were years of halcyon, peaceful and careless ease. They were, of course, years when, quite apart from the German menace, domestic differences were bringing the nation to the verge of civil war. Party politics were more bitter than they have ever been before or since, and the Union naturally enough had its political debates and numbered aspiring politicians among its officers. Indeed it recorded some amusingly surprising verdicts over those years. At the time of their institution in 1903 it refused by a considerable majority to welcome the Rhodes Scholars. In one of its last debates before the war, at the end of May 1914, it condemned the policy of the Triple Entente of Britain, France and Russia as 'unnecessary and unnatural'. The vote, given in May, no more prevented the young men from going to war in August then the more famous vote not to fight for King and country prevented them from going to the Second World War in 1939. In June of 1914 the German Ambassador visited Oxford to attend a banquet in celebration of the hundred years of peace between the two countries and 'the *wahleverwandtschaft* between German *geist* and Oxford *kultur*'.

But Ronald Knox, according to this contention the Union's most representative figure, was never at all involved in politics. As he says of himself in his *Spiritual Aeneid*, 'I passed chiefly for a Conservative, though it was not necessary for a speaker to belong consistently to any party. I voted No Confidence in the Government with Mr. Wyndham, Home Rule with Mr. Redmond, Socialism (dare I admit it?) carried off my feet by the eloquence of Mr. Philip Snowden.'

In fact, though he forgot it, he not only supported Socialism when advocated by Philip Snowden but on another occasion on December 5, 1907, actually moved a motion, 'That this House would welcome the advent of a Labour Government'. His main interest was of course in religion, but the rule against theological motions was still in force at the Union and he never dreamed of introducing religion there whether directly or indirectly. His predominance at the Union arose solely from the fecundity of his wit and paradox. Philip Guedalla, alone perhaps of the officers of that period, could rival Ronald Knox in epigram and paradox. Guedalla had a great reputation and he was followed about by a sort of Roman *claque*, who passed along to the outside world his latest epigram, whispering in awe, 'Have you heard Guedalla's latest?' But Guedalla—it is often said, and, I think, truly —never outgrew his Union style. He remained a permanent undergraduate throughout life, with little important to say and often sacrificing meaning to manner. Ronald Knox's progression was very different. *Reunion All Round* and *Absolute and Abitofhel* in his early years as a Don showed amply that he was still the master of satire, but with the years he passed on triumphantly to deeper things.

If we may judge from the University papers the outstanding figure of the earlier years of the century was William Temple. The reporters of the *Isis* and *Oxford Magazine* contain tribute after tribute to him. He was a Socialist in a Union that even under the influence of his eloquence could only muster 37 votes in favour of Socialism. The *Isis* congratulated the Union on its tolerance in permitting such a debate at all. 'It is indeed,' it wrote, 'a notable sign of the times, a sign of what may be called, according to the individual's point of view, advance or retrogression, not only that the Union should have tolerated such a debate but that no less than thirty-seven out of one hundred and nineteen voters should have recorded their votes in favour of Socialism. We can quite imagine that in the old days of the Union horse-play a speaker who had the temerity to advo-

cate Socialism might have met with an unpleasant reception.'
But, as it was, 'Mr. Temple's vigour and unconventionality
carried all before him. An enthusiastic House was given a
glimpse into the beautiful Socialist paradise where there is
no middle class and of which Mr. Temple is the managing
director.' The *Isis* idol on him the next term when he was
President, wrote, 'His indeed is the *mens vasta in corpore vasto*.
By the age of six he had mastered Kant and other philo-
sophers in quick succession—Hegel, Nietzsche, Royce and
Spencer received his discriminating patronage. His originality transcends them all. His staple food is chocolate cream.'
It was then the custom that the President should never leave
the chair to take part in a debate. To the general delight
on February 4 Temple broke this custom. 'After the fourth
speaker had finished,' recorded the *Isis*, 'the greater part of
the House rose to leave, until suddenly they became aware
that the President was going to speak. Immediately everyone
returned and supporters of the motion (one condemning the
importation of Chinese labour into South Africa) cheered
loudly when they found that the President was advocating
their side.' After his Presidency Temple returned to make a
speech in favour of Church Establishment

In 1913 the House elected its first American President—
W. J. Bland—to be killed five years later on the Western
Front. 'Father Bland', he was called by his friends. The *Isis*
idol gave a doubtless apocryphal account of his manner of
election. 'Father Bland happened to be walking up and down
Cornmarket Street with a friend on Thursday evening and
went into the Union to see what the crowd was about; it
happened to be a debate, so he spoke. No great effect was
produced as he spoke rather late, and the audience (another American) wanted to speak as well. Time tells with
merit and within two terms Father B. had made a great hit,
vociferating with a voice of no mean order, helped out by a
patriotic accent, he became by turns teller, paper speaker,
member of Library Committee. Needless to say when he
was elected he was chosen to fill the first place and the

following term saw him Secretary. His career onwards was upwards from Junior Treasurer to Junior Librarian, and then, tactfully giving way to a well known Balliol cricketer (Lord Monckton) he allowed himself to be nominated for the last and highest office. This he received not by some inordinate vulgar majority, but he 'chose to be elected by some nine votes over a very capable young speaker from Christ Church (Gilbert Talbot).'

Mr. Macmillan's politics in those days oscillated between Liberal and Labour. On October 31, 1912, he joined with Mr. Harry Strauss, now Lord Conesford, in approving 'the main principles of Socialism'. On February 27, 1913, he condemned the public schools. 'He preferred the lethargic libertine,' it was reported, 'to the bureaucratic busybody.' On April 24, 1913, he supported Harry Strauss in another motion in favour of Socialism and on December 5, 1913, he spoke against F. E. Smith in support of a motion expressing complete confidence in Her Majesty's (Asquith's Liberal) Government. 'Mr. M. H. Macmillan (Balliol) was hardly logical and rambles badly,' reported the *Isis*. 'Mr. M. H. Macmillan (Balliol) was macabre. And a good thing, too,' it reported of another debate—with what exact meaning I cannot say. 'In many ways a model paper speech, but just as a hint for the more distant future we may recommend a little more originality of thought.'

Perhaps the most vivid picture of what life was like in the Union buildings, as opposed to what it was like in the Union debating hall in those years, has been given us by Mr. Victor Gollancz in his book to his grandson, *My Dear Timothy*. 'Better than anything were the long slow winter afternoons, spent amid the haze of tobacco smoke in the Reading Room upstairs. The armchairs were deeper than any in the world, the fires like fires in a railway engine. I was always amazed by the prodigality of the attendants with these fires; they flung on great bucketfuls of coal, one after another, and when you thought they had finished they had only just begun. I would sit there from lunch till nearly seven, reading, dozing, eating much hot buttered toast; and as likely as not the Britter would be snoring nearby. The Britter was one of those oddities that Oxford has always collected, like the man with a big square face who, three decades ago, could be seen any day in the Broad, baring his teeth and screaming at passers-by. The Britter was very old and very round and dressed like a better-to-do labourer; Britter was short for the British Working Man. He was the world's first authority on the Basquish verb. He had been appointed, I believe, ages before my time to teach the subject. He had no pupils.'

CHAPTER EIGHT

THE TWENTIES

THE FIRST WORLD WAR brought an interruption of Oxford
life and consequently of the Union's life far more drastic
than any before known and also far more drastic than that
of the Second World War. In the Second World War the
Government encouraged students to complete a portion of
their undergraduate studies before drafting them into the
forces. In the First World War at its beginning, when
recruitment was still voluntary, any fit man was accepted
with no questions asked about the occupation that he was
leaving, and undergraduates were naturally among the
most enthusiastic of volunteers. Later, when conscription
was imposed, boys were taken straight from school at seven-
teen and a half and their University studies were postponed
until the war was finished. In the first terms after the outbreak of war there were still a few undergraduates about,
who thought it right to finish their courses and take final
schools before volunteering. After the war's first year
Oxford's undergraduate population was almost reduced to
a handful of neutrals and the unfit. Sydney Ball, of St.
John's, the Society's Senior Treasurer, rendered the Union
invaluable service by looking after its finances. A few rooms
were still kept open for the benefit of life members, but the
debates came to an end. No officers were elected. The debating hall was used for lectures to the Officers' Training
Corps. The greater part of the premises was turned into an
Officers' Mess.

With the end of the war the undergraduates came back
to Oxford. It took many soldiers a little time to get

demobilised, but by October 1919, what with the demobilised soldiers and the ordinary intake from the schools, Oxford had over four and a half thousand undergraduates—more than ever before in its history. It was a very different Oxford from that of former years—and by consequence also a very different Union. Whereas previously the overwhelming majority of undergraduates had always been boys straight from school, only just relieved from school discipline, not having yet undertaken the responsibility of earning a living, now of course a substantial proportion of the undergraduates had been a few months before facing death in the trenches. The tale was told of an ex-Brigadier freshman who was rebuked by a Don who had held the rank of a Second Lieutenant, for walking on a forbidden stretch of grass. The Brigadier accepted the rebuke with a smile, but in general it was obviously not possible to impose upon such men the discipline that might be imposed upon boys straight from school. At the Union it might have been expected that there would be a greater sense of responsibility in debate, a greater maturity of opinion than in normal times. Perhaps that was so, but it is hard to say because, the nightmare of the war at last ended, there was in those years at Oxford and the Union as elsewhere, a great reluctance to talk about the experiences of the war. Whatever the future might hold, every one felt, at least we should never see another World War. Why then should we think about war?

Party politics during the war had been in abeyance. With the armistice and with the election of November 1918 they came back in strength and therefore, partly because of their intrinsic importance and partly because of their novelty, undergraduates, or at least those of them who frequented the Union, threw themselves into the party game with enthusiasm. The first post-war elections took place in the Trinity term of 1919. In order to familiarise the new undergraduates with the Society's habits, Dr. Nathaniel Micklem, ex-President of 1911 and then resident in Oxford as a tutor at Mansfield College, took the chair at the first debates as Acting-President and earned general applause and gratitude by his conduct of them. The *Oxford Magazine* recorded that 'had it not been for him members would have floundered in ignorance of the ancient forms and procedure, and it would have been impossible for such an extraordinary recovery to be achieved in one term.' Officers were elected for the Michaelmas term in which the Union's full life began again. In those elections Mr. Henry Andrews, today the husband of Miss Rebecca West, was elected Secretary, Mr. Constantine Gallop, afterwards to be Master of the Bench of the Middle Temple and a Labour candidate, at the time a Liberal, was elected Junior Treasurer. The future Professor J. B. S. Haldane, who stood considerably to the left of Liberalism, was Librarian and for the Presidency Hore Belisha as the Liberal candidate defeated Dr. C. R. S. Harris, soon to be a Fellow of All Souls, who stood for the Conservatives.

The Union began its post-war life in a blaze of enormous and high-minded enthusiasm. The general election of November 1918 had not shown the British nation in an extravagantly idealistic mood. But there was an instant—perhaps excessive—reaction of shame against its crudities. In the nation at large Coalition candidates at by-elections lost their seats by majorities as exorbitant as those with which at the general election such candidates had won them. At Oxford young men came back from the trenches, determined to build a new world, in which there should never again be another war, and went to the Union in enormous numbers to say so. Lord Robert Cecil came down to the Union to champion the League of Nations and carried his motion by 924 votes to 99—a total vote only exceeded by that given to Lloyd George before the war. He made, according to the *Isis*, 'a magnificent speech which was enthusiastically received by a crowded house'—the more crowded because its members were swelled by an influx of non-members who had paid no subscription but forced their way in without right. Among these gatecrashers was an undergraduate from Christ Church called Anthony Eden, who expressed himself greatly impressed by Robert Cecil's speech but who never, I think, visited the Union again or paid it a subscription. But the interest in listening to debates dropped rapidly and only one hundred and sixty-six voted at the Presidential debate of June 1920.

The Asquithian Liberals, as will be remembered, were almost extinguished at the general election of 1918. Mr. Asquith himself lost his seat. Yet immediately afterwards as electors at by-elections turned against the Coalition Government, Liberals won a number of seats. The spirit of revolt against the Establishment that breathed over the nation at large, characteristically breathed nowhere more potently than among Oxford undergraduates. Undergraduates were not yet ready in significant numbers to embrace the newly rising Labour party. That was too alien to their origins, but many of the brightest among them turned to Asquithian Liberalism and during these first years after the war the majority of the Union's officers were Liberals. Their political opponents naturally enough took the occasion to make well-seasoned jokes about Oxford as the home of lost causes.

The reporters were also of the left. An undergraduate journalist is seldom capable of writing an objective report and then, as later, the Union reports were patently biased against Conservatives—so much so as largely to detract from their value. The pre-war reports had, when they saw fit to be extravagant, been extravagant in their straightforward insolence. 'Mr. T. D. Robb must speak again. Mr. L. A. Farsons is under no such obligation,' was a specimen of their wit. The post-war journalists undoubtedly made a dead set, conscious or unconscious, at Maxwell Fyfe, then the leading Conservative speaker, and perhaps had a share in responsibility for the misfortune that he never attained the Presidency. 'Mr. D. P. M. Fyfe (Balliol) delivered himself in a voice quivering with emotion, an imperialist of imperialists. His attitude was calculated to alienate political manners. An earnest but not a very good speech.' One can, I think, guess at the politics of the writer and wonder what sort of a Conservative speech would not have alienated him.

Visitors were rather more common immediately after than before the war, though of course far less common than in modern times. Men in public life were anxious to see what this new post-war Oxford was like and the Union was anxious to hear the leading figures of the day. Whereas before the war it had never been the custom to have more than one visitor in a term, now two were often invited—one for the Presidential and one for one of the other debates. Old officers deplored the innovation—particularly Sir John Simon. He reiterated his argument that the honour of addressing the Union should only be allowed to the very leading figures of the day and that with more frequent visitors speakers of the second rank would be bound to receive invitations. Simon, who was himself at that time one of Asquith's leading lieutenants and one of the most vigorous and virulent of the critics of Lloyd George's Government, had a special aversion to Coalition Liberal politicians who were holding office in the Government. He regretted an invitation which was given to one such member, Dr. McNamara, a Coalition Liberal, who was at that time one of Lloyd George's Ministers, and indeed there were plenty of undergraduates who thought that Dr. McNamara was not a man of sufficient distinction and reading to justify such an honour. The *Isis* wrote, deliberately mispronouncing his name:

> It would be odd to find Dr. McNamara
> In the Radcliffe Camera.
> It would be still odder
> To find him in the Bodder.

In the Trinity term of 1920 the Union entertained a distinguished visitor from outside the ranks of the politicians —G. K. Chesterton, who debated before it on Divorce. The rule against theological motions was still in force, and, although of course there are plenty of arguments about divorce on the secular plane, it is not very easy to deploy a full case if one is not allowed to avert to the purely Christian conception of marriage. Certainly Chesterton was not a man who would, left to himself, have dreamed of discussing such a subject without bringing in religion. He therefore spoke under something of a handicap. The debate suited well Mr. Beverley Nichols who had been Librarian of the term before and was then standing for the Presidency. Mr. Nichols called himself a Liberal but he was not deeply interested in party politics. He was far more at home on a general social topic. Chesterton chanced in one of his books to have made a characteristic quip against the proposal that drunkenness should be recognised as a cause for divorce. It would be far more reasonable, he argued, that a wife should be allowed to divorce her husband for being a teetotaller than for being a drunkard. Mr. Nichols was able to quote this sentence and to deplore the flippancy with which Chesterton had treated the subject. Chesterton in reply defended himself, and the House was in general impressed by his sincerity but Mr. Nichols had been given, and had taken, his opportunity, and as a result he was elected President.

During his Presidency Mr. Nichols had two visitors. The first—for the Presidential debate—was Winston Churchill, then Secretary of State for War in Lloyd George's Government, to defend the record of the Government. No exception could possibly be taken to such an invitation, and Churchill, according to the *Isis*, made 'one of the most impressive speeches in the Union we have heard for some time', carrying by 663 votes to 351 a motion in support of the Coalition Government to which the House, unswayed by his oratory, would probably have been opposed. Mr. Nichols' other visitor was a far more controversial figure. Horatio Bottomley is today remembered as one of the great English criminals. Of course at the time of his invitation to the Union neither the President nor anybody else was aware of the full scale of his activities. Still there was at the least no secret about it that his financial reputation was not of the highest. He himself in the course of his speech told the House with light flippancy that he had never lived in such affluence as when he was an undischarged bankrupt. There were many members who shook their heads sadly and told one another that Horatio Bottomley was not the sort of man who ought to be invited to the Union.

Horatio Bottomley had been an Independent Member of Parliament before the war. During the war he was the editor of *John Bull*, an intensely jingoistic paper, which posed as the soldiers' friend and poured its abuse on any whose patriotism was in any way more mitigated than its own. He was a strong critic of party politicians and the party system and demanded in place of the rule of politicians what he called, without very clearly defining its meaning, a Business Government. In the election of 1918 Bottomley stood for Hackney and had the largest majority of any elected Member who stood against a candidate with a Coalition coupon. The motion on which he was invited to speak to the Union was one condemning the party system. Maxwell Fyfe (afterwards Lord Kilmuir), who was then Junior Treasurer and Hore Belisha, who had recently gone down and returned for the evening as a guest, spoke on the other side. Bottomley was at the time one of the best known of public figures and his appearance drew an enormous crowd. But his speech, though not unpleasant, was superficial and a little too obviously cheap. Hore Belisha had before the debate taken advice from friends whether he should use the famous words, 'There are more things in heaven and earth, Horatio.' They advised against as being too obvious. However Hore Belisha in the event got carried away and found the line tripping off his lips. There was an immense burst of applause and he astutely sat down without completing the quotation with its second line. The next day Belisha and Bottomley travelled back together in the train and Bottomley made to Belisha proposals about how he should invest his money.

Mr. Nichols was succeeded as President by Mr. Beechman, then the most prominent of Oxford's Asquithian Liberals, afterwards to be for a time a National Liberal Member of Parliament. After Mr. Beechman came Mr. Ramage, who was also by profession a Liberal.

After Mr. Ramage the Presidency came to Mr. Kenneth Lindsay, interesting as the first representative of the newly nascent Labour party to sit in the chair. There had been Presidents before who had at any rate flirted with Socialist opinions. But a Socialist opinion before 1914 was still only a personal opinion, and, as such to be encouraged in the world of Oxford and the Union along with all other eccentricities. There was not at that time any question of a Socialist Government and therefore of Socialist opinions being of any practical importance. After the election of 1918 the Labour party was the official Opposition at Westminster. There were dark speculations at Oxford, as elsewhere, as to what a Labour Government would do if it came to power. Would it impose upon the Universities drastic bureaucratic control as the price of financial assistance? The undergraduates from Grammar Schools often did not greatly fear such control. Some of them indeed even welcomed the prospect of it. But the majority of undergraduates still came from Public Schools and they were not as yet quite adjusted to the new dangers. Labour, it was said, would abolish the Public Schools. What exactly that meant, how they would abolish them was not indeed clearly known, but the fear for their schools probably bulked larger in the minds of the undergraduates straight from such schools and whose total experience of life was life at such a school than did more general questions of egalitarianism and nationalisation. Anyway, the majority of undergraduates, or at any rate of vocal undergraduates, combined their love of novelty with their dislike of any novelties that might interfere with their own chosen ways by espousing the Liberal party, confident that that party would indeed introduce reforms but not reforms that were to their own inconvenience.

The British Workman

Herbert Jackson, known as the 'Britter' or the British Workman, on account of his dress, who was a well-known frequenter of the Library in the years before and immediately after the First World War

ABOVE   Members of the Union Committee in 1914. Mr Macmillan
is second from the left on the ground, Lord Monckton,
ex-president is the last on the right seated on the ground. The
President was Mr Wedderburn. To his right is Sir Austen
Chamberlain, guest of the evening

BELOW   On November 22, 1922, Dean Inge debated the
Motion 'That this House would welcome a return to Victorian
ideals'. The Motion was defeated by 417 votes to 333

The issue that aroused the deepest passions at that moment was the issue of reprisals in Ireland. Majorities at the Union oscillated. A little later when Sir Henry Wilson was assassinated, Union undergraduates, like everybody else, were deeply shocked, and an especial motion expressive of their horror was passed by the Union. An Irish peer at Christ Church, who was suspected of Sinn Fein sympathies, was ducked in Mercury. F. E. Smith—Lord Birkenhead as he had by then become—used often to come over from his home near by, listen to and intervene in the Union's debates. On one occasion he intervened with characteristic power and sarcasm in favour of the Government's Irish policy. But most often the Union's verdict was in favour of Irish freedom. At the very beginning of the repressive campaign Grattan Esmonde came down and made a flamboyant speech as an Irish rebel, demanding to be treated by an English audience as an enemy and not as a guest. The Union took the characteristically Oxonian revenge of cheering him to the echo and voting for him by a large majority. On another occasion W. B. Yeats, who at that time lived in Oxford in the Broad, made an eloquently poetic speech condemning reprisals against Henry Lygon, the Liberal Lord Beauchamp's strongly Conservative brother, and won the verdict. The Union could generally be called upon to support what might vaguely be called the progressive motions. Whether it would go so far as to vote Labour was less certain. However under Mr. Beechman's Presidency in the Hilary term of 1921 Ramsay MacDonald, then not even a member of Parliament, came down and asked the House to welcome a Labour Government. He appeared in a dinner jacket and black tie in place of tail coat and white tie which were usual at that time even for guest speakers. He addressed the House as 'my friends', apologising for his lack of familiarity with its customs, and won general sympathy and the vote of a majority at the debate's close, much to the dismay of Maxwell Fyfe, then the Junior Treasurer and the only Conservative among the Society's office-holders, who wondered

L

audibly whether there was any limit to the follies which the Society would embrace. As a result, when his turn came to stand for office, the Society elected Mr. Lindsay as the first Labour President over a Liberal opponent. Mr. Lindsay, a handsome young man, a Soccer Blue, in addition to being an officer of the University Labour Club, a moderate among Labour politicians and a political champion, according to a reminiscence of Mr. Beverley Nichols, of clean teeth, proved himself very amply worthy of his honour.

Among other guests of that era Asquith spoke not very successfully. Lloyd George defended the Treaty of Versailles against Pringle, an Asquithian M.P., before a crowded House and won a verdict on a motion that would probably have been defeated without his advocacy. Dean Inge, then a very widely read journalist, drew a surprisingly enormous House of seven hundred and fifty voters for a debate on Victorianism which was in a sense hardly a debate as the Dean prided himself on his hardness of hearing, sat on the front bench rather than on the Committee bench as is the usual custom, and was careful not to prejudice his case by reference to any observation that might have been made by any other speaker. Hilaire Belloc spoke, hampered or assisted by a practical joker who filled his water glass with gin. Lord Birkenhead was continually speaking—sometimes with and sometimes without invitation. He would walk in in the middle of a speech and then intervene as it occurred to him, often pulling to pieces somewhat brutally the stammering observations of some poor undergraduate. The habit came to be somewhat resented. The Union is essentially the under-graduates' debating society and it is a mistake for older members, whatever their technical rights, to intrude themselves without invitation. The *Oxford Magazine*, as well as Sir John Simon, was becoming critical of the stream of visitors. 'The Union,' it complained, 'is a debating society and not a gallery for ex-Cabinet Ministers,' and for a time it ceased reporting its meetings.

For a time in 1921 Union life was largely dominated by the

antics of Dr. Farnell, the Rector of Exeter and Vice-Chancellor. A Brighter Union Society was founded by Gerald Gardiner subsequently himself to be President of the Union. It consisted of many officers but only one member, Dr. Farnell, member *malgré lui*. Its duty was to rag off Union debates by such devices as putting a bell under the President's chair so that every time he moved he summoned one of the Society's servants who came to ask him what he wanted. Farnell foolishly attempted to impose on post-war undergraduates a discipline similar to that of pre-war years—sent down editors of papers, banned theatre programmes, made a fool of himself by suspecting without reason that a box of chocolates that were sent to him had been poisoned and calling in the police, and finally banned Bertrand Russell from addressing the Labour Club. The incidents are only of importance because they forced the Union to ask itself whether it had a duty to act as the representative of the undergraduates and to protest against authority's attacks on undergraduate freedom—an issue which we shall find coming up in one form and another again and again.

The atmosphere of the Union in the post-war world was less offensively English than it had been twenty years before. As will be remembered when the Rhodes Scholarships had been instituted, the Union had passed a motion deploring the arrival of the Scholars in Oxford. In the Trinity term of 1922 an American, Mr. Carson of Oriel, was elected President. He had, as we have seen, had a predecessor before the war and the fact of his election was in a way less remarkable than the cause of it. At the end of the war the United States had, as will be remembered, passed a constitutional amendment establishing prohibition as the law of their land, and there were in England, as in other European countries, some who hoped and some who feared that American prestige would be such that the American experiment, or something like it, would spread to other lands. Liberal opinion in Great Britain, still largely under the influence of the Nonconformist vote favoured, if not prohibition, at least local

option. Politicians and metaphysicians vied with one another
to argue whether prohibition was an interference with liberty
or whether every drunkard did not really by his higher self
and his real will prefer sobriety, and whether by compelling
him to be sober the State was not in truth saving him from
himself and conferring upon him the higher liberty. Whatever the rights of such an argument, at least it is certain that
they were widely canvassed in the world of the early 1920s
and that in these first years of the American experiment
prohibition was a very much livelier issue than it is today.
Few, I fancy, at that time would have prophesied that forty
years later there would have been no further restrictions on
the sale of liquor. Equally it is certain that, whatever the
rights of such an argument, the very great majority of undergraduates and of frequenters of the Union were opposed to
prohibition. Drink was then, as now, a part of the pattern of
University life and I fancy that there was probably more
drinking than there is today. Yet Mr. Carson, when he was
Junior Treasurer, proposed and succeeded in carrying a
motion in favour of prohibition—and that, though the leading speaker against the motion was Mr. Douglas Woodruff
who had the deserved reputation of being by far the wittiest
speaker of the day at the Union. Why a House that by no
means consisted entirely of teetotallers voted in favour of
prohibition it would be hard to say. Perhaps it was because
those who favoured prohibition favoured it more earnestly
than those who opposed it and therefore took the trouble to
go to the debate and vote, while the lovers of wine found
more congenial ways of indicating their preference than by
listening to a debate about it. Perhaps it was that there is
always among Union audiences, as among other English
audiences, a lurking feeling that earnestness ought to be
honoured above flippancy, and some, it may be, who did not
especially accept Mr. Carson's conclusion yet felt a duty to
pay a tribute to his earnestness. *Isis* recorded with some
truth at the time of Philip Guedalla's defeat for the Presidency by a less amusing candidate that the Union generally

prefers to vote for people who slightly bore it. However that may be, Mr. Carson first won his debate and then, when the time came for his election, he won the Presidency.

Mr. Carson's Presidency had twelve months before been preceded by another American invasion. In general debating does not bulk very large in the curriculum of American Universities. Such as it is, it is looked on essentially as a contest between two rival teams. Judges give their verdict not on the merits of the question but on the merits of the debaters—which side has debated better. It is more, as it were, a parody of a law court than, as in England, a parody of Parliament. But it is generally considered only as 'a minor sport'. A small College in the state of Maine, Bates College, had, however, the astute conception that, while they could not hope to rival better established Colleges in more generally regarded activities, if they specialised in debating, they might win victories in that field and thus, as the phrase goes, put themselves on the map. The policy met with some success in America and then, in 1921, their debating coach conceived the notion of challenging Oxford to a debate. The challenge was accepted and towards the end of the Trinity term the Bates team came over to debate at Oxford. The motion for debate was: 'That this House opposes the American policy of non-intervention in European affairs.'

The debate quite frankly was not altogether a success, as not sufficient trouble had been taken beforehand by either side to discover what was the conception which the other side had of a debate. If three debaters had come over to Oxford from, say, Cambridge, two of them would have been put upon the one side and one on the other. They would have exchanged their quips and their opinions and at the end there would have been a vote on what were conceived to be the merits of the question. A motion would have been accepted or rejected. There would have been no question of Oxford or Cambridge winning. The American conception of the debate was quite different. The Americans came over as a team. They had with meticulous care and with intensive coaching worked out exactly the case which they were in collaboration to present. Speakers said not 'I say' but 'Bates says!' They came armed with a card index which would provide for them the rebuttal with the answer to any conceivable point that their opponents might raise. As the Englishmen were speaking there was a constant click-click from the other side of the House as Bates turned up the appropriate point in their card index. They were deadly serious. They expected the verdict to be awarded not on the merits of the motion but on the merits of the debaters. By contrast the Oxford speakers, of course, appeared casual, flippant and inconsequent. Each of them said what it came into his head to say without caring too much whether it tallied with what another speaker might have said before. They cracked jokes some of which were of an only marginal relevance. Factually they were far less well prepared than the American speakers and in American eyes were shockingly indifferent to their lack of preparation. They had no notion that it was Oxford which was on trial against Bates. So far as anything was on trial, it was the opinion of the audience on the merits of the question.

Yet the outcome of that debate was of practical importance. Bates issued an invitation to a return contest in America. The invitation was accepted. It was thought that, while they were visiting Bates, the debaters might as well also debate against a number of other East Coast Colleges. American Colleges meet a little earlier in the autumn than does Oxford and a team went over consisting of Edward Marjoribanks, Mr. Quintin Hogg's half-brother, Mr. Kenneth Lindsay and myself, who was then the Secretary. In addition to Bates we visited Columbia, Yale, Harvard, Princeton and the University of Pennsylvania. This was the forerunner of many other debating trips from the Union. Two years later there was a more extended trip, of which I was also a member and in which my colleagues were Mr. Douglas Woodruff and Mr. Malcolm Macdonald. We had all three then gone down and were therefore under no obligation to get back to keep a term. We debated our way right over the American Continent and then travelled on to New Zealand and Australia, thus taking a year to debate our way round the world. There have been frequent tours in later years to America, though the experiment of an Australian tour for some reason does not seem to have been repeated. There have been a few return visits of American debaters to Oxford, but the American visit to England is not so easily arranged as the English visit to America. On the one hand English audiences are not willing to pay to listen to a debate or lecture. It is therefore not easy to finance an American debating tour of England. On the other hand Britain has, of course, only a handful of universities. Whereas the English debater in America can travel from university to university almost indefinitely, the programme of the American debater in Britain must necessarily be very limited. These tours, for the Union debaters who have been lucky enough to be selected for them, have certainly been both highly educative and highly enjoyable. It is a great opportunity for a young man thus to be able to travel over the country.

What lessons in debating have been learnt from them is less certain. Oxford debaters remain unshakeable in their belief that a debate is only tolerable if it is an individualistic and fairly light-hearted expression of opinion. Perhaps they are too obstinate in their prejudices and might have done better to have been willing humbly to learn some lessons from the Americans with their team-contests and card-indexes and parody of the law courts, but, rightly or wrongly, it must be confessed that they have not been ready to learn. Oxford debating has not been at all influenced by its contact with America and, even where attempts were made, as they sometimes were made, to hold debates in America in accordance with what was known as 'the Oxford plan', they were not really very successful. The 'Oxford plan' was so utterly unfamiliar to the American debaters that they could not really debate in accordance with it. The debates tended to be at cross purposes, and the decision at the end of them a confusion. An Oxford debate ends, with a division in which the auditors give their votes for what they conceive to be the merits of the question. In America judges give their verdict as to which side has debated better, irrespective of the merits of the question that they have supported. When, as sometimes happened in America, the vote was thrown open to the audience and they were invited to vote in Oxford fashion on the merits of the question, the notion was so unfamiliar to them that they did not grasp it and many of them imagined themselves to be judges awarding the verdict to the better debaters. It was difficult at the end to know what people had voted about or to interpret their conclusions.

Mr. Carson was succeeded as President by Edward Marjoribanks, himself beyond doubt destined for a brilliant political career had it not been for his early death. Marjoribanks was a proof that the Union, though at that time predominantly Liberal in its political opinions was willing to recognise merit irrespective of party. For he was a die-hard Tory, though of a highly intellectual type. After Marjoribanks, Mr. Douglas Woodruff, the present editor of the *Tablet*, perhaps the most brilliant of all the Union's wits of the era, became President.

If the election of Mr. Carson to the Presidency was evidence that the Union could rise superior to insular prejudices, the career of Mr. Bandaranaike there taught a more equivocal lesson. Mr. Bandaranaike was the son of a very distinguished Ceylonese Christian of strongly imperialist sympathies. Indian undergraduates often came to the Union and voted—especially of course when an Indian issue was at debate as it was from time to time in those days of the Montagu-Chelmsford reforms. There were not many of them who attempted to play a prominent part in its debates. Doubtless difficulties of language deterred. But Bandaranaike was by his upbringing less inhibited. From his first arrival he threw himself with enthusiasm into the Union debates. He was a brilliant speaker and popular among the members of the Union. He spoke at the beginning of his career, as was but natural, as his father's son, generally on the Conservative side. On February 8, 1923, I proposed a motion: 'That the development of the Eastern races of the Empire lies in development on eastern and not on western lines'. Bandaranaike opposed it. He was then a Westerner. At the appropriate time he stood for the Committees, and was elected. In the Michaelmas term of 1923 he served as Secretary. In the Trinity term of 1924 he was Junior Treasurer. He stood, as the Junior officers usually do, for the Presidency, but he was defeated. He was defeated by Scrymgeour Wedderburn, as he then was—the present Earl of Dundee and afterwards one of the representatives of the Conservative Government in the House of Lords. Scrymgeour Wedderburn, then perhaps a more defiantly imperialistic Conservative than he would call himself today, was indeed in every way a very suitable candidate. He had been Junior Librarian when Bandaranaike had been Junior Treasurer. Plenty of candidates before and after Bandaranaike have stood for the Presidency and been defeated and there was no kind of reason why a voter should not most properly prefer Scrymgeour Wedderburn to Bandaranaike. Yet there was some reason to think that the word had gone out among the old life-members who lived around in Oxford that it would be undesirable that the Union should have a President who was not white, and it was rumoured that they turned up in some numbers and recorded against him a sufficient number of votes to ensure his defeat. If so, it was a manoeuvre of complete legality but of doubtful propriety.

The Union is a club which many join as life members. If such life members live in Oxford, it is entirely proper that they should use the club's amenities—its dining room and Library and the like. There is no reason why they should not attend its debates, but naturally enough very few of them in fact do so. Not many mature men would be likely to get any very great pleasure out of listening week after week to undergraduates debating, and life members as a rule only attend very occasionally if there happens to be some guest speaker whom they are anxious to hear. The debating of the Union is an activity carried on, and rightly carried on, by under-graduates for undergraduates. Though no rule forbids the election of a senior life member to office it would in fact be inconceivable that anyone today should stand for office except during his residence in *statu pupillari* or perhaps im-mediately after he had taken his degree. That being so, it is doubtful whether it is desirable that life members who have not attended the debates should vote in the election of officers and clearly highly undesirable that life members who have not attended the debates should form themselves into a bloc to vote for extraneous reasons against a candidate. The ballot is secret and canvassing is forbidden and can therefore only be carried on under the rose. It is very difficult to say whether there was in fact any such bloc of life members who went to the Union to vote against Bandaranaike. There was certainly some diehard muttering, but what it amounted to it is hard to say. But it is certain that Bandaranaike believed that there was such a bloc against him, and this belief was at any rate one of the influences which caused him in his closing months at Oxford to reject his father's 'loyalist' political principles, to renounce Christianity for Buddhism and to become a very strong nationalist. His political career in Ceylon was, of course, built on the nationalist principles of which he remained the champion right up to the time of his final assassination.

As has been said, the Union has always claimed continuity with its predecessor, the United Debating Society, and there-fore claimed 1823 as its founding year. Its Jubilee was cele-brated in 1873 and it was natural when 1923 came round that all preparations should be made for a centenary cele-bration. There was to be an appropriate debate on a Thurs-day evening in October, in which what might be called the distinguished ex-officers of the second class were to take part and on the Friday there was to be a banquet in the Town Hall at which the Society's most distinguished members would speak. Unfortunately it so happened that in the chances of politics the Prime Minister, Baldwin, a Cambridge man, dissolved Parliament that autumn and named the Thursday of the week after the Union celebrations as polling day. There would clearly be no chance of getting the leading politicians of the day to a banquet at the very height of a general election campaign, and it was therefore necessary to postpone the Union celebrations until the next term.

The subject chosen for debate was whether civilisation had progressed during the last hundred years. Professor Gilbert Murray, who in his undergraduate days had been a frequent speaker but had never held office at the Union, proposed the motion. John Buchan, President in 1899, opposed it. Other ex-officers such as Dr. A. J. Carlyle, President of 1888 and in 1923 Senior Treasurer—Ronald Knox, E. C. Bentley, the author of *Trent's Last Case* and President of 1898, Philip Guedalla, President of 1911—all took part in the debate. The next day there was the banquet. The Archbishop of Canterbury, Randall Davidson, who had been a member of the Union but had never taken part in its debates, said Grace. As speakers to the various toasts there was a galaxy of talent such as could hardly have been found anywhere else in England at that date—Asquith, Lord Curzon, Lord Birkenhead, Archbishop Lang (then Archbishop of York), Sir John Simon, Hilaire Belloc and others all spoke.

As advertisement of the talent which the Union over its years had fostered, the centenary celebrations were an outstanding success. The debate, it is true, was not, and from its nature hardly could have been, on its own merits one of the Union's outstanding debates. The motion was not one to which anyone would naturally give a clear-cut verdict of Yes or No and the festive mood of the speakers was not one which inclined them to deal at one another the hearty blows which are necessary for a successful debate. The banquet was perhaps a little marred by an unfortunate misunderstanding. There was a problem of accommodation. Not more than five hundred could be seated on the floor of the Town Hall and more than five hundred applied for tickets. The suggestion was therefore made that the press be invited to report the proceedings from the gallery upstairs. The suggestion was made by the undergraduate organisers in innocence but in ignorance. They did not take in that it was a rule of journalism that the press must be allowed fully to participate in that which they are asked to report. The unfortunate result was that the journalists thought that, since the President would not give way and allow them to join the other diners on the floor, etiquette allowed them no alternative but to refuse to report the occasion. *The Telegraph* alone, whose leader-writer was E. C. Bentley, an ex-President, was persuaded to relax from the strict rigor of their rules and mention the event.

The Union suffered the penalty of its own riches—as no doubt it had done fifty years before. It is not really tolerable to listen to more than one or two after-dinner speeches. Yet with such a wealth of distinction it would not have been possible without insult to have had a short toast list. One or two of the speakers, both undergraduate and graduate, might perhaps have been omitted, but the leading statesmen of the day could not be denied their hearing. Nor, though vague hints about short speeches were dropped, was there in fact any way of imposing a rule of brevity. Politicians are long-winded, and, though the speeches did not go on quite as long as fifty years before, they started later, and the age was one of more impatient listeners. It was two in the morning before the diners left the table. The general verdict was that the occasion was more memorable than the oratory.

Lord Curzon, the Chancellor, made, it was generally agreed, a happy speech devoted to the task of congratulating himself on being himself rather than any of the other ex-Presidents. In good after-dinner style he contrasted his own official position as the Chancellor of the University with that of the President of the Union, which has 'no official existence' in the University; 'it is not even mentioned in the monument of literary style, the Oxford University Calendar. Its President is not prayed for from St. Mary's pulpit on Sundays, much as I am sure he stands in need of that arbitrary aid to continued existence'. 'Yet', he said, 'the Union is an indispensable feature' in Oxford life. But by general agreement the best speech of the evening was that of Lord Birkenhead. He confessed that he was a barrister but said that he had not always been irrevocably destined to that profession. There was a time when his parents had thought that 'a career more suited for my talents and abilities might be found in the Church', where he thought that he 'might have risen to the position then occupied by Dr. Randall Davidson'. As he alleged, 'by a strange chance I once discussed this very office with his present Grace, the Archbishop of Canterbury, and we both agreed that this promotion might have been possible, if, adopting a metaphor borrowed from the world of golf, I could have kept on the pretty between the holes'.

CHAPTER NINE

BETWEEN THE WARS

CHRISTOPHER SCAIFE WAS President at the time of the Union's centenary. He was succeeded by Gerald Gardiner, (now Lord Gardiner) destined to a high legal career. Gardiner succeeded to the tradition of Ramage in coming to the Presidency of the Union from the Presidency of the O.U.D.S. The Union was perhaps in a certain mood of reaction from celebrations and politics. The motions seem to have been more bizarre than ever before or since—such as for instance, 'That this House attributes to supernatural causes what are commonly known as psychic phenomena'—and Union life is perhaps at this period mainly notable for the *Isis* reports of it which were then being written by Mr. Evelyn Waugh. Gerald Gardiner emphasised his connection with the drama by holding a debate on the interesting motion: 'That Shakespeare did not mean Hamlet to be mad.' The *Oxford Magazine* recorded, 'Mr. H. Hylton Foster (Magdalen) made a very promising speech. He regarded Hamlet as a very ordinary mortal, being apparently of the opinion that there were few undergraduates so eccentric as not to murder their uncles from time to time.' Gerald Gardiner, if it is not offensive to recall it, was with the exception of Oakley the only President to be sent down during his term of office. His offence was in no way connected with the Union. He was also deputy editor of the *Isis*. Miss Dilys Powell wrote a vitriolic pamphlet on the state of the Women's Colleges which the *Isis* published. The heads of the Women's Colleges took exception to this and prevailed on the Vice-Chancellor to send Gerald Gardiner down. He had already taken his degree. So the punishment was not of great moment.

Birkenhead in the course of his speech at the Centenary Banquet recounted that in his time the intellectuals presumed to despise the Union. 'Whenever you deal with any particular period in the history of the Union,' he said, 'you always find that the intellectuals of the period disparage it as a contemptible institution. When I was at Oxford and used to speak at the Union, as I speak today, we were always told that it was an inferior place. There have always been a few intellectuals who have refused to take part in the debates. Lord Morley never spoke until he had become a figure in the larger sphere of public life. Lord Randolph Churchill never opened his mouth in this hall until he again was the leader of a great section of the Unionist party. I cannot help thinking that both would have been the gainers had they been debaters in this hall. Lord Morley would have gained in flippancy. Lord Randolph Churchill would have gained in earnestness.' The details of the indictment were inaccurate. Morley did speak as an undergraduate—though unsuccessfully. Randolph Churchill only did not speak because he was expelled for not paying his subscription. What was more surprising was the general burden of it, for most people have thought that, whatever might be said of the Union at almost any other period of its history, the Union of Smith, Simon and Belloc was not a Union that could be said to be boycotted by the intellectuals.

Yet certainly that could be said of the Union of the late 1920s. The Dons thought that it encouraged a cheap smartness which was affected only by those who were incapable of real academic distinction. The intellectual leaders of Oxford, like David Cecil and Edward Sackville West, who rotated around Sir Maurice Bowra, never went to it. Among Sir Maurice Bowra's clientèle who never went to the Union, was Hugh Gaitskell. His fellow Wykehamist, Mr. Crossman, contrived substantially to avoid both Sir Maurice Bowra and the Union. So a little later did Mr. Harold Wilson. Sir Alec Douglas Home, I do not think it is unfair to say, absented himself from the Union without being an intellectual. It was notable that, when Mr. Roger Fulford succeeded in persuading Sir Maurice Bowra, and Robert Bernays succeeded in persuading Anthony Asquith to speak there, their presence on the paper attracted a quite different sort of undergraduate who would never have dreamed of going there for an ordinary debate to hear a politician.

It is now over forty years since the Union's centenary, and there is one obvious difficulty in contrasting those forty years with their predecessors. In so far as the purpose of the Union is to be a nursery of statesmen, we can measure statistically its success during its earlier years. For we know to what greatness its speakers subsequently attained. It is indeed certain that in more recent years it has still proved itself capable as the first stepping stone to power. Look through the list of its officers and you will find name after name that was afterwards to attain some post or other of political importance. But exactly how great is the greatness that awaits them? Whether among those names there is, as is more than probable, anyone who is destined to be added to the list of the Union's four Prime Ministers, it is not yet possible to say, as the bearers of those names are in the great majority happily still with us, their careers unfinished.

From Gerald Gardiner the Presidency passed to Scrymgeour Wedderburn, the first Conservative President except Edward Marjoribanks since the war, perhaps mainly famous in Oxford history as the bogus Professor Heythrop who took the chair for George Edinger when he gave his hoax-psychology lecture under the pseudonym of Emil Busch. After Wedderburn came Robert Bernays, to be a National Liberal Member of Parliament and to be killed in an aeroplane accident in Italy during the Second World War. It was with his Presidency that the Society passed the first of a number of motions in favour of the abolition of capital punishment. After Bernays came the present Mr. Justice Lloyd Jones. After him Lord Molson. Then Sir Gyles Isham, like Ramage and Gerald Gardiner, combining the Presidency of the Union with the Presidency of the

O.U.D.S. and in his case adding to it also the editorship of the *Isis*. Then Lindley Fraser, afterwards of the B.B.C.— then Lennox Boyd—then Roger Fulford. As can be seen, it is a formidably respectable list. It was during Lennox Boyd's Presidency that Lord Birkenhead came to unveil the bust of Curzon, who had recently died. There were some who thought that the bust should not be accepted on the ground that Curzon had never been Prime Minister, but fortunately a more generous and less mechanical standard prevailed.

A higher proportion of the Union officers has, I fancy, gone into politics than in earlier times. If so, this is because in the new world of fewer independent incomes and more intense competition the modern undergraduate is more concerned with what will be useful to him in his career, the careless dilettante who does what amuses him without thought of advantage is less common than before 1914. The critics of the Union complain that those who frequent it are a clique. It is very much as a hunting ground for not very attractive or edifying careerists that the Union appears in the earlier pages of Mr. Fulford's amusing *Right Honourable Gentleman*. The hero-villian obtains the Presidency by promising to fill with gin the glass of his rival who cannot speak without alcoholic refreshment, and in fact filling it with water and thus spoiling his rival's speech, but I do not know that Mr. Fulford pretended that this refinement of gamesmanship was ever practised in real Union life on a candidate. He derived the conceit, I fancy, from the fact that Belloc really was given gin in place of water—a transposition which in that case caused the speaker no embarrassment whatsoever.

Under Sir Gyles Isham the first woman Don, Miss Grier, President of Lady Margaret Hall, spoke at the Union, debating on education against Lord Eustace Percy, who was at the time President of the Board of Education. The invitation to Miss Grier was, it seems, a last minute invitation owing to the failure of another speaker and she did not acquit herself very impressively. On the whole Miss Grier, as female Dons sometimes are, was a set-back to the cause of women. A

M

year later, addressed not by a female Don but by a female undergraduate, Miss Sutherland, the Union under Lennox Boyd debated and carried the motion: 'That the Women's Colleges be levelled to the ground.' 'There is no question,' reported the *Isis*, 'that the Union's standard is higher than at any time since the war.'

The memory of Dr. Farnell's follies had perished and Gerald Gardiner's fate was treated both by the victim of it and by the Union largely as a joke rather than as a scandal. Relations with the University authorities had for a few years been tranquil. Then in Isham's Presidency a quarrel flared up. Two undergraduates, Stephenson, an Australian Rhodes Scholar from Queen's, and Thomas, a Welshman from Merton, were summoned before the Vice-Chancellor, Wells of Wadham, incidentally also the Union's Senior Treasurer, and told that they would be sent down unless they gave an undertaking that they would take no part in politics. Their alleged offence was that they had befriended Indian Nationalists and the objection of the Union to the Vice-Chancellor's action was not so much to the action in itself but that it was alleged that he had acted on the request of Lord Birkenhead, who was then Secretary of State for India. In somewhat characteristically Oxford fashion it was never clearly established whether this was so or not—and it might seem to be the nub of the controversy. For many Oxonians would be more concerned at the general fear that the University authorities were prepared to take instructions from London politicians than they would be at the particular fate of a couple of somewhat undisciplined undergraduates. The Union debated the matter and censured the Vice-Chancellor, but a poll was demanded, and life members rolled up to reverse the verdict. Gyles Isham, the President, was unashamedly relieved at the reversal, fearing that the authorities might otherwise have taken measures against the Union, but, whatever the merits of the undergraduates, whatever the truth about Birkenhead's representations to the Vice-Chancellor, the Union surely is and ought to be the

Society of the undergraduates and whatever their technical rights, it is intolerable if life members come in to reverse the votes of the undergraduate members.

After Fulford the Presidency went to Playfair Price. He had been a Liberal, but at the time of the General Strike had dramatically announced his conversion to the Conservative party. He believed strongly in preserving the dignities—not to say the pomposities—of life and was, I fancy, the only President who habitually brought a top hat with him to the Society's debates. Playfair Price was succeeded by Malcolm Brereton, another Conservative, a charming and a witty speaker whose early death was a great loss to many friends and to the nation's life. He was of the old school, though a worthy representative, but a wind of change was then blowing over the Union. Since the first burst of earnestness immediately after the war, the Union had settled down into a tradition of flippancy and epigrammatic speaking. The tradition had been inherited or at least revived from before the war. Its originator, more than any other single man, was, I suppose, Philip Guedalla. The post-war epigrams at their worst were little better than copies of his witticisms. At their best they perhaps contained rather more meaning, but their critics complained, and sometimes had a right to complain, that the meaning often seemed something of an afterthought to the verbalism. Douglas Woodruff was the supreme master of the phrase that was merely funny, such as 'The trouble about a good all-round man is that he can so easily be squared', although he was also the master of very much more than that, and Michael Franklin made a good contribution with his 'Animals have tails, but human beings are left to form their own conclusions'. There were plenty of other examples of that sort of wit that were less felicitous and one could perhaps after a time tire of it. But anyone would have to be very pompous or very priggish who denied the right of undergraduates to a little innocent amusement. Still the obvious truth is that there is no single right way of debating, but that debates are only tolerable if the manner of them changes from time to time. So it was doubtless because a new type of undergraduate was finding his way into the Union in the second half of the 1920s that a revolt against the traditional Union manner set in. The old snobbery was thought to have reduced itself to an absurdity when in 1928 the King of Greece was invited to take part in a debate as a visitor. The King, defending the thesis, 'That an athletic education was more important than an aesthetic', was obviously entirely without any intrinsic qualification to contribute to the debate. He could not even speak English properly. Traditionalists and radicals agreed that the invitation was an unworthy move which brought the Society into ridicule.

At about the same time the *Isis* took up the question of Union elections. It alleged that, in spite of the rule against canvassing, there were notoriously in certain Colleges—it instanced in particular Worcester and St. John's—'caucuses' which herded members from these Colleges to vote for their candidates at elections, irrespective of their merits. The accusation was doubtless, and doubtless in a large measure always has been, true of all Colleges which took an interest in the Union. It was certainly true of my day that all Balliol members were expected to go to the polls to vote for a Balliol candidate and what exact amount of reminder of this expectation was required to constitute canvassing was a problem which only the subtlest of metaphysicians could be expected to answer. From time to time both before and after this *Isis* article accusations of canvassing have been brought. It has always been found wiser to drop them. I remember forty years ago a presidential candidate telling me how on the eve of polling day he chanced to be walking down a dark alley when his opponent of the morrow, not recognising him, taking him affectionately by the arm, said, 'You will be a dear and vote for me tomorrow, won't you?' The rule against canvassing serves, I think, its purpose in that it prevents absurd extravagances such as candidates setting up committee rooms, which we might get if there were no rule.

It is beyond human nature to expect that a candidate's friends will not take a certain amount of trouble to see to it that his friends' friends go to the poll on election day. What law can prevent an undergraduate from saying to another undergraduate, 'I hope that A. beats B. for the Presidency' and, if challenged, giving the reasons why he thinks this desirable? At what point does the giving of reasons become canvassing?

Allied to the problem of canvassing was now, and on two of the subsequent occasions, the problem of reporting. There were three occasions on which it was discovered that candidates for office were reporting the debates for one of the papers under a *nom de plume* and, as was alleged, giving a more favourable account of their own speeches than of those of their rivals.

The *Isis* was at this time in general very critical of the Union. In an editorial of June 12, 1929, it wrote, 'Everyone not connected with the place regards it as a joke, a joke that was never very good but is rapidly becoming worse. A Union debate is nearly always a lethargic and depressing affair, which not even the excuses that are offered for it can entirely condone.' But the opinion of the undergraduate is not necessarily representative just because he writes it in a newspaper.

At any rate there grew up round the end of the decade a group at the Union which clamoured for more serious and earnest motions. Mr. Michael Stewart and Mr. Roger Wilson were its two most prominent members, and they were both elected President in 1929. When Mr. Osbert Lancaster came down to debate about the ethics of duelling, they insisted on interrupting the debate, moving the adjournment and demanding that the House debate unemployment instead. Mr. Randolph Churchill came up in the Hilary term of 1929. His arrival was heralded by a great fanfare of trumpets from the London press announcing that he proposed to attain the Presidency of the Union in a shorter time than any other undergraduate. Mr. Roger Wilson was

then President. He called Mr. Churchill in his first debate at
11 p.m. and allowed him three minutes instead of the usual
two allowed to a non-paper speaker. There was an impression that Mr. Churchill thought—it was not very clear why—
that he had been unfairly treated. He came back at the
presidential debate and asked a number of questions of the
President about the Society's heating system, culminating in
the inquiry whether it was possible to introduce more hot air
into the Chamber. He spoke once in a subsequent debate on
the paper but did not survive long at Oxford and his presidential ambitions were never achieved.

It was perhaps Mr. Stewart and Mr. Wilson more than
any others who were responsible for introducing into the
Union a note of greater moral earnestness. It was doubtless
the inevitable consequence of the changed times, of the
appearance in Oxford in larger numbers of a new type of
undergraduate from a new type of school, with a more direct
acquaintance with poverty and with the problems of unemployment than their predecessors. But if there was a
reaction to moral earnestness it must not be imagined that in
those years moral earnestness was found only on the left.
On the contrary, sandwiched in between Mr. Stewart and
Mr. Wilson as Presidents came Quintin Hogg. Quintin
Hogg's career at the Union was, as may be imagined, marked
by eloquence and brilliance. As may equally be imagined,
there was also an incident when he was the centre of protest
and disturbance. After he had completed his term of office
at the Union and when he was a Fellow of All Souls', he returned to the Union and made some interruptions at the
presidential debate of March 6, 1930, in which Mr. Winston
Churchill was speaking against the Labour Government.
His conduct annoyed the *Oxford Magazine* which wrote, 'Mr.
Hogg is easily the best speaker and has easily the best brain
in the Union. It is a pity that, when he comes to the Society
merely as a speaker, he should see fit to behave like a nine-
year old schoolboy.' Undeterred by rebuke, Mr. Hogg the
next term came to a debate on India on the motion: 'That

this House would have broken the Salt Tax,' and moved an amendment that the debate he adjourned until after the publication of the Simon Report. Amusingly enough in view of what was to happen at the King and Country debate a few years later Quintin Hogg was violently opposed on this amendment by Randolph Churchill who was one of the paper speakers and did not wish to miss his opportunity. When his amendment was rejected, Quintin Hogg stalked out of the House, followed by some hundred sympathisers.

Mr. Wilson's Presidency was notable not only for the introduction of left-wing politics but also for the Society's first unqualified debate on birth control. Marie Stopes had come down to address a meeting on birth control seven years before but had only been allowed to speak in Ruskin Hall. Several of the Dons even now greatly disapproved of Mr Wilson's enterprise and refused to take part in the debate. When the Union had discussed this problem in the previous decade it had only done so in the very guarded form of expressing alarm at the population problem—a motion which anyone could support or oppose whatever he might think to be the remedy. Mr. Wilson was the first Oxford President who dared ask the Society to give a clear verdict on this problem. The praise or blame for his bold policy can neither of them however be fairly ascribed to his Socialistic principles, for he was on this point merely following in the footsteps of the Cambridge Union which a few years before had debated the same question under the Presidency of Mr. Selwyn Lloyd, then an Asquithian Liberal.

CHAPTER TEN

KING AND COUNTRY

OVER THE NEXT years the Union had a number of Presidents whose names have since become familiar, but the hero of that period was the Indian speaker Mr. Kabir, who never got beyond Librarian. He made his farewell speech on the motion: 'That this House condemns the Indian policy of His Majesty's Government,' and the *Isis* recorded 'The passing of Mr. Kabir from the Union is very much like the passing of an epoch. The charm of his personality has won him universal popularity and the quality of his speaking has brought him nearer the Presidential peak of Everest than any Indian has ever climbed before.' The *Oxford Magazine* recorded, 'The Union loses one who has done more than any other to influence its opinions on India and (incidentally) to sustain the debating reputation of the Society.' Whatever Mr. Kabir's responsibility it was certainly true that at a time when interest in Indian affairs throughout the nation was lethargic, Indian debates were always curiously popular at the Union.

In the Michaelmas term of 1932 the House elected as President the nephew of Field Marshal Smuts. By then the Union seemed quite to have recovered from its brief fear of progressive opinion into which it, like so many of the British public, had been thrown by the collapse of the second Labour Government, and in an impressive debate in which Duff Cooper spoke on the one side and George Lansbury on the other declared for a Socialist Government by 316 votes to 247. The debate was a triumph for Lansbury. The Union, according to the *Oxford Magazine*, was 'completely

carried away by Mr. Lansbury's speech. Its obvious sincerity, the force of its delivery and its delightful joviality left
the House no other course but to pass the motion.' It is a
sign of the changed times that it should be an orator of such
a type who could at that date sway the Union.

Mr. Smuts, a Liberal, was succeeded by Mr. Hardie, a
Labour man, and it was under his rule that the Union held
what was perhaps the most famous—or, if it be preferred, the
most notorious—debate in its history—the debate in which it
carried by 275 votes to 152 a motion 'that in no circumstances
would it fight for King and country'. This motion played so
large a part in shaping the reputation of the Union in the
eyes of many throughout the whole world who knew little
about the Society that it is worth while telling the story of it
in some detail.

At the end of the first meeting of the Standing Committee
in the Hilary term of 1933 the President, Mr. Hardie,
asked for any suggestions of possible subjects for debate.
The Junior Librarian, Mr. David Graham took a half sheet
of notepaper and wrote down this motion. The President
said, 'My dear chap, this is a very good motion, but
you can't really suppose you will get any one to speak in
favour of it.' Yet, on consideration, Mr. Hardie decided
that it was such a good motion that it certainly ought to be
debated, but, thinking that no undergraduates would be
found to support it, he thought that in order to give it a
chance it was essential to enlist a powerful guest speaker.
There was no difficulty in getting a guest speaker to oppose
the motion. Mr. Quintin Hogg, as we have seen, had been a
few years beforehand the ablest Conservative speaker in the
Union and was at that time still resident at All Souls'. He
accepted the invitation to speak. He not only accepted the
invitation to take part but also accepted the President's offer
of hospitality beforehand, and he does not appear at that stage
to have made any protest. Mr. Hardie's main concern at that
time was, however who he could get to support the motion.
After some failures he eventually got Professor C. E. M.

Joad. The debate was opened by Digby of St. John who spoke of Armistice Day as 'a bad and bitter joke', and claimed that 'Soviet Russia alone for peace had rid itself of its war-mongering clique'—a quaint description from a pacifist mouth of Stalin's policy. In the debate none of the under-graduate speakers was particularly outstanding, but both Hogg and Joad made very effective speeches. Hogg's basic argument was that 'the unilateral disarmament of Britain would render us impotent to prevent war in other parts of the world'. Joad was mainly concerned to paint a vivid picture of what he alleged would happen in the event of another war. 'Within half an hour,' he maintained, 'a single bomb from an aeroplane could poison every living thing within an area of three quarters of a mile.' To the contrary 'an invading army which met with no resistance would appear ridiculous to the military mind. All orders given by the invaders would be systematically disobeyed and, though a few leaders would be shot, the casualties would be infinitesi-mal compared with those in a war.' It was a surprise when the motion was carried by 275 votes to 153. But at that stage no one thought that the debate would have any great reper-cussions. 'I hope this gets into the press,' said the President to the Librarian as they left the hall.

There was no particular reason why it should have done so to any notable extent. There was no sort of novelty in the Union passing what the patriotic would consider unpatriotic motions. As we have already seen, shortly before the First World War the Union had passed a motion deploring the policy of the Triple Entente. In 1927 the Cambridge Union had passed by 213 votes to 138 a motion almost identical with that of the Oxford Union, 'That lasting peace can only be secured by the people of England adopting an uncompromising attitude of pacifism', and no breath of notice was taken of it. When this Oxford debate was an-nounced it aroused no journalistic interest. No London paper sent a reporter to the debate. The *Oxford Mail* alone covered it and its representative reported; 'I don't think it was particularly interesting or inspiring.' The next day, Friday, there was little about the debate in the press. Papers merely reported the bare result, as they usually do. It was only on Saturday that there appeared in the *Daily Telegraph* a letter signed 'Sixty-Four', of which the President alleged— without contradiction—that the author was J. B. Firth, a member of the *Telegraph*'s staff, in which the vote was alleged to be the product of 'Communist cells in the Colleges'. Then the *Daily Express* took up the running and on the Monday ascribed the vote to 'practical jokers, woozy-minded Communists and sexual indeterminates'. *The Times* spoke of 'a children's hour'. Lord Winterton declared that 'of those of his Oxford contemporaries who had been officers of the Union he could not recall one who had subsequently distinguished himself in public life'—an evidence of a surprising recollection. The *Manchester Guardian*, alone keeping its head, said that 'a worse exhibition of newspaper hysteria it would be hard to find'.

Even then the matter might well have blown over and been soon forgotten had not Mr. Randolph Churchill formed the determination to come down and move a motion in Private Business to expunge the motion from the Society's records. To the next debate on February 16 Mr. Malcolm Macdonald had already been invited as a guest and the President declined to allow his visit to be interrupted, but he agreed to allow Mr. Churchill and his friends to move their motion on March 2. But at February 16's debate, just as Mr. Karaka, the Secretary, had finished reading the minutes, a gang of undergraduates pushed their way in through the doors, seized the minute book, tore out the page recording the debate and afterwards burnt it at the Martyrs' Memorial. 'Some of our number,' one of them told the *Evening Standard*, 'are supporters of Sir Oswald Mosley's Fascist party.' The House then proceeded to Mr. Malcolm Macdonald's debate.

On March 2 the Private Business motion was moved. It was moved by Lord Stanley of Alderley and supported by

Frank Pakenham, at that time still, of course, a Conservative. By then contrary to the expectations of those who were to move it the opinion of the House, angered by the attack on their minute book and the ill-informed abuse of the London press, was thoroughly hostile to the threat of external bullying and many undergraduates who had no sort of sympathy with pacifism, as, for instance, the President of the Conservative Club, had come determined to refuse meekly to allow external pressure to alter the record of the Union's decision. The House was packed. One thousand tickets were issued. Undergraduates with false beards forced their way into the Chamber. Stewards patrolled ineffectively. Lord Stanley began, 'I am not Hitler,' and his half-finished sentence was greeted with loud, if somewhat idiot, laughter. A stink bomb was let off. The President then got up and made a dignified explanation of what had happened and why, whatever the merits of the House's decision, it would be quite improper to alter the minutes at external dictation. He was listened to in silence. Then Mr. Randolph Churchill got up. It was quite clear that the feeling of the House was overwhelmingly against him. His supporters tried to withdraw the motion. The President—his one stumble during the evening—was inclined to permit withdrawal. Mr. Dingle Foot pointed out that it was not permissible to withdraw a motion, once it had been moved, save by leave of the House, and the House angrily refused leave. It insisted on a division and on the division Mr. Churchill's motion was defeated by the overwhelming majority of 750 to 138.

While the resolution of the Cambridge Union passed, as such things so often do pass in our day of hit-and-miss journalism, totally unnoticed, while it never occurred to a less sensational age that the opposition of the Oxford Union to the Triple Entente was a material factor in encouraging the Kaiser to violate Belgium's neutrality, 'the Oxford resolution', as it was called, was taken up as a sort of symbolic expression of pacifism, debated as such and passed or rejected over the coming years in numerous universities, particularly in America. In so far as the effect was bad, the responsibility for that bad effect was entirely with the newspapers and with the opponents of the resolution who ensured for it greater publicity by their inept attempts to get it reversed.

It should not have been difficult to foresee that a demand from life members from London that the Union reverse its decision would in fact rally to the cause of the Union many members who had no sympathy at all with the original motion. This is manifestly what happened. The comparatively narrow majority on the original motion may have represented opinion on the merits of the question. The overwhelming majority against Mr. Churchill was obviously swollen by people who did not clearly know what they thought about pacifism but knew very clearly what they thought about the intervention. Mr. Churchill himself apparently came a few years later to admit as much. The *Oxford Magazine* in 1936 records that while Mr. Churchill, of course, continued to condemn what seemed to him the folly of the Union's vote, yet, 'as Mr. Churchill handsomely admits, the steps taken by himself and his friends to undo the mischief were unhappy in their result, as they only spread the news of the Union's crime still further with the final result of horrible mischief'. The Oxford papers fought this second battle on the side of the Union entirely as a battle of resistance against an attempt to bully Oxford from outside. The *Isis* thought that Mr. Churchill and Lord Stanley of Alderley were lucky to have got away with it as lightly as they did. The *Oxford Magazine*, while it thought that more practical advocates of Mr. Churchill's views might have made a better impression, yet condemned the *Daily Express* for having grossly misrepresented Mr. Hardie's views and claimed that the second debate was 'a notable triumph for Mr. Frank Hardie. He spoke with great clarity and power and—after one slip—he handled the question of procedure well.'

There were those in the subsequent controversy who objected to the introduction of the word 'King' into the motion.

They found in it a tang of disloyalty. The phrase 'King and Country' was introduced into the motion simply because that was the phrase of the recruiting posters of the previous war. Mr. Brian Farrell, now Wilde Reader in Mental Philosophy at Oxford, alone during the debate criticised the monarchy. But, apart from him, the speakers were not concerned with the question of republicanism and monarchy. Indeed it is very strange that the Oxford Union, which has at one time and another debated every issue from the existence of God downwards has only on one occasion debated the monarchy and that was on February 17, 1955, when it rejected by 193 votes to 109 the motion: 'That this House looks forward to a Republican Britain.' The 'King and Country' debate was on the personal issue a great deal less offensive than a debate a few years later when the House expressed its preference for the Red Flag over the Union Jack—a debate which passed quite unnoticed.

The motion of the 'King and Country' debate was supported not only by unconditional pacifists but also by those who argued that they would support a war demanded by the League of Nations but would not support a purely nationalist war. On December 6, 1934, the House carried by 151 votes to 60 a motion 'That in the opinion of this House the League of Nations should be able to enforce its decisions, where necessary, with full military measures.' Such a faith, as events were to prove, may well have been disastrously naïve, and Professor Beloff who was at the time as an undergraduate acting as a teller for the Ayes at the first debate, has recorded that: 'on reflection I now think it was an extraordinary piece of folly' to have supported the motion. He goes on, 'I think it's ridiculous to suggest that if it hadn't been for the debate Hitler wouldn't have gone to war. But it was one of the things that made it plausible for Ribbentrop and other people to report back that Britain wasn't ready to fight.' This may be a pertinent comment on the repetitions of the Oxford debate elsewhere some few weeks later, but it is important to remember that at the time of the Oxford debate Hitler had been only a few weeks Chancellor of Germany. There was in the debate no suggestion on the part of those who opposed the motion that, if we went to war, it was Germany who would be the enemy. Mr. Quintin Hogg gave as an example of a place where we might use our influence and where without armaments we would be unable to do so—Manchuria. Mr. Steel-Maitland, who spoke first in opposition to the motion, devoted his speech to the necessity of our being strong enough to stand up to Russia. The young men, who tore the page out of the minutes, in so far as they were Fascists, were presumably persons who thought that we should be allied with Germany against Russia. The whole controversy of the moment was entirely on the assumption that Russia was the enemy, and it is notable that when some years later at the very time of Munich on November 10, 1938, Joad opposed the motion: 'That war between nations can sometimes be justified', in a debate which again aroused no interest, he was supported by two Conservatives, one of them Sir Arnold Wilson, himself soon to be killed in action. The left wing speakers in that second debate denounced appeasement with scorn.

Mr. Winston Churchill, it is said, on hearing of the Union's motion, proclaimed that on no account would he ever speak in such an assembly again, though whether at that date he thought of Russia or of Germany as the potential enemy or whether it was a merely paternal rather than a political pride which objected to the Assembly, some of whose members had threatened to throw his son into the river, it would be hard to say. Some years later in an article in *Public Opinion* Lord Mottistone claimed that Churchill had 'actual proof' that the Union's vote had 'a direct influence' on Mussolini's decision 'to come in on Hitler's side', but as far as I am aware Sir Winston never confirmed Lord Mottistone's statement. A year later, when Mr. Karaka was President, the Union took its revenge, if revenge it can be called, on Winston Churchill when instead of a debate the President staged a mock trial of Churchill before the Court for the Suppression of Current

Menaces 'in that he has constituted, and does constitute, a menace to the world'. Mr. Michael Foot prosecuted and Churchill was condemned by 175 votes to 55. 'The President, having passed sentence of elevation to the peerage, the House adjourned at 10.20. p.m.'

It is always one of the curiosities of history that events have consequences wholly different from those that have been foreseen for them. It is unlikely that the Union's motion had any material effect in bringing on the Second World War. It is much more arguable that it was one of the material causes of women being admitted as members of the Union. Yet for all that the arguments for admitting women into the Union once they had been admitted to degrees were intrinsically overwhelming, whenever the suggestion was made, it was always voted down, and indeed it was difficult to get the male members to give it even serious attention. The reason was, of course, that few of them gave serious attention to the financial position of the Union. One consequence of the Union's resolution about 'King and Country' was a considerable drop in membership. By the time that the press had done its worst the Union had been given the reputation, deservedly or undeservedly, of a place inhabited by long-haired and careerist cranks. Both among undergraduates and among life members there were found some who were unwilling any longer to be associated with it—sufficient to bring about a drop in membership and a financial situation of some gravity. Women, if not desirable in themselves, were at least preferable either to insolvency or to a higher subscription. It was after the 'King and Country' debate that there began a running battle which continued off and on for some thirty years and has only been finally settled in our time, whether women should be admitted into the Union. That battle had its ups and downs. For a considerable period both undergraduates and life members were opposed but the broad outline of the pattern by the end was that the undergraduates were in favour of their admission and the life members were against it. It is possible to repre-

Oxford Union Society.

Thursday, 9th February, 1933,

at 8 p.m.

QUESTION FOR DEBATE.

" That this House will in no circumstances fight for its King and Country."

Moved by MR. K. H. DIGBY, St. John's.

Opposed by MR. K. R. F. STEEL-MAITLAND, Balliol.

MR. D. M. GRAHAM, Balliol, Librarian, will speak third.

THE HON. QUINTIN HOGG, Christ Church and All Souls, Ex-President, will speak fourth.

MR. C. E. M. JOAD, Balliol, will speak fifth.

TELLERS.

For the Ayes.	*For the Noes.*
Mr. M. Beloff, C.C.C.	Mr. R. G. Thomas, Brasenose.

Christ Church,
    4th February, 1933.

F. M. HARDIE,
President.

Agenda for the Union debate on Thursday, February 9, 1933

ABOVE   During the war it was impossible to maintain the Society's central heating and stoves had therefore to be introduced during the winter debates. The member fourth from the left is Sir Edward Boyle

BELOW   The Debating Hall. On the left are the busts of three ex-Prime Ministers, Asquith, Gladstone and Salisbury who held office in the Union. On the right are the busts of Simon, Birkenhead and Curzon

sent that battle as a battle between the generosity of youth
and the conservativism of middle age. A more realistic consideration was perhaps that undergraduates had still to pay
their subscriptions and life members had already paid once
and for all. For the alternative to admitting women was, of
course, to raise the subscription.

In the middle of the 'King and Country' controversy the
customary election for officers took place and Mr. Anthony
Greenwood, who had spoken in favour of the 'King and
Country' motion, was elected President. The rising star at
that time was Mr. Michael Foot, then still a Liberal. He was
triumphant alike in serious and in light debate. On a
motion: 'That this House prefers Fascism to Socialism,' *Isis*
records, 'Mr. Michael Foot was as usual terrific. He
trampled on Socialism and Fascism in turn, choosing as his
special victims Sir Oswald Mosley and Mr. G. D. H. Cole.
The Liberal party in Oxford is safe while the Librarian is at
the helm.' The next week in the Eights' Week debate:
'That this House flatly refuses to view anything with concern, apprehension or alarm, Mr. Michael Foot, the most
brilliant all-round speaker in the Union, made a superb
speech which everyone enjoyed.' At the end of the term,
though it was only his sixth term, he was elected President.

The Union finished this term by carrying by 107 votes to
87 the motion: 'That this House has no use for conventional
morality.' One of the most interesting of the developments
of the Union in modern times is the increasing frankness of
its motions. As we shall see the old prohibition on theological notions was after the war to be abolished and in recent
years we have had frank debates on, and indeed votes against,
the existence of God. The House over the years by ambiva-
lent motions felt its way towards, and then frankly faced by
an outspoken motion, the question of birth control. 'Conventional morality' might mean anything or nothing. It was
a motion which anyone might support or anyone might
oppose according to interpretation. Nevertheless the critics

N

of the Union naturally found in it confirmatory evidence of their belief that the Union was in an unhealthy state.

The Secretary, of the Trinity term of 1934, was Schlepegrell, of University—the only German ever to hold office there. He was very popular and on his departure at the end of the term *Isis* wrote, 'It is with great sorrow that we must bid him good-bye.' He was an anti-Nazi, though a patriotic German, and was afterwards shot by Hitler. It was owing to his eloquent advocacy that in this term the House carried by 125 votes to 25 a motion: 'That the acceptance of the German claim to arms equality is essential to the preservation of European peace.'

During the next two terms the House was presided over by Rhodes scholars—one from South Africa and one from Canada. Politics were debated and there was the usual stream of visitors—Lord Altrincham, Monsignor Knox, Father D'Arcy, Sir Stafford Cripps, Lady Megan Lloyd George, Herbert Morrison—but the House was becoming increasingly occupied with its own domestic financial problems. In the Michaelmas term of 1934 a vote was taken in Private Business to admit women to the Coffee Room, but so momentous a revolution required a poll of the Society for its authorisation and life members could vote in polls.

On January 26, 1935, the Union, which in the previous June started to serve luncheons, threw open its rooms also for dinners. One had been able to dine at the Cambridge Union for some years and even life members have stomachs. The proposal was considered less revolutionary and likely to be profitable. Indeed there were some life members who thought and hoped that the profits of the Dining Room might be sufficient to make possible the continued exclusion of the women. The *Oxford Magazine* took the occasion to publish an article, making it clear that, while it had no objection to Dining Rooms, it had the strongest objection to women being allowed into them. Yet in spite of the life members and of the *Oxford Magazine* the poll went in favour of the women. The President, Mr. David Lewis, now a very able member of the New Democratic party in Canada, a little surprisingly ruled that the majority was not sufficient to justify so revolutionary a change. However, in the next term it so chanced that all the main officers were Labour men. The President was J. P. Hickerton, now a Baptist Minister in the North of England. Mr. Hickerton ruled as against his predecessor that only a simple majority was required to obtain the admission of women to the Dining Rooms and only thirty-nine members refused to support him in this interpretation of the rules. The simple majority having been obtained in the poll of the previous term, Mr. Hickerton therefore merely declared women admitted and the problem was thus solved.

In the Michaelmas term of 1935 Mr. Brian Farrell was the President. Of all the speakers in the famous 'King and Country' debate Mr. Farrell remained throughout the subsequent furore and indeed, as far as the evidence of an article in *Town* in April 1963 goes, remains to this day, the most unrepentant and the most detached. It was his opinion that the 'King and Country' motion was a very cleverly phrased motion because it brought into the same lobby the total pacifists and those who thought that we should only fight at the behest of an international authority. Therefore he thought it of interest to have a motion which would divide these two schools of thought and staged a debate that: 'The Government's acceptance of collective security does not justify its claim to rearm.' It was, it will be remembered, the time when the Peace Ballot had shown an enormous majority throughout the nation willing to give general support to the League of Nations, but a very much smaller majority willing to support the League of Nations if it should call for military sanctions. It might be asked how there could be collective security if there were not any arms to support it, and the pure pacifist who rejected both collective security and rearmament was in some ways in a more logical position. However that may be, when the issue was posed in this way, three things were discovered—first, that opinion in the Union was very evenly divided—the motion was carried by 112 votes to 106—second, that in spite of some rather half-hearted attempts by Fleet Street to reopen the campaign against the Union, neither in Oxford nor in London did the matter arouse much interest. It was a poor House and the debate was sparsely reported. Obviously the overwhelming desire was not to have the raging controversy reopened. Thirdly, the Power against whom the rearmers thought it desirable to arm was at this date not, of course, Russia as two years before, nor Germany as two years later, but Italy. Having refused to rearm, the House then, the next week, proceeded by 147 votes to 90 to demand the abolition of the death penalty. Curiously enough, in spite of its shifting personnel and oscillation in party allegiance, the Union has been consistently throughout its history the opponent of capital punishment.

Mr. Farrell returned again to the topic of birth control. One trouble about the public debate of sexual questions is that, though sex is indeed a serious subject, it is also a funny subject and all the high-minded agnosticism in the world will not prevent its being funny. 'A revolution in the rubber trades has had a profound influence on sexual morality,' announced Mr. Farrell. It was true enough and pertinent enough, but neither truth nor pertinence could prevent the 'girlish giggles' with which the announcement was greeted and which Mr. Farrell attempted a little too portentously to rebuke.

By Michaelmas, 1936, the House was at last turning anti-German. On Mr. Edward Heath's motion it refused to return the German colonies and two weeks later in Private Business censured the Proctors for their refusal to allow the University Peace Council to lay a wreath on the War Memorial on Armistice Day, and in Public Business censured *The Times* as 'unworthy of its position as the leading English newspaper'.

The Hilary term of 1937 saw a debate in which Mr. Michael Foot, by then a convert to Socialism, moved a little surprisingly: 'That this House expresses its undying faith in politicians.' At another debate of this term Harry Pollitt, the Communist leader, was a guest and an enthusiastic Conservative threw down a stink bomb from the gallery. Mr. Ian Harvey picked it up with an expression of disgust and carried it from the Chamber, to show that responsible Conservatives did not approve of such antics. The Union played the Cambridge Union at rugby football and defeated it in spite of the fact that a high proportion of both teams took time out to be sick on the touch line. That evening it debated and carried the motion: 'That sport is either murder or suicide.'

Christopher Mayhew, President in the Hilary term, was succeeded by Mr. Anderson, who was at that time a Conservative, although he has since gone to Canada and is thought to have become a Communist. Professor Joad, who at that time enjoyed a reputation as lecturer at large to the nation which is not today remembered, and had established himself as a sort of permanent visitor to the Union, like Guedalla, never quite got over being an undergraduate and he gave the impression that he was more interested in getting a laugh than in expounding a consistent philosophy. A typical Joadism from this term was: 'After the war they carved up Europe into small pieces and called that making the world safe for democracy. Really it was only making it very difficult for stamp collectors.'

Oxford by this time was becoming a little bored with the excessively political, excessively intriguing young men of the Union and division figures in the debates were consistently lower than they have ever been before or since. Mr. Ian Harvey had built up and made efficient the Conservative machine. The Labour Club was eight hundred strong and had incessant meetings. But the average undergraduate found this continuous playing at politics and talking of politics day in, day out, both childish and tiresome. This was probably the period when the Union was most unpopular with undergraduates at large. The *Isis* wrote during this term: 'Oxford politics have strangled the Union. Their petty machinations have ruined real freedom of speech. As an office-hunter advances in seniority, his politics become more important. He must denounce capitalism without appearing an absolute revolutionary. If he is a Socialist he must not appear in evening dress or he would lose twenty votes. At any rate his tie must be a made-up one to show his contempt for bourgeois prejudices.' There was some truth in this criticism. Irresponsibility is the occupational fault of the undergraduate and it is up to a point attractive. A too careful careerism—a superstitious worship at the altar of the bitch goddess—is an odious absurdity. Few things in this world are more firmly closed than the closed mind of the professional progressive undergraduate. Max Beloff, almost alone, showed himself at this time of independent mind, championing the admission of women and opposing the abolition of evening dress for officers. Puzzled progressives did not know whether he was on their side or against them, and, though he was the most brilliant speaker of his day, thought it safer not to elect him President. The most popular figures at the Union at that time were its frank and unambitious buffoons—first among them perhaps a man from Hertford who professed himself a supporter of General Franco and proclaimed his faith week after week, whatever the motion. He would announce, 'I have now thought of thirty-seven reasons for supporting General Franco. . . . I have now thought of seventy-nine reasons for supporting General Franco', and so on as ingenuity suggested to him additional reasons while time marched on.

Under the next President, Mr. Fyfe, the political obsession of the Union was directly attacked by a motion in Private Business. At the Oxford Union, as indeed in the nation at large, there are political periods and non-political periods. Over many years no clear issue divides party from party. The nation's Government carries on in humdrum fashion. The ordinary citizen feels under no great obligation to commit himself. Then arises some great question. Everyone takes sides and politics are the order of the day. In this way the years before the war were intensely political years and their nature was amply reflected in the Union. But, while political, they were politically depressing years. Few could view them with much optimism. It was difficult for anyone to doubt that the world was drifting towards the appalling catastrophe of universal war. The supporter of the Government could not with much conviction persuade himself as the crises crowded on one another that Chamberlain's policy was likely to succeed. The most that he could say was that it was the only policy which held out any possibility of success and that there was no alternative to it. The Opposition thundered against appeasement, but there was all too much reason to believe that they were taking advantage of irresponsibility and that, if they should be faced with power, they would not find it easy to say what they would do and that the alternative policy, even if it was adopted, would not be very likely to be successful. In such a situation it was inevitable that the Union should hold political debates, and it was equally inevitable that those debates should produce a wearisome reiteration of the same old arguments, that they should be intensely depressing as it became increasingly obvious that none of the policies recommended had any prospect of being adopted and that undergraduates in increasing numbers should take the only remedy against depression that was open to them by staying away from the debates. In November of 1937 in Fyfe's Presidency a motion was introduced to make it mandatory on all Presidents to have at least one non-political debate a term. The motion was defeated on practical grounds. Who was to define what was a non-political motion? But the motion showed all too clearly that many undergraduates were becoming very bored and restive with debates of any sort, whether on political or non-political topics. It was all too much like fiddling while Rome was getting ready to burn.

Under the new President, Mr. Walton, a Liberal, full attention was paid to the demands of the non-political. There were indeed little but non-political motions: 'That the Law is an

Ass,' 'That this House deplores modern morality'—a motion even less precise than that in condemnation of conventional morality a few years before—'That freedom of the press under present conditions is an illusion.' Mr. Edward Heath, the rising star of the stern and bending Tories, moved that 'this House regrets the decline of frivolity'. But the change in the type of debate did not attract any larger audiences and Union officials were becoming increasingly concerned about the Society's financial position. The *Isis* estimated that the 'King and Country' motion had lost the Society £1,000 a year in subscriptions. Conventional parents and guardians were no longer prepared to consider a subscription to the Union an expenditure deserving subsidy. The only remedy, thought the *Isis*, was to admit the women.

In the elections the Union swung decisively from the non-political to the political and elected as its President Mr. Philip Toynbee, then a Communist. He brought back politics into the Union but sought to attract the crowds by bringing them back in a colourful and original form. He brought down Mr. Gollan, the Secretary of the Young Communist League, and put up to debate against him Mr. Bird, the Society's Steward, an ex-soldier. But neither Mr. Walton's tactics nor those of Mr. Toynbee gave much sign of solving the Society's financial problems and in Private Business on May 13 Mr. Mayhew moved a motion, calling for the only possible remedy—the admission of women to the debates in return for a subscription. But the House defeated the motion by twenty votes and, when a poll was demanded, the requisite hundred and fifty signatures were not forthcoming. The proposition therefore for the moment fell into abeyance.

Mr. Toynbee was succeeded by Mr. Wood, an Australian Liberal, under whom the House condemned Munich under the somewhat question-begging motion of disapproving 'of the policy of peace without honour', and more amusingly also voted against Joad, when he opposed the motion: 'That war between nations can sometimes be justified.' The vote was amusing because in this debate, unlike that of five years before, Joad, as has already been said, was supported in his pacifism by two Conservatives and opposed by a Socialist and a Liberal. But, whatever the views of other Conservatives, there was one among them at any rate—Mr. Edward Heath —who had no pacifist inclinations. He moved a motion condemning the Conservative Government: 'That this House has no confidence in His Majesty's Government.' 'As for Mr. Chamberlain's foreign policy,' said Mr. Heath, 'it could only be described in the maxim, If at first you don't concede, fly, fly, fly again.' In the next crisis he supposed 'that Mr. Chamberlain would turn all four cheeks at once'. Mr. Heath carried his motion by 203 votes to 163 and as a result was elected President.

Mr. Heath had a very successful term of office, almost all the debates running over one night. A motion opposing the recognition of General Franco was, it is amusing to notice, proposed by Mr. Biggs Davison, whose political principles were at that time of the extreme left. The rule against theological motions still stood but it was decided that it did not prevent a general debate on religion and a motion, 'That a return to religion is the only solution to our present discontents' was carried by the surprisingly large majority of 279 to 94.

After Mr. Heath came Mr. Hugh Fraser. His term of office was memorable for the ninth and last appearance of Monsignor Ronald Knox at an Eights' Week debate. Monsignor Knox was leaving Oxford and would not have appeared again, war or no war. His speech was, as had been all his previous speeches, according to the *Isis*, 'not a success but a triumph'. This was the first Union debate to be broadcast. But a larger cloud hung over Oxford and undergraduates had little heart to give themselves to Union debates. At the Presidential debate there were only a hundred present at the beginning and only forty when Alan Fyffe, the principle guest, got up to speak. Mr. Frank Giles, the present foreign editor of the *Sunday Times*, was elected President but he was not in Oxford to serve his office by the time that the next term opened.

CHAPTER ELEVEN

WAR AND AUSTERITY

———————————

THE SECOND WORLD WAR was by no means so complete an interruption of Oxford life as the First. Whereas in 1914 the young were allowed and encouraged to respond to the invitation of war and rushed off at once to the recruiting offices so that by the time that the Michaelmas term of that year was due to begin the University in the traditional form had virtually ceased to exist and remained non-existent throughout the war, in 1939 a more experienced Government pursued a more considered policy. It was judged important that education should not be ruthlessly abandoned. It was thought that those who were destined for a university career should have some experience of it before they were allowed to go into the forces and they were encouraged to come up for one year. The result was that, while Oxford and other Universities were very diminished places in comparison with their peacetime life, they did not come to an end. There were still undergraduates, though many fewer than usual. Games were played, dinners eaten and the University institutions were allowed and encouraged to carry on as best they could. As we have seen, in the First World War the Union as a debating society came wholly to an end. Its rooms were turned over to the military. Throughout the Second World War it continued as a club and it continued to hold its debates.

Naturally it could only carry on under some difficulties. When the undergraduates assembled in October 1939 all the four officers who had been elected at the end of the Trinity term had gone off to the war. Acting officers had to be appointed to carry the Society through its first wartime term. After the first term officers were elected as in normal times, but with the great majority of undergraduates only up for a year or so there was no possibility of living out a full Union career. The elections continued, but sometimes, it must be confessed, were a little peculiar. The elections that were held in June 1941 for the Michaelmas term's President were annulled for irregularities established by a commission of inquiry and Mr. Kenneth Riddle, the President, resigned. Towards the end of the war the Union elected its first Continental President Mr. Weisweiller—an Austrian but one who had been at school in England. As one looks through the names of those who held office during the war there are as many distinguished names in it as in any other period, which would seem to prove that as a discoverer of merit selection by chance is as effective as selection by ballot. For certainly officers were elected, of necessity, by voters who had much smaller experience of their capacity than in normal times.

The Union during the war also laboured under other handicaps—or at least was compelled to follow other policies than those of normal times. In the nature of things guest speakers were less easily come by and those of them who were in uniform could not make controversial political speeches. So long as the party truce was in force it was not easy to get two politicians to come and speak against one another on a political motion. This, though considered a disadvantage at the time, probably turned out in the end to be an advantage. Again the nature of the war made it difficult to find lively motions. There were no party issues in the ordinary sense. It would not have been possible to debate the rights and wrongs of the nation's cause, even had enough speakers to make a debate been willing to speak against the war. The Union was hardly qualified to discuss questions of strategy or the conduct of the war. On the other hand the times were such that there was little appetite for the purely frivolous motions of the pre-war Eights' Week debates, or indeed even for serious motions that were not topical. I remember returning home on leave, shortly before the German surrender in Italy, to be confronted with an invitation to debate the rights and wrongs of the Battle of Marston Moor. I did not feel strong enough for such an argument at such a time, nor, I imagine, did many others. I cannot remember whether the motion was ever debated.

Some motions about post-war policies could be and were concocted, but such debates tended to be repetitive and depressingly hypothetical, the life was taken out of the party clubs and organisations when there were no national party politics. Conservatives, who on the whole do not like politics, dropped party organisation. Socialists like politics and therefore continued to involve themselves in bewildering and incomprehensible combinations. The right-wing Socialists had broken with the old Labour club, when the Communists infiltrated into it, and formed the Democratic Socialist club. When the Communists infiltrated there, the regular Socialists broke again and formed the Labour Party Association, but these intrigues were of little interest to any but the intriguers. Among undergraduates, as in the nation at large, those who were discontented with the national management of affairs tended in the closing years of the war to give their support to the new Commonwealth party, which had a quite considerable following at the Union.

Union debates during the war laboured under another disability. The University authorities were not willing to take the risk that the Union should bring the University into discredit by passing motions which would bring down on them the wrath of Security. The chances of a Union speaker revealing some secret which would be of value to the enemy were not perhaps large, though not altogether negligible as a number of the Union members either were or had been in the forces and presumably on occasion in contact with secrets. But, though the real motive was doubtless the desire to prevent trouble, the plea of Security could not be derided and the University authorities were able

to make the condition of allowing the Union debates to be
continued that all motions should first be submitted to the
Proctors for approval. The Proctors were as a general rule
reasonable enough but they were always nervous about any
motion that appeared to impinge upon the conduct of the
war. They vetoed, for instance, a motion: 'That in the
opinion of this House lack of initiative rather than lack of
resources is retarding the Allied prosecution of the war.'
Whether the discussion of such a motion would have im-
perilled the nation's security is perhaps a matter of opinion.
It must be confessed that it was a motion which a casual
collection of undergraduates was almost ludicrously unqualified to discuss. Again there was some argument and
controversy when the Union wished to debate a motion
condemning American support of Admiral Darlan, the ex-
Pétainist French Admiral who had set himself up in North
Africa and who was soon afterwards assassinated. In face
of the ban the Union substituted the motion: 'That in the
opinion of this House there is no sweetness in the desert air,'
and by agreement between the speakers under the guise of
discussing the motion spent the evening talking about
Admiral Darlan. The undergraduates thought that they
had been very clever and amusing and had made fools of the
Proctors. But the Proctors are not quite such fools as undergraduates imagine. The Proctors were doubtless well aware
that there was plenty of room for difference of opinion, and
plenty of difference of opinion, throughout the nation as in
the Oxford Union, about the wisdom of American policy
in Africa at that time. It may well be that some of the Proctors themselves in their private capacities shared these
hesitations, and it can hardly be that they greatly objected
to undergraduates airing opinions that could at that date be
heard in any bus or tram in the land. There was no very
large probability that any of the crisper epigrams of the
Union debate would be reported back to Hitler or to
Roosevelt or that, if they were, they would spread alarm
and despondency in the White House or encourage the

Germans to persevere obstinately in their resistance. What the Proctors minded was obviously not what was said in the debate but the wording of the motion. With wartime restrictions on newsprint there was little prospect that the debate would be extensively reported in any paper. There was just a chance that the motion and the vote might be reported and, if it should get back to Washington—as well it might in garbled form—that the Oxford Union had voted without qualification against American policy, the result might have been unfortunate.

The most impressive debate of the war years was one on a motion calling on the Government to admit Jewish refugees from Germany. The motion was: 'That in the opinion of this House His Majesty's Government is doing everything in its power to rescue the victims of Hitlerite terror.' The debate is interesting reading today because it reminds us, as we have so easily forgotten, how little at that time the man-in-the-street, which was from this point of view the undergraduate in the Union, knew about Hitler's policy towards the Jews. We all knew of course that in Nazi Germany Jews were persecuted. We had read stories about Viennese intellectuals who were compelled to get down on their knees and scrub the paving stones. We were duly shocked. But it was not until after the war—until Nuremberg—that the world at large had any conception of the full horror of the story. So in this Union debate the opening speeches ambled along a conventional pattern. The one side argued that it was reasonable that the Jews should wish to get out of Germany. The other side complained that some of the refugees had been ungraciously insistent that British policy should be devoted entirely to rescuing refugees. If the Germans did not like Hitler, it was argued, they should not have allowed him to come to power. We had enough trouble owing to Hitler in defending ourselves. We could not be expected to put ourselves to unlimited further trouble in rescuing other people. In particular we could not allow unlimited immigration into this country to the upset of our economy and society. The arguments for control of immigration are familiar. We need not recount them, but what reads so strangely today is the light tone of the opening speeches of the debate as if this was a topic on which argument was evenly balanced and appropriate for the exchange of Union quips. The explanation is, of course, that the speakers, like the vast majority of the inhabitants of this country at that time, did not know, and could not have known, the facts of the situation.

The guest speaker of that evening was Mr. Victor Gollancz. When his turn came to speak he began by saying that he took no exception to the tone in which the debate had so far been conducted. Nevertheless he did beg the House to remember that it was just possible that their decision that night might influence Government policy. He then explained the reality of the issue and to such effect that, when he sat down, his opponents withdrew their case. The mover rose in his place and said, 'Mr. President, I can no longer vote as I intended. I wish to cross the floor,' and all but a handful of those who had been supporting him followed him. For the only occasion, I fancy, in the Union's history a motion in Public Business was passed unanimously.

Perhaps the most colourful of the Union's wartime Presidents was Mr. Cameron Tudor of Keble, who presided in the Michaelmas term of 1942. He was the Union's only Negro President, although, as we have said, forty years before the Union had had a Negro Treasurer. He exercised in the Chamber a pleasant and astringent wit, but it is, I think, fair of him as of other wartime officers to say that he encountered less opposition in his ascent of the tree than he would have encountered in normal times. Those few who for a medical reason or because of a neutral nationality did not get called up for the forces were of course at a special advantage as permanent fixtures of a Society the greater number of whose members were very obviously no more than transient and embarrassed phantoms.

The years immediately after the war were again, though

for a very different reason, very untypical years in the Union's history. Oxford, instead of being half-empty, was overfull as the servicemen returned from the war to finish their courses and, as after 1918, provided a type of under-graduate very different from that of normal times. They had fought in the war. Many of them had held responsible and commissioned rank. Among those who went to speak at the Union were at least five or six who had been candidates—albeit, of course, unsuccessful candidates—at the 1945 General Election. I do not think that there had been any such in the Oxford of 1918 or 1919. Therefore I think that it is fair to say that the young men of this war generation quite deliberately refused to consider themselves as typical undergraduates or their Union as a typical Union. In the future, for all they cared, Oxford might well revert to its traditional irresponsibility. For the moment they occupied a special position in which they were entitled to speak with authority on behalf of a generation. They did not want to revive the pre-war custom of having guests at every debate. They thought that they were capable of providing their own arguments and that a guest should be a rare luxury with which they could easily dispense. They discussed earnestly the shape of things to come. It was all a little pompous and a little splendid. It was in many ways preferable to the custom of other generations both before and after that who have thought too servilely of a Union career as a way of meeting influential people from London. But what is odd—and, I fancy, unique in the Union's history—was that this high-mindedness was combined not, as might have been expected, with left-wing politics but with a strong reaction to the right. The Union, of course, in this only reflected a general trend of national opinion among the young.

When the results of the 1945 election came through, there were many—some to rejoice and some to bewail—who thought that this was the end of conservativism in England. It did not seem an unreasonable prophecy. It certainly seemed less improbable than what did happen. What did

ABOVE   Nehru's visit. On March 9, 1961, Mr Nehru visited the
Union and debated the Motion that 'Ambition is the Last Refuge
of the Failure'. Mr Philip Whitehead, the President of the day, is
seated between Mr Nehru and Mrs Pandit

BELOW   The newly built cellars

Alexander Munro's carving of King Arthur and his Knights over the
side door of the Union forecourt, formerly the entrance

happen, as we all know was that, though the Labour Government was able to hold its seats at by-elections, yet Conservativism was very soon able to appear to many of the young as a more attractive creed than Socialism. In all parts of the country recruits flocked to the young Conservatives far more readily then they did to the young Socialists. It was indeed a Conservativism with a new look. The young generation did not sigh for the old feudal days and the return of the rule of 'the squire and his relations'. They wanted to strike off the shackles of bureaucracy and help the Conservatives to 'set the people free'.

How much sincerity there was in these slogans, where the truth lay in the debate of parties is of course a matter wholly outside the terms of reference of this book. But the interesting discovery was that, if the pre-war undergraduate had been so often left wing it was not because he intrinsically preferred left to right but because in perversity he liked to be 'agin the Government'. It was only necessary to change the Government from right to left and almost instantaneously you changed the undergraduate from left to right. In the first years after the war the Union voted pretty steadily Conservative. It was not in opinion die-hard Conservativism. It was essentially the Conservativism of Mr. R. A. Butler which delighted in depicting the Conservatives as more progressive than the Socialists, but there were occasions when it made up for moderation of opinion by rudeness of manner—as when Sir Hartley Shawcross, then the Socialist Attorney General, was shouted down. In comparison with either its predecessors or its successors the Union of those years was puritanical. Where the pre-war Union had repudiated conventional morals and the Union of a later day was prepared to deny the right of either State or University authority to concern itself with what it called 'private morality', the post-war Union a little priggishly refused to accept a copy of the poems of Oscar Wilde with which Mr. Montgomery Hyde wished to present it.

Politics apart, the first year after the war was an anxious

o

time at Oxford. As everyone remembers, the end of the war in the country at large did not bring a relief of austerity but an intensification of it. American lend-lease was brought to an end. Rations were cut down. The returning soldiers after 1918 had for the most part returned from the direct physical danger of the trenches. Minor inconveniences palled before the overwhelming joy of being alive. In the Second World War there were far fewer British casualties. A far smaller proportion of the ex-servicemen came back from great physical danger. They came back instead from a condition of ration-privilege in order to share the austerity of their civilian fellow citizens. The war had gone on two years longer than the previous war. There were more men therefore to crowd back to the Universities and they were two years older than their predecessors of the other war—in two years of a greater hurry to obtain the qualifications which would enable them to pursue their civilian careers. More of them were married than in 1918. The Government claimed—and on the whole with justice—that it was generous to the Universities and generous to the returning undergraduates. Yet even a generous bureaucracy demands an inordinate amount of form-filling and even an efficient bureaucracy succeeds in losing, or mislaying, or muddling a certain proportion of its forms. The result was that there were many undergraduates whose Oxford pleasures were marred by uncertainty and controversy and correspondence about their grants. There are those who will say that the undergraduate is still menaced by such anxieties, and to a large extent that is true. But with the passage of time a less fallible machinery has been worked out. It is easier for the undergraduate today to discover where he stands. The year after the war was a year of exceptional anxiety and uncertainty.

This anxiety and uncertainty meant that, while it was easy enough to start up the Union's debates on a note of high seriousness, it was much more difficult to get its social life going again. It was easy enough to open the bar. It served little purpose if the drink behind it ran out, as it often did in those months not only at the Union bar but at every bar in England. Alcohol is an essential lubricant and the unoiled undergraduate finds discussion intolerable. Union debaters were reduced to speaking on cocoa, and it is not surprising that under such depressing auspices the post-war Union, while it succeeded in being edifying and high-minded, singularly failed to be popular or fashionable. The risk was that the post-war undergraduate would drop the habit of going to it.

The man to whom, more than any other, is due the credit of putting the post-war Union on its feet was Mr. Roger Gray. Mr. Gray had been at the outbreak of the war one of the senior boys at Wycliffe School in Gloucestershire. He left school and, like other undergraduates, went up for a short time to begin his undergraduate studies at Oxford—at the Queen's College. There, as early as the Michaelmas term of 1940, he served a term as Junior Treasurer—by nomination because the elected Treasurer, Mr. Crisp of Balliol, had been called up for military service. He then went into the army whence he returned after V.E. Day. In those times there were a number of people who served terms of office at the Union which were separated from one another by a span of years—such as would hardly be possible in normal times. Mr. Anthony Crosland, for instance, was Junior Treasurer in 1940 and President in 1946, Mr. Wigoder, Junior Treasurer in 1941 and President in 1946. Mr. Gray's career was in this respect similar. He was elected President in the Hilary term of 1947.

Mr. Gray was himself a strong Conservative, but, though the Union was predominantly Conservative at that time in its opinions, election to its offices did not run along party lines. The Conservatives were much more impartial with their votes than the Labour undergraduates had been before the war. Mr. Gray had indeed Sir Edward Boyle as his Secretary, but his Junior Librarian was the Hon. G. E. Noel and his Junior Treasurer Mr. Anthony Wedgwood Benn.

Up till then the post-war undergraduates had on the whole a little complacently and without much effect been content to wait for the mountain to come to Mahomet. They had held their high-minded debates, and taken the line that it was for undergraduates to decide whether they saw fit to come to them or not. If the undergraduates did not attend, the loss, thought the speakers, was theirs. Mr. Gray was, I think, the first of the post-war Presidents to decide that, if the Union was to regain its pre-war prestige, it was necessary to go out and fetch people to it. In the Presidency of Mr. Crosland in the Trinity term of 1946 a financial appeal had been launched, which was successful, and a sum of money was raised which not only cleared off the inevitable losses of the war but left the Union in a stronger financial position than it had enjoyed in its slightly parlous pre-war days. It remained for Mr. Gray to restore its social prestige.

The Union, of course, dated back to the days of amateur status. In the Victorian times, when Members of Parliament were still unpaid, Presidents of the Union were also expected to be gentlemen who entertained the Union's guests out of their private pockets. As long as the guests were only one or two a term, the matter was not of great moment. Between the wars the custom grew up of having guests every week or almost every week and of having a supper after every debate. The Presidency under the new order was often in the occupancy of men of small means. If the dilemma was to be avoided that worthy candidates would have to refuse the Presidency simply because they could not afford it—which, it was generally agreed, would be intolerable—it was necessary to give the President something in the way of an entertainment allowance, but, as happens so often with English reforms, when a principle was conceded, it was, to begin with, only conceded in as niggardly a form as possible. A Presidential entertainment allowance was granted, but it was fixed at only £15 a term—a sum which by no means covered the President's expenses even in pre-war days and which was wholly insufficient with the higher prices of the years after

the war. Mr. Wedgwood Benn, when he was Mr. Gray's
Junior Treasurer, initiated a campaign for raising the
President's allowance. Some battling was necessary before
this campaign met with success and Mr. Gray did not wait
for its success. He began to entertain a great deal more
lavishly than his predecessors and he used this entertainment
as a bait to attract to the Union a number of Oxford personalities who had not previously thought of frequenting it.

Of these beyond question the most colourful was Mr.
Kenneth Tynan. Mr. Tynan's natural home was not the
Union but the O.U.D.S. He had never thought of going to
the Union until Mr. Gray persuaded him. But he was in
many ways the outstanding undergraduate of the post-war
years and his career at the Union, which led him eventually
to the Secretary's chair in the Michaelmas term of 1948, had
its inevitable effect on the Union. It was not a wholly good
effect. At that time Tynan was not deeply interested in
politics. The theatre that he preferred was what he himself
called 'the theatre of the fantasy and shock . . . I revered
poetical plays about the death of kings'. He had not yet
come to feel that 'no theatre could flourish until there was an
umbilical connection between what was happening on the
stage and what was happening in the world'. It was not
a handicap to the Union that one of its leading figures should
be a man prominent in other walks of University life and
not immersed in the game of party politics. Nor was it
a handicap that he should be a dynamo—acting, writing,
producing, editing the *Cherwell*—whose energies were not
nearly satisfied by his merely Union activities. Nor again
was it a handicap that one of the Union's officers should be
an exhibitionist and an extrovert, a public character in the
street with his purple doe-skin suit and his gold satin shirt.
He infuriated the rugger toughs, it is true, who burnt him in
effigy in the Broad and would have gone on to debag him
in propria persona had he not had the presence of mind to sink
to the ground with a cry of 'Christ, my hip, it's gone again,'
whereupon they gathered round and carried the supposedly

wounded hero back to his rooms. Such adventures and such exhibitions are the common stock-in-trade of the conventional unconventional Oxford character, and, although there is no compulsion on every Oxford character to behave and to appear like this, it is essential that in each era there should be some characters of such a sort. He was no more flamboyant and no more remarkable than was Harold Acton a little less than thirty years before. Such characters there must be, and it is doubtless good—indeed even essential—for the Union that it should sometimes harbour characters who are remarkable outside its walls.

Yet the cobbler must obstinately stick to his last. The Union is a debating society or it is nothing. A debate is an entertainment where people strive to persuade or to amuse by making speeches at one another. The speeches should be enlivened by humour, and who is to say what jokes are good and what jokes are bad? But the entertainment should come by way of speech and repartee. It is not that a debating society is necessarily a better place than a music hall but simply that everything should be itself and not another thing. It may be an excellent plan to sleep under a hedge, but sleeping under a hedge is not a form of architecture. It is the purpose of a debating society to debate and it is frustrated of its purpose where gimmicks are introduced pretendedly to enlighten, but in fact to prevent, debates. If the officers choose to dress up in pink hunting coats instead of evening dress for the Eights' Week debate as they did in the years immediately after the war, there is no harm in that, for the uniform does not prevent debate. But it was to be deplored when in the years before the war a custom grew up of undergraduates playing musical instruments in the Chamber in order to strengthen their case against being called up for military service. The Union's guests have, I am afraid, not been guiltless of such antics. Monsignor Knox before the war in an Eights' Week debate donned a gas-mask to illustrate a comic turn. Mr. Christopher Mayhew in more recent years brought down a baboon to support him in his criticism of Independent Television. Miss Nancy Spain filled the gallery with some more human supporters, armed unfortunately with musical instruments.

Mr. Tynan's tactics did tend to transform the Union from a debate into an entertainment turn and his influence on undergraduate life was so great that he has lit a candle that to this day has unhappily not been wholly put out. When he spoke to a packed house on the motion: 'That this House would rather be a dustman than a Don,' he had himself carried into the Chamber in white tie and tails, lying on a Corporation dust-cart. At another time he persuaded the whole House to leap to its feet and cry, 'I am big, strong, powerful'. Undergraduates are terrified of being what are today known as 'square' and therefore few of them have the courage to protest against such antics, to refuse to take part in them or not to laugh at them, but, though they are well enough for once, they easily become a habit and when they do so are almost unendurably boring.

In 1948 when Sir Edward Boyle was President the Union had to take an important decision. Under the Town and Country Planning Act there was a possibility that schemes for the replanning of Oxford might result in a threat to the Union premises. The decision which the Union had to take was whether it should put itself under the University. Such submission would enable it, in the event of threat, to plead that it was an educational institution. Would it carry with it an even greater threat to its independence? There had, as we have seen, been in the Union's earliest years a time when the University authorities were by no means favourable to it. But the general view both of legal advisers and of ex-officers who were circularised was that the chance of the University in any serious way seeking to curtail the freedom of the Union were in modern times negligible, whereas if they did at any time wish to take any action against any unruly member, they could always take that action against the undergraduate, whether the Union was nominally subject to the University or not. The verdict was therefore that the advantages of recognition as a society of the University were real, the advantages of proclaiming a verbal independence mainly meaningless. The decision was taken with little opposition that the Union should incorporate itself into the University and thus enjoy the advantages of a charitable organisation for the purposes of compensation were they to be displaced in some future planning scheme. But up to the present they have, of course, not been displaced, nor indeed has anything been done about Oxford's traffic save to make the congestion of the Corn worse by the destruction of the Clarendon and the substitution for it of a gigantic multiple store

After Sir Edward Boyle's term of office the House elected as President Mr. Seymour Hills of St. Catharine's, an ex-apprentice printer, ex-Ruskin College student, ex-ranker of thirty-seven. It is a commentary on the changed nature of the Society that it should have been prepared to elect such a candidate and that Mr. Hills should have been prepared to accept office. Mr. Hills was succeeded in the Presidency by Peter Kirk, the late Member for Gravesend. At the election at the end of his term there was for the only time in the Union's history a tie—between Faber of Christ Church, a Conservative, and Donald of the same College, a Socialist. Faber sportingly stood down on the ground that it was Donald's last term, but the term after was elected to succeed him.

The battle against the women was maintained with curious success. From time to time over those post-war years their admission was proposed but always defeated. This time they were defeated overwhelmingly by 311 votes to 98. It looked as if the Union and the House of Lords might be the two last assemblies in the country to remain obstinately male.

Apart from the admission of women the main political controversy of those days was whether the Union should consent to have its debates broadcast or televised. The arguments on each side were the usual ones. As has been recorded, an Eights' Week debate had already been broadcast before the war. In November 1950 the Union decided against allowing a debate with Cambridge to be televised but three weeks later agreed to a debate on the rearmament of Germany being recorded for the B.B.C.'s European programme. Some strange, if petty, precedents were established over the next year. Three members of the Wedgwood Benn family—the father and two sons—took part in a debate. The Union elected an American, H. E. Shuman of New College as its President, and an ex-President of the Cambridge Union, Norman St. John-Stevas as its Secretary. The women were defeated again. The Union agreed to serve breakfasts. A team from Oxford went to the United States and debated in Massachusetts against convicts. At last on February 23, 1953, obstinate resistance crumbled and the Union agreed to be televised. It was, it seems the first debating society in the world to submit itself to such an ordeal as a result of which, the Secretary announced the next week to the House, 'The President (Tyrell Burgess) has received 34 proposals of marriage and 61 other proposals.' The speakers in this debate were Lord Dundee and Lady Megan Lloyd George.

CHAPTER TWELVE

THEN AND NOW

As we come towards recent years, the story must for a number of reasons be told in a somewhat different way. As one turns over the pages of past records the main interest lies frankly in the discovery of what was said and done by those who were afterwards to rise to eminence. Few undergraduate epigrams are so pointed or epithets so cogent that they are worth exhuming simply for their own sake, if he who coined them is a person of no interest. We estimate the vigour or the lack of it in the Union in the various past decades. There again our judgement is clearly in part coloured by the subsequent careers of those who were at that date prominent there. It is indeed possible to discover plenty of contemporary testimony that Simon and Smith and Belloc were remarkable figures in their undergraduate days. We the more confidently accept that testimony because from their subsequent careers, it seems, inherently probable. It is amusing even when we discover those destined later to eminence speaking in their undergraduate days for causes the opposite of those which they would later espouse, Mr. Macmillan for instance speaking as a Liberal or as a Socialist —and we can expect those whose so very distant past is thus exposed—if indeed exposure be the right word—to take it in good part, but an undergraduate in current years moving from one political position to another and wondering what effect this transference may have on his political future would perhaps take less kindly to a gentle record of his chops and changes, while the record would at the same time be of little interest to the world at large.

One can marshal the evidence of those who have left records and pass verdicts on the past—at least record that such
debates were thought good debates and such debates thought
bad, that it was reported that so-and-so spoke well and
so-and-so spoke ill. It is much less easy to do this in print
concerning the immediate present, and that for a variety of
reasons. First, it is peculiarly difficult to form any reliable
judgement which can compare the health of the Union at
one period and at another. In the House of Commons there
are always a few Members and a few journalists in the Press
gallery who have been there for a generation or more. They
can compare from their own experience the giants of today
with the giants of yesterday. We may perhaps sometimes be
a little sceptical about the accuracy of their evidence, but at
least they are witnesses and a substantially reliable picture
can at any rate be obtained by balancing their evidence, one
against another. But in the Union there is at any given
moment virtually no undergraduate who remembers the
officers of more than three years. Even the press reports are
written by undergraduates whose memories are similarly
short. A visitor perhaps comes down from time to time to
listen to or to take part in a debate, and he compares the
Union as he finds it with the Union as he remembered it.
But no visitor is invited at the most more than about once in
three years or so. His impressions, comparing one visit with
another, are of some value but of limited value. Were the
speeches that night typical? Or were they particularly good?
Or particularly bad? If there was some unconsidered horse-
play or an excess of interruptions, does that happen every
week? Or was it an exception? It is very difficult to get a
certain and satisfactory answer to such questions.

Indeed it is quite impossible to give any generalised
answer that will hold good over even quite a short period of
years, because the orderliness, vigour, amusement and
general health of the Union's debates depend so much on the
President of the day, and the President, of course, changes
from term to term. Here again is an important difference

between the Union and the House of Commons. The health of the House of Commons depends very much on the Speaker of the day. But not only is the Speaker a mature man whereas the President is an ʼundergraduate, or near-undergraduate. The Speaker holds his office for a term of years. He has time to feel his way, to develop a technique, to retrieve, it may be, early mistakes. The President of the Union is only in the chair for eight debates. This is in all probability his first exercise of responsibility. The Speaker of the House of Commons has been selected—whether by entirely unanimous vote or not—as one who, it is hoped, will be generally accepted by all parts of the House. He is probably someone who in his previous years has played an honourable but not a bitterly controversial part in the affairs of the House nor one of quite the first prominence.

The President has arrived at the chair as a result of a contest at the end of the previous term against the second most prominent figure of the day at the Union. Probably not far short of half the voters at that contest expressed their opinion that he should not be President. Until he was elected President, he was always an aspirant—first from the floor to one of the Committees, then from the Committee to one of the junior officers, then from the junior office to President. If he was not ambitious of office, it is unlikely that he would have attained it, for there is always a sufficiency of ambitious young undergraduates at the Union and aspirants do not have to be dragged protesting to the chair, and, if he was ambitious, then, human nature being what it is, it is unlikely that he has not been at some pains to curry favour with voters and to show himself both in debate and in private life as perhaps a little bit more accommodating and smiling to audiences and casual acquaintances than sheer sincerity would demand. Then, on attaining the Presidency, he is at once elevated above the throng. There is no further honour that the Union can pay him. In that respect he has nothing more to gain or lose. On the other hand he must have a natural ambition to make a success of his term of office.

Suddenly he has to turn round and exercise discipline as a magistrate over those before whom up till now he had presented himself as a candidate, seeking their favour, and he has to succeed at once, for, if he mismanages his first debate or two, eight weeks are not a long enough time in which to retrieve such a mistake and impose a new mastery, and his presidency will prove a failure.

Perhaps it would be better to adopt the Cambridge system by which only the Secretaryship is contested and, once elected Secretary, the candidate progresses thence to the Vice-Presidency and the Presidency without opposition. As it is, at Oxford quite frankly plenty of Presidents do fail. One, anxious not to get the reputation of a prig and kill-joy, allows too much rope to the buffoons who are trying to rag off the debate. Another, anxious not to be thought a tyrant, does not call the interrupters to order as soon as he should. Other Presidents make the opposite mistake—show too crudely from the first that Henry V is no longer Prince Hal and come down too abruptly, whether in committee or in debate, on those who had the previous term been their equals, and muttered comments complain that the new young President is giving himself airs. Those who care to attend a debate at all wish the motion to be debated. They may welcome a little light relief and a modicum of horse-play but it very soon becomes tiresome, and the ordinary Member of the House wishes to see in the chair a President who has the courage and the tact to keep order and to pre-serve them from the intolerable tedium of the persistent in-terrupter or the professional buffoon. He despises the President who has not the wit or the courage to perform his task. Yet the President's task—that of holding the balance, of being firm without being pompous or tyrannical—of carrying the House with him without appearing to curry to it —is not an easy one. This constitutes an additional difficulty if one seeks to answer the question whether the Union today is better or worse than it was at some past date. There is not only the difficulty of finding a witness competent to make the comparison, when the whole personnel of the Union changes every three years. There is the difficulty that the Union goes up and down not so much from period to period as from term to term in accordance with the competence of the President. Even for as short a time as a year it is not really possible to say whether the Union is in good health. One term can make it, or one term can mar it.

Times do not change very rapidly at Oxford and in many ways the Union of the last years is very much the same as it has been through the generations. Its outward forms are much the same. The only great change there is is that the battle of the women has at last been won. By the 1960s it was no longer difficult to get a vote in their favour on the floor of the House but for such a change a poll could be demanded and in a poll a two-thirds majority was required. The life members rolled in to oppose and in November, 1962 the women just failed to get their requisite majority. 903 voted for them and 459 against. Mr. L. R. Reed, the Junior Treasurer, resigned in protest. In February next they came back and this time carried the day with 1,034 votes to 427. A last ditch attempt was made to exclude them by blackballing all women candidates, but the day of the black ball was gone and that effort did not meet with success. Yet the women's victory has up to the present been more of principle than of practice. It is admittedly too soon for a final judgement, but the number of women who are interested enough to attend Union debates is small. There have not up to the present been enough of them much to affect the Union, which remains predominantly a man's Society. Women can of course now be elected to its offices, but as yet no woman has been so elected.

The most notable mark of the modern Union is beyond question that it allows motions of much franker challenge to traditional custom than was allowed in previous ages. As we have seen, throughout the greater part of the Union's history theological motions have been banned. In spite of that the Society has from time to time invariably found a way of debating motions that common sense would have called theological. Even in the middle of the nineteenth century it discussed monasticism, a discussion that, one would have thought, could hardly have been sensibly possible without some consideration of what one believed to be the nature of God and His relationship to Man. Just before the Second World War the House debated and overwhelmingly asserted the importance of religion. In 1950 the theological ban was removed. There is no longer of course the predominant interest in the affairs of the Church of England that there was in the last century. There have indeed been two debates on its disestablishment in recent years, one in January 1956 and one in February 1963. In both, disestablishment was carried by fairly comfortable majorities, but neither debate aroused great excitement. The issue, in so far as it is an issue, is today very different from what it was in Victorian times. In Victorian times disestablishment was demanded by Nonconformists and was placed at the head of radical political programmes. It was resisted by the united body of the Anglicans who raised against it the battle-cry of 'the Church in danger'. But in both of these modern debates Anglican clergymen were found to speak on both sides and the argument was mainly an argument between clergymen as to whether disestablishment would or would not be in the best interests of the Church of England. Where a religious denomination has been challenged in debate in the Union in modern times, that denomination has usually been the Church of Rome. The debates have not been directly whether the tenets of the Church of Rome are true or false. Since only a small minority of the Union's members are Catholics, the result of a debate on that direct question would be a foregone conclusion. But motions have been drafted condemning the Catholic Church as the enemy of freedom or progress—motions which of course many who are not themselves Catholics but who believe that the Catholic Church, while not the repository of ultimate truth, is nevertheless on the whole a force for good, might well oppose. The wordings of these motions have varied slightly—'That the world would be a better place without the political power and influence of the Roman Catholic Church'—'That the oppressive political influence of the Roman Catholic Church in many countries and its unreasonable social doctrines in all countries justify our condemnation of this institution'—'That in the opinion of this House the Roman Catholic Church is a bar to intellectual and social progress'—'That the Roman Catholic Church is a major menace to freedom of thought and conscience in the Western world'—but they all amounted to much the same. The vote of the House has in all these debates gone against the Roman Catholic Church, but, whereas in the first of these debates in 1955 the Church was voted down by a comfortable majority and in the second in 1957 and third in 1961 by a very large majority, in the fourth such debate, on March 8, 1962, it was only defeated by 216 votes to 210. What was the reason for this? It can hardly be claimed that it was evidence of a wave of revival of religious feeling in the Union, since at about the same time the Union was repudiating belief in God, but that last Catholic debate happened to be a Presidential debate, and one of the Presidential candidates—who was indeed elected President at the subsequent poll—Mr. John McDonnell, was a Catholic. It was generally agreed that he made a particularly impressive speech. Perhaps the vote was a personal tribute to him. But also by that time John XXIII was on the Papal throne whereas at the three previous debates Pius XII had still been alive. Was ecumenicism at work? There is no way of apportioning responsibility for the Church's increased popularity as between Mr. McDonnell and Pope John. Some cynics indeed have even been so unkind as to notice that this fourth debate at which the Church polled so much more strongly was the only one of the four where no priest spoke on its behalf.

Other motions, as I have indicated, have made a more direct attack on religion. With the ban on theology withdrawn the House at first, as it were, reconnoitred the position by raising questions just short of the fundamental question of the existence of God. On May 12, 1955, it debated and substantially defeated by 349 to 224 the motion 'That the methods of science are destructive of the myths of religion'. The word 'myth' it might be thought was somewhat question-begging. The B.B.C. was going to broadcast the debate but somewhat mysteriously at the last minute banned its own broadcast on the ground that a general election was going on and the B.B.C. was therefore precluded from broadcasting controversial political matter other than the party political broadcasts. On November 1, 1956, the Union rejected by a similar majority the motion: 'That the modern man does not require religious belief in order to be moral.' On May 22, 1950, it rejected the motion: 'That a belief in God is not necessary for the enrichment of human experience,' but by February 1959 it had come round to believing 'That Science has demolished the myths of religion,' and on May 3, 1962, facing the issue without any sort of equivocation, voted by 295 votes to 259: 'That this House does not believe in God.'

On so-called 'progressive' topics it has narrowly approved of the extension of facilities for abortion and disapproved of euthanasia. It has several times unequivocally condemned capital punishment, but its most outstanding majorities have been for the repeal of the Homosexual Laws—587 to 87 on November 21, 1937, and 390 to 72 on February 4, 1960. It had already been established before the war that birth control was a debatable subject, but the convention then still was that all that was under discussion was the use of contraceptives within marriage. This made the debates always somewhat unreal since but few undergraduates were married or acquainted in any but a notional way with the problems of marriage. On the other hand the question whether they might indulge in pre-marital sexual activities was a very real one to them and the availability of contraceptives had a good deal of bearing on it. It was therefore perhaps inevitable in the modern mood that the House should go

P

forward from the debates on birth control or divorce to debate in February of 1961 the central question of chastity. The motion asserted: 'That the Christian ideal of chastity is out-moded', but it was voted down by 302 votes to 227. On June 6, 1963, the critics of traditional views returned to the attack and debated: 'That the State and University authorities should have no part in the enforcement of individual adult morality.' It was an ill-worded motion because it raised two different issues. The main field of 'individual adult morality' upon which the State was debatably entrenched was homo-sexuality. The House had already on a number of occasions expressed its strong opinion in favour of the abolition of these laws and it was on that aspect of the problem that the visiting speaker, for the motion, Mr. Montgomery Hyde, mainly dwelt. On the other hand neither University nor College authorities have ever been at all anxious to spy upon the moral habits of undergraduates and rarely, if ever, take cognizance of any conduct that is not positively forced on their attention. Mr. Brock, an ex-Proctor, argued that it was not practicable that the authorities should do less than they now did—that lodging house keepers and parents alike in-sisted on some minimum of control and that, if the University entirely abdicated its authority, the only result would be that the police would interfere more. The result of an ill-attended and unsatisfactory debate was that the motion was carried by 112 to 95.

The Union is by no means universally popular in modern Oxford. Many undergraduates will not join it. Many will not attend its debates. Many attend a few debates when they first come up and then decide to leave it alone, and the officers of recent years have been far from complacent about the reasons for its unpopularity. Members—or some of the members—they say, are themselves much to blame. They complain of what Mr. Michael Beloff, a recent President, has called in a memorandum of criticism 'left-wing McCarthyism' —that is to say, an ill-mannered refusal to give a decent hearing to any opinions other than those of the conventional left wing. Since there had been some years of Conservative Government at Westminster, the left wing was naturally in the majority at the Union. Indeed the curious result of twelve years of Conservative rule was that not only was there a left-wing majority but that a considerable proportion of the so-called Conservatives were in vigorous revolt against their own party line. When, for instance, in 1959 Mr. Macmillan came down to the Union for the unveiling of his bust, a Conservative leader tried to get the House to adjourn in protest against the Government's detention of Dr. Banda. The President, Mr. Trattner, rather foolishly allowed the motion to go to a division, when on a show of hands it appeared that the majority was in favour of the adjournment. Mr. Macmillan had however passed up a whispered message by way of the Librarian that, if the motion were passed, he would feel compelled to leave the Hall. The President therefore declared the motion not carried.

Buffoonery, it is alleged, has almost reduced the traditional Eights' Week debate to a cabaret show and, if the old epigram and verbal paradox of other days is no longer amusing to the present generation, it would be better, they say, to scrap the Eights' Week debate altogether. Debates are often marred by incoherence. Interruptions should only be indulged in on rare occasions and when genuinely necessary to challenge a mis-statement or to demand evidence—never merely to express a contrary opinion. A stream of interruption—demands that the speaker deal with some point other than that with which he happens to be dealing—destroys the possibility of intelligible debate.

On top of that it must frankly be confessed that Lord Simon's prophecy has been fulfilled. The custom of providing visitors for every debate has meant that a high proportion of visitors are persons of no special distinction and sometimes with no great experience of debating. Some of the visitors themselves have foolishly co-operated in buffoonery. An invitation to the Union is no longer the extreme compliment which it was when it was only offered to statesmen of the first eminence. A good many who are invited refuse invitations. Others more unpardonably accept them and then throw them over for subsequent engagements. Presidents sometimes invite rebuff by a failure of public relations which causes them to invite visitors to come down and speak on a side opposite to that on which they have expressed opinions or, even worse, on subjects in which they have never shown themselves remotely interested.

The life of a President of the Union today is enormously different from that of past generations—perhaps largely because the President has now so much more business of entertainment and of arranging visitors. Today for one short term the President finds himself equipped with all the paraphernalia of a business executive on a scale which he will not enjoy again for many years, if ever, private office, messengers, private telephone and the like, and the reason is simple necessity. He has his own telephone because he has to do such a lot of telephoning. It could not be otherwise. I cannot recollect ever telephoning to anybody when I was President of the Union.

Perhaps the most serious of the Union's problems today is the adjournment motion. The rules provide the possibility of a member moving the adjournment. The intention behind the rule was, of course, that that motion should only be used when for some very special reason it was thought necessary to interfere with the House's normal business, which is to debate matters of public interest in Public Business. Thus— to take a random example from past years—when Mr. Gladstone, the Society's most distinguished member, died on a day on which it had been planned to hold a light-hearted Eights' Week debate, it was obviously only decent that the House should adjourn rather than hold such a debate. In 1922 the adjournment of the House was moved in order to express its support of Mr. Lloyd George's stand in the Genoa Conference which was then being held. There were some who thought that Lloyd George's conduct would have been a quite proper subject for a debate in Public Business,

but that it was no special concern of the Union to express as
its own an opinion on a topic on which there was room for
difference of opinion and on which there was no reason for a
special Union view. However, the majority thought otherwise and passed the motion. It would be difficult to believe
that it did any especial good, but at the same time it probably
did not do much harm—provided that the example of it was
not frequently followed. But of recent years the habit has
grown of moving such motions at most frequent intervals.
They delay and interrupt Public Business. They are a great
nuisance. Two speeches and a ten-minute debate are not
sufficient to enable anyone to express a balanced or valuable
view. It is hard to see what purpose they serve except to give
advertisement to their movers.

These adjournment motions are of different sorts. Some
are on account of the death of some generally respected per-
sonage—an ex-officer of the Society, a monarch and so on.
Such motions are obviously proper enough and one may expect
them to be passed unanimously and without debate, though
a member was found so ill-conditioned as to raise a technical
objection to a motion of respect on the death of John XXIII.
There are motions of protest against some action of the
University authorities—such as the motions which we have
recorded in previous pages in criticism of Dr. Farnell or of
Wells of Wadham, when he was Vice-Chancellor for his
attempt to exact from two undergraduates a promise that
they would refrain from political activities. In recent years
there have been motions of protest against the punishment of
undergraduates, both male and female, who have been
found guilty of sexual offences. There have been motions of
protest against a Proctorial censorship of the *Isis* on one
occasion and of the *Oxford Circus* on another. The Union
cannot in any way claim to be the undergraduates' Parliament with a general mandate to speak for all undergraduates.
The majority of undergraduates do not belong to it. If anybody has the right to speak in the name of all the undergraduates it is the Students' Council. Still the Union is one

of the recognised organs of undergraduate opinion. If it should set itself up week after week to carry out an inquisition into the policy of the Proctors or of the Vice-Chancellor it would rapidly make itself ridiculous, but there is a case for its expression of opinion on some particular action of the authorities, where it feels strongly that injustice has been done. But what purpose can possibly be served by moving the adjournment of the House to protest against China's invasion of India, against the United Nations' policy in the Congo, against General de Gaulle's policy in Algeria, against the Government's treatment of Chief Enahoro, against Dr. Banda's detention, it is hard to see. Such subjects would if selected, have made proper subjects for debate in Public Business, but they were not subjects on which there was in any way a Union view. Those who passed the motions could, if they wished, say that they expressed the view of the majority of members who happened to be present in the Union at that moment. They could not possibly say any more than that and it is not very easy to see what purpose could be served by saying that. It is the rule of the Union that the Secretary should write to any person referred to in an adjournment motion to inform him of its contents, but it is hardly to be expected that Mao-Tse-Tung or General de Gaulle, Mr. Henry Brooke or U Thant would be deeply impressed by the reception of such a letter.

The fourth class of adjournment motion is the purely comic, such as that which congratulated the people of Ecuador on having three Presidents in one day. Recently a humorous ex-officer put upon the board a notice deploring the recent atrocities in Turkey and asking all who would support a motion to that effect to append their names. There had, as it happened, been no noticeable atrocities in Turkey at that time of which anybody had heard. Nevertheless, needless to say, a considerable number of names were appended. Of these joke motions it is sufficient to say that, if members were not already so profoundly wearied by the motions that did not pretend to be funny, they might with more patience endure those that did make this pretence.

Mr. Rose and Mr. Ziman in their *Camford Observed* complain of the modern undergraduates that they 'lack intellectual self-confidence' and I have not pretended that I do not regret the extent to which at the Union and elsewhere they have allowed themselves to become dependent for their entertainment upon London visitors. It is the complaint of Mr. Rose and Mr. Ziman that, though Oxford and Cambridge have indeed changed in modern times, they have not changed nearly enough and certainly, while the Oxford Union is, as has been often said in this volume, a parody of Parliament, it is in many ways a parody of the Parliament of 1864 rather than that of 1964. The Union debates with their encouragement of variety of opinion, with their free vote at the end, with their lax rules of procedure, are, if they be reminiscent of anything, reminiscent of a Parliament that has for long vanished from Westminster. Mr. Rose and Mr. Ziman dismiss it contemptuously as merely one of the discreditable frivolities of Oxford life. 'Some of the Dons,' they write, 'are still enthusiastic in their encouragement of athleticism, of the Union, of wine-bibbing rowdiness, of boys being boys, of every kind of tomfoolery, irrespective of the claims of work. They wantonly pander to that popular mythology.' The Union does not in their catalogue appear in a very high class, and it is indeed true that of Oxonian politicians who have attained a first rank since the war Macmillan had indeed his Union career, but Attlee, Eden, Gaitskell, Home and Wilson never had much truck with it. The Union changed remarkably little, considering the change of times, between 1823 and 1914. By 1914, though the proportion of Union orators who were going forward to Holy Orders was, of course, much less than a century before, it was still substantial and the potential ordinand was still often the Union's most lively orator. The top hat was by the later date relegated to the very ceremonial occasion, but clothes were still formal and collars stiff. The boys from public schools, though they had not the monopoly of the Union, still generally set its tone. The motions at the end of that period did not differ greatly from those which had been debated at its beginning.

If we may judge from motions, the Union has changed a great deal more in the last forty years of its life than it changed in the first ninety, and the largest changes have been in the last few years. The change has been in the frankness of the motions that are today admitted. Yet, changing thus, it has merely changed with the general fashion of the day. Oxford is here merely doing as the world does.

In general when every allowance has been made for extravagances and frivolities, I am sure that the verdict of Mr. Rose and Mr. Ziman is wrong. The Union must not indeed take itself too seriously, but at the same time it would be an appalling evil if the 'tomfooleries' which these authors denounce should all perish from undergraduate life. It is a good thing that there should survive a place where the young are encouraged to parade their opinions and to parade them in a light-hearted fashion.

PRESIDENTS

1823

D. Maclean	*Balliol*	Hon. T. A. Powys	*Christ Church*
Hon. A. W. Ashley	*Christ Church*	J. Bramston	*Oriel*
J. C. Colquhoun	*Oriel*	Viscount Ingestre	*Christ Church*
J. Wilson Patten	*Magdalen*	R. Durnford	*Magdalen*

1824

R. C. Dallas	*Oriel*	Hon. J. A. Stuart-Wortley	
E. Vernon-Harcourt	*Christ Church*		*Christ Church*
Hon. H. G. Vane	*Oriel*	R. I. Wilberforce	*Oriel*
T. F. Hodges	*New College*	D. C. Wrangham	*Brasenose*
H. B. Baring	*Christ Church*	A. J. Lewis	*Trinity*
Viscount Mahon	*Christ Church*	H. H. Dodgson	*Christ Church*
C. Des Voeux	*Oriel*	Hon. J. C. Talbot	*Christ Church*

1825

N. H. Macdonald	*Oriel*	E. E. Villiers	*Merton*
H. W. Torrens	*Christ Church*	Hon. C. A. Murray	*Oriel*
S. Wilberforce	*Oriel*	W. Trower	*Christ Church*
R. Durnford (*bis*)	*Magdalen*	R. A. Hornby	*Oriel*
W. J. Blake	*Christ Church*	F. Calvert	*Christ Church*
Hon. T. Vesey	*Christ Church*	J. R. Wood	*Christ Church*

VICE-PRESIDENTS

1823

J. C. Colquhoun	*Oriel*	Viscount Ingestre	*Christ Church*

1824

E. Vernon-Harcourt	*Christ Church*	A. J. Lewis	*Trinity*
C. Des Voeux	*Oriel*		

1825

H. W. Torrens	*Christ Church*	R. A. Hornby	*Oriel*
Hon. T. Vesey	*Christ Church*		

TREASURERS

1823

H. B. Baring	*Christ Church*	T. W. Carr	*Brasenose*

TREASURERS

1824

T. W. Carr	*Brasenose*	J. A. Stuart-Wortley	*Christ Church*
S. Wilberforce	*Oriel*		

1825

F. Calvert	*Christ Church*	W. J. Blake	*Christ Church*
N. H. Macdonald	*Oriel*		

PRESIDENTS

OF THE OXFORD UNION SOCIETY

1826

H. H. Dodgson	*Christ Church*	E. E. Villiers	*Merton*
D. C. Wrangham	*Brasenose*	R. A. Hornby	*Oriel*
R. Durnford	*Magdalen*	N. H. Macdonald	*Oriel*

1827

D. Smith	*Christ Church*	E. T. B. Twisleton	*Trinity*
H. Tufnell	*Christ Church*	W. R. Courtenay	*Christ Church*
J. Pearson	*Balliol*	H. Merivale	*Trinity*

1828

F. Trench	*Oriel*	A. Grant	*New College*
D. Smith (*bis*)	*Christ Church*	C. Baring	*Christ Church*
T. B. Hobhouse	*Balliol*		

1829

H. W. Wilberforce	*Oriel*	H. E. Manning	*Balliol*
T. D. Acland	*Christ Church*	H. W. Wilberforce (*bis*)	*Oriel*
H. W. Moncrieff	*New College*		

1830

Hon. S. Herbert	*Oriel*	W. E. Gladstone	*Christ Church*
J. M. Gaskell	*Christ Church*		

1831

Hon. J. Bruce	*Christ Church*	J. E. Lyalls	*Balliol*
J. Anstice	*Christ Church*	Earl of Lincoln	*Christ Church*

1832

G. K. Rickards	*Trinity*	W. G. Ward	*Christ Church*
R. Palmer	*Trinity*		

234

PRESIDENTS

1833

E. Cardwell	*Balliol*	E. Massie	*Wadham*
A. C. Tait	*Balliol*		

1834

R. Lowe	*University*	W. Sinclair	*St. Mary Hall*
C. Marriott	*Oriel*	J. Adams	*Christ Church*

1835

W. G. Ward (*bis*)	*Balliol*	E. Cardwell (*bis*)	*Balliol*
J. M. Capes	*Balliol*		

1836

T. Brancker	*Wadham*	W. N. Tilson-Marsh	*Oriel*
J. R. Cornish	*Christ Church*		

1837

H. W. Cripps	*New College*	J. A. Hessey	*St. John's*
G. R. Moncrieff	*Balliol*		

1838

W. H. Ridley	*Christ Church*	H. Highton	*Queen's*
W. C. Lake	*Balliol*		

1839

G. R. Moncrieff (*bis*)	*Balliol*	W. E. Buckley	*Brasenose*
H. W. Sullivan	*Balliol*		

1840

J. B. Blackett	*Christ Church*	C. T. Arnold	*Magdalen Hall*
G. Rawlinson	*Trinity*		

LIBRARIANS

1830

T. D. Acland	*Christ Church*

1831

G. K. Rickard	*Trinity*	E. Massie	*Wadham*
B. Harrison	*Christ Church*	R. G. Alston	*Christ Church*

1832

L. D. De Visme (formerly Goldsmid) *Balliol*

LIBRARIANS

1833

R. Palmer	*Trinity*	E. Cardwell	*Balliol*
T. W. Allies	*Wadham*	R. Lowe	*University*
G. K. Rickards (*bis*)	*Trinity*		

1834

G. K. Rickards (*ter*)	*Trinity*	G. C. Pearson	*Christ Church*

1835

W. Sinclair	*St. Mary Hall*	T. Brancker	*Wadham*
W. G. Ward	*Balliol*		

1836

J. R. Cornish	*Christ Church*	G. Mellish	*University*
W. N. Tilson-Marsh	*Oriel*		

1837

G. R. Moncrieff	*Balliol*	E. C. Woollcombe	*Oriel*
G. C. Fowler	*Pembroke*		

1838

W. C. Cotton	*Christ Church*

1839

W. C. Lake	*Balliol*	J. E. Bode	*Christ Church*

1840

J. E. Bode (*bis*)	*Christ Church*	F. Courtenay	*Exeter*

TREASURERS

1826

Hon. J. A. Stuart-Wortley		H. Merivale	*Trinity*
	Christ Church	H. Tufnell	*Christ Church*
R. A. Hornby	*Oriel*	J. R. Wood	*Christ Church*

1827

N. H. Macdonald	*Oriel*	D. Smith	*Christ Church*
F. Trench	*Oriel*		

1828

T. B. Hobhouse	*Balliol*	H. Tufnell (*bis*)	*Christ Church*
C. Wordsworth	*Christ Church*	H. W. Wilberforce	*Oriel*

TREASURERS

1829

J. D. Harding	*Oriel*	Sir J. Hanmer	*Christ Church*
T. D. Acland	*Christ Church*	J. M. Gaskell	*Christ Church*

1830

J. Odell	*Christ Church*	A. H. D. Acland	*Christ Church*
H. W. Moncrieff	*New College*		

1831

A. H. D. Acland (*bis*)	*Christ Church*	C. H. Oakes	*Merton*

1832

F. J. H. Reeves	*Merton*	W. H. Brandreth	*Christ Church*
W. G. Ward	*Christ Church*		

1833

W. H. Brandreth (*bis*)	*Christ Church*	G. E. Bruxner	*Christ Church*
W. G. Ward (*bis*)	*Christ Church*		

1834

G. C. Pearson	*Christ Church*	J. M. Capes	*Balliol*
E. Marjoribanks	*Christ Church*		

1835

W. L. Hussey	*Balliol*	G. Mellish	*University*

1836

G. Mellish (*bis*)	*University*	G. R. Moncrieff	*Balliol*

1837

J. A. Hessey	*St. John's*	W. C. Lake	*Balliol*

1838

S. H. Northcote	*Balliol*	W. E. Buckley	*Brasenose*
H. Highton	*Queen's*		

1839

F. W. Robertson	*Brasenose*	C. T. Arnold	*Magdalen Hall*
G. B. Northcote	*Exeter*		

1840

G. Rawlinson	*Trinity*	R. C. Powles	*Exeter*
R. Congreve	*Wadham*		

SECRETARIES

1826

R. Durnford	*Magdalen*	D. Smith	*Christ Church*
R. A. Hornby	*Oriel*		

1827

H. Tufnell	*Christ Church*	W. J. Crichton	*Merton*
J. Pearson	*Oriel*	T. B. Hobhouse	*Balliol*

1828

C. Puller	*Christ Church*	T. D. Acland	*Christ Church*
W. K. Hamilton	*Christ Church*		

1829

W. B. Smythe	*Corpus*	H. W. Wilberforce	*Oriel*
H. E. Manning	*Balliol*	J. M. Gaskell	*Christ Church*
E. V. Neale	*Oriel*		

1830

J. M. Gaskell (*bis*)	*Christ Church*	J. E. Lyalls	*Balliol*
W. E. Gladstone	*Christ Church*		

1831

S. C. Denison	*Balliol*	W. F. White	*Trinity*
G. K. Rickards	*Trinity*	W. E. Jelf	*Christ Church*

1832

A. C. Tait	*Balliol*	E. Massie	*Wadham*
E. Cardwell	*Balliol*		

1833

W. H. Brandreth	*Christ Church*	T. Brancker	*Wadham*
H. Barne	*Exeter*		

1834

A. R. Campbell	*Balliol*	J. R. Cornish	*Christ Church*
F. W. Faber	*Balliol*		

1835

J. R. Cornish (*bis*)	*Christ Church*	G. K. Morrell	*St. John's*
W. Tilson-Marsh	*Oriel*		

1836

H. W. Cripps	*New College*	W. H. Ridley	*Christ Church*
T. Phinn	*Exeter*		

SECRETARIES

1837

| G. L. Browne | St. John's | F. Poynder | Wadham |
| C. Campbell | Exeter | | |

1838

| H. W. Sullivan | Balliol | H. Fox | Wadham |
| W. E. Buckley | Brasenose | | |

1839

| C. T. Arnold | Magdalen Hall | R. Congreve | Wadham |
| J. B. Blackett | Christ Church | | |

1840

| C. C. Lempriere | St. John's | J. Clements | Oriel |
| R. C. Powles | Exeter | | |

OFFICERS FROM 1841

OFFICERS FROM 1841

1841

H.	W. Clerk	*Trinity*	J. Clements	*Oriel*
E.	P. Parnell	*St. John's*	M. Portal	*Ch. Ch.*

1841–2

M.	E. K. Karslake	*Ch. Ch.*	M. Portal	*Ch. Ch.*
H.	H. Cotton	*Ch. Ch.*	E. B. James	*Queen's*
E.	J. G. Cazenove	*Brasenose*	S. Lucas	*Queen's*

1842–3

M.	J. E. Gladstone	*Magd. Hall*	P. Parnell	*St. John's*
H.	J. L. Patterson	*Trinity*	W. H. Scott	*Trinity*
E.	A. Pott	*Balliol*	H. Tickell	*Queen's*

1843–4

M.	A. Pott	*Balliol*	H. M. White	*New*
H.	R. Lawson	*Ch. Ch.*	J. F. Mackarness	*Merton*
E.	M. Osborn	*Balliol*	A. Pott	*Magdalen*

1844–5

M.	P. Cumin	*Balliol*	A. Pott	*Magdalen*
H.	J. Conington	*Magdalen*	R. Lawson	*Ch. Ch.*
E.	R. J. Simpson	*Oriel*	F. R. Sandford	*Balliol*

1845–6

M.	R. Thornton	*St. John's*	R. J. Simpson	*Oriel*
H.	C. H. Stanton	*Balliol*	R. J. Simpson	*Oriel*
E.	G. O. Morgan	*Balliol*	C. H. Stanton	*Balliol*

1846–7

M.	M. Blackett	*Ch. Ch.*	C. H. Stanton	*Balliol*
H.	W. Congreve	*Wadham*	G. Ward Hunt	*Ch. Ch.*
E.	W. K. R. Bedford	*Brasenose*	G. Ward Hunt	*Ch. Ch.*

1847–8

M.	G. R. Portal	*Ch. Ch.*	H. Hayman	*St. John's*
H.	F. Meyrick	*Trinity*	G. R. Portal	*Ch. Ch.*
E.	R. A. Benson	*Ch. Ch.*	G. R. Portal	*Ch. Ch.*

1848–9

M.	Lord R. Cecil	*Ch. Ch.*	F. Meyrick,	*Trinity*
H.	J. R. K. Ralph	*Queen's*	G. D. Boyle	*Exeter*
E.	G. W. Latham	*Brasenose*	Lord R. Cecil	*Ch. Ch.*

OFFICERS FROM 1841

TERM	SECRETARY		TREASURER	
		1849–50		
M.	A. Mitchell	*Ch. Ch.*	Lord R. Cecil	*Ch. Ch.*
H.	F. Lygon	*Ch. Ch.*	Lord R. Cecil	*Ch. Ch.*
E.	F. R. Johnstone	*Exeter*	E. B. Lomer	*Oriel*
		1850–1		
M.	C. H. Pearson	*Exeter*	F. Lygon	*Ch. Ch.*
H.	B. B. Rogers	*Wadham*	F. Lygon	*Ch. Ch.*
E.	G. J. Goschen	*Oriel*	F. Lygon	*Ch. Ch.*
		1851–2		
M.	T. F. Wetherell	*Brasenose*	C. H. Pearson	*Exeter*
H.	C. H. Collier	*Oriel*	T. F. Wetherell	*Brasenose*
E:	A. G. Butler	*University*	G. J. Goschen	*Oriel*
		1852–3		
M.	F. A. Stapley	*Wadham*	G. J. Goschen	*Oriel*
H.	H. M. Jackson	*Trinity*	G. J. Goschen	*Oriel*
E.	F. M. Stopford	*Ch. Ch.*	G. Lushington	*Balliol*
		1853–4		
M.	G. C. Brodrick	*Balliol*	G. Lushington	*Balliol*
H.	G. J. Brown	*Ch. Ch.*	G. Lushington	*Balliol*
E.	C. A. Turner	*Exeter*	R. E. Bartlett	*Trinity*
		1854–5		
M.	A. Johnston	*University*	R. E. Bartlett	*Trinity*
H.	P. F. Eliot	*Trinity*	R. E. Bartlett	*Trinity*
E.	A. S. Thompson	*Wadham*	D. C. Lathbury	*Brasenose*
		1855–6		
M.	A. S. Thompson	*Wadham*	W. F. Wilberforce	*University*
H.	K. Smith	*Brasenose*	W. F. Wilberforce	*University*
E.	A. O. Rutson	*University*	E. K. Bennet	*University*
		1856–7		
M.	J. S. Tyack	*Exeter*	E. K. Bennet	*University*
H.	C. E. Turner	*Lincoln*	E. K. Bennet	*University*
E.	P. P. Fogg	*Jesus*	C. S. C. Bowen	*Balliol*
		1857–8		
M.	H. Wace	*Brasenose*	C. S. C. Bowen	*Balliol*
H.	H. Le Poer Wynne	*Oriel*	P. P. Fogg	*Jesus*
E.	W. E. Neale	*St. John's*	P. P. Fogg	*Jesus*

TERM	LIBRARIAN		PRESIDENT	

1849–50

M.	J. Earle	*Oriel*	W. H. Milman	*Ch. Ch.*
H.	W. H. Stowe	*Wadham*	J. R. K. Ralph	*Queen's*
E.	W. H. Stowe	*Wadham*	E. H. Knatchbull-Hugessen	
				Magdalen

1850–1

M.	H. J. S. Smith	*Balliol*	E. B. Lomer	*Oriel*
H.	H. J. S. Smith	*Balliol*	A. Mitchell	*Ch. Ch.*
E.	W. W. Shirley	*Wadham*	H. J. S. Smith	*Balliol*

1851–2

M.	W. W. Shirley	*Wadham*	F. Lygon	*Ch. Ch.*
H.	C. E. Johnston	*Oriel*	W. W. Shirley	*Wadham*
E.	C. E. Johnston	*Oriel*	H. N. Oxenham	*Balliol*

1852–3

M.	A. Watson	*Brasenose*	C. H. Pearson	*Exeter*
H.	A. Watson	*Brasenose*	J. Fitzgerald	*University*
E.	A. Watson	*Brasenose*	B. B. Rogers	*Wadham*

1853–4

M.	E. S. Beesly	*Wadham*	G. J. Goschen	*Oriel*
H.	F. Harrison	*Wadham*	A. G. Butler	*University*
E.	F. Harrison	*Wadham*	G. Lushington	*Balliol*

1854–5

M.	F. Harrison	*Wadham*	G. C. Brodrick	*Balliol*
H.	J. H. Bridges	*Wadham*	R. E. Bartlett	*Trinity*
E.	G. C. Brodrick	*Balliol*	J. H. Bridges	*Oriel*

1855–6

M.	W. J. Stephens	*Queen's*	D. C. Lathbury	*Brasenose*
H.	W. J. Stephens	*Queen's*	C. A. Turner	*Exeter*
E.	W. J. Stephens	*Queen's*	W. F. Wilberforce	*University*

1856–7

M.	J. Mitchinson	*Pembroke*	J. Oakley	*Brasenose*
H.	J. Mitchinson	*Pembroke*	P. F. Eliot	*Trinity*
E.	T. R. Halcomb	*Brasenose*	J. Mitchinson	*Pembroke*

1857–8

M.	F. St. John Thackeray	*Lincoln*	T. R. Halcomb	*Brasenose*
H.	F. St. John Thackeray	*Lincoln*	T. W. Fowle	*Oriel*
E.	F. St. John Thackeray	*Lincoln*	C. S. C. Bowen	*Balliol*

TERM	SECRETARY		TREASURER	

1858–9

M.	J. F. Dickson	*Ch. Ch.*	P. P. Fogg	*Jesus*
H.	W. Salting	*Queen's*	H. L. Harrison	*Ch. Ch.*
E.	C. C. Puller	*Balliol*	H. L. Harrison	*Ch. Ch.*

1859–60

M.	H. M. Robinson	*Pembroke*	F. M. Beaumont	*St. John's*
H.	M. F. Farrell	*Exeter*	F. M. Beaumont	*St. John's*
E.	G. W. Butler	*University*	F. M. Beaumont	*St. John's*

1860–1

M.	E. B. Key	*Lincoln*	A. O. Hardy	*Trinity*
H.	G. A. M. How	*Brasenose*	A. O. Hardy	*Trinity*
E.	A. Robinson	*University*	A. O. Hardy	*Trinity*

1861–2

M.	T. F. Dallin	*Merton*	O. W. Tancock	*Exeter*
H.	C. H. Waller	*University*	O. W. Tancock	*Exeter*
E.	O. A. Vidal	*Trinity*	O. W. Tancock	*Exeter*

1862–3

M.	H. F. O'Hanlon	*Brasenose*	A. Robinson	*University*
H.	F. H. Jeune	*Balliol*	A. Robinson	*University*
E.	W. C. Benett	*Ch. Ch.*	A. Robinson	*University*

1863–4

M.	J. L. Strachan-Davidson	*Balliol*	F. H. Jeune	*Balliol*
H.	W. Sanday	*Trinity*	F. H. Jeune	*Balliol*
E.	W. G. F. Phillimore	*Ch. Ch.*	R. Robinson	*Worcester*

1864–5

M.	W. B. Duggan	*Lincoln*	R. Robinson	*Worcester*
H.	J. E. Tinné	*University*	R. Robinson	*Worcester*
E.	R. H. Spearman	*Oriel*	E. S. Talbot	*Ch. Ch.*

1865–6

M.	H. D. Russell	*Wadham*	E. S. Talbot	*Ch. Ch.*
H.	H. G. Shee	*Ch. Ch.*	W. G. F. Phillimore	*Ch. Ch.*
E.	A. A. Elliott	*Queen's*	Lord Francis Hervey	*Balliol*

OFFICERS FROM 1841

TERM		LIBRARIAN		PRESIDENT	

1858–9

M.	E. Moore	*Queen's*	E. K. Bennet	*University*
H.	E. Moore	*Queen's*	A. V. Dicey	*Balliol*
E.	E. Moore	*Queen's*	A. O. Rutson	*University*

1859–60

M.	C. H. O. Daniel	*Worcester*	P. P. Fogg	*Jesus*
H.	J. R. King	*Merton*	E. Moore	*Queen's*
E.	J. R. King	*Merton*	H. L. Harrison	*Ch. Ch.*

1860–1

M.	Æ. J. G. Mackay	*University*	F. M. Beaumont	*St. John's*
H.	J. R. Magrath	*Queen's*	K. E. Digby	*Corpus*
E.	J. R. Magrath	*Queen's*	T. H. Green	*Balliol*

1861–2

M.	J. Bryce	*Trinity*	J. R. Magrath	*Queen's*
H.	J. Bryce	*Trinity*	Hon. Auberon Herbert	*St. John's*
			A. H. Beesly	*Wadham*
E.	C. Burney	*Corpus*	J. Bryce	*Oriel*

1862–3

M.	E. C. Boyle	*Trinity*	O. W. Tancock	*Exeter*
H.	W. Berkley	*Trinity*	R. Bosworth Smith	*Corpus*
E.	W. Berkley	*Trinity*	Hon. R. C. E. Abbot	*Ch. Ch.*

1863–4

M.	I. Bywater	*Exeter*	A. Robinson	*University*
H.	I. Bywater	*Exeter*	W. A. Fearon	*New Coll.*
E.	I. Bywater	*Exeter*	F. H. Jeune	*Balliol*

1864–5

M.	C. P. Ilbert	*Balliol*	A. A. Clive	*Lincoln*
H.	C. P. Ilbert	*Balliol*	A. Robinson (*bis*)	*New Coll.*
E.	C. P. Ilbert	*Balliol*	R. Robinson	*Worcester*

1865–6

M.	E. Caird	*Merton*	C. P. Ilbert	*Balliol*
H.	E. Caird	*Merton*	E. S. Talbot	*Ch. Ch.*
E.	E. Caird	*Merton*	G. A. Simcox	*Queen's*

TERM	SECRETARY		TREASURER	

1866–7

M.	A. Macmillan	*Brasenose*	Lord Francis Hervey	*Balliol*
H.	A. Brown	*Ch. Ch.*	W. Lock	*Corpus*
E.	C. L. Tupper	*Corpus*	H. G. Shee	*Ch. Ch.*

1867–8

M.	J. S. Cotton	*Trinity*	H. G. Shee	*Ch. Ch.*
H.	C. T. Cruttwell	*Merton*	C. T. Redington	*Ch. Ch.*
E.	R. F. Dale	*Queen's*	C. T. Redington	*Ch. Ch.*

1868–9

M.	E. Harrison	*Balliol*	C. A. Fyffe	*Balliol*
H.	J. A. Bryce	*Balliol*	C. A. Fyffe	*Balliol*
E.	N. Dawes	*St. Alban Hall*	A. H. Turner	*Ch. Ch.*

1869–70

M.	W. M. Sinclair	*Balliol*	A. H. Turner	*Ch. Ch.*
H.	C. R. MacClymont	*Balliol*	A. H. Turner	*Ch. Ch.*
E.	E. Ashmead-Bartlett	*Ch. Ch.*	J. A. Bryce	*Balliol*

1870–1

M.	D. F. Schloss	*Corpus*	J. A. Bryce	*Balliol*
H.	F. A. Hyndman	*St. John's*	W. M. Sinclair	*Balliol*
E.	M. H. Gould	*Trinity*	J. S. Cotton	*Trinity*

1871–2

M.	R. G. Matthew	*Wadham*	J. S. Cotton	*Trinity*
H.	W. S. Parker	*St. John's*	J. S. Cotton	*Trinity*
E.	S. C. Dudley Ryder	*Keble*	H. H. Asquith	*Balliol*

1872–3

M.	H. A. Venables	*New Coll.*	H. H. Asquith	*Balliol*
H.	J. T. Nance	*New Coll.*	H. H. Asquith	*Balliol*
E.	F. S. Pulling	*Exeter*	M. H. Gould	*Trinity*

1873–4

M.	C. G. Whitby	*Keble*	M. H. Gould	*Trinity*
H.	E. B. Ottley	*Keble*	H. A. Venables	*New Coll.*
E.	G. R. Parkin	*Non-Coll.*	H. A. Venables	*New Coll.*

TERM	LIBRARIAN		PRESIDENT	

1866–7

M.	J. L. Strachan-Davidson	Balliol	W. Awdry	Queen's
H.	J. L. Strachan-Davidson	Balliol	W. Sanday	Trinity
E.	J. L. Strachan-Davidson	Balliol	Lord Francis Hervey	Balliol

1867–8

M.	M. Creighton	Merton	J. L. Strachan-Davidson	Balliol
H.	M. Creighton	Merton	R. S. Copleston	Merton
E.	M. Creighton	Merton	E. S. Talbot (bis)	Ch. Ch.

1868–9

M.	W. B. Duggan	Lincoln	M. Creighton	Merton
H.	W. B. Duggan	Lincoln	C. T. Redington	Ch. Ch.
E.	W. B. Duggan	Lincoln	R. S. Copleston (bis)	St. John's

1869–70

M.	H. de B. Hollings	Corpus	C. A. Fyffe	Balliol
H.	H. de B. Hollings	Corpus	W. B. Duggan	Lincoln
E.	H. de B. Hollings	Corpus	A. H. Turner	Ch. Ch.

1870–1

M.	W. Lock	Magdalen	J. A. Doyle	All Souls
H.	W. Lock	Magdalen	T. H. Grose	Queen's
E.	W. Lock	Magdalen	H. A. James	St. John's

1871–2

M.	C. T. Cruttwell	Merton	W. Lock	Magdalen
H.	C. T. Cruttwell	Merton	J. A. Bryce	Balliol
E.	H. P. Richards	Wadham	H. M. R. Pope	St. John's

1872–3

M.	E. W. B. Nicholson	Trinity	C. T. Cruttwell	Merton
H.	E. W. B. Nicholson	Trinity	W. M. Sinclair	Balliol
E.	H. W. Lloyd-Tanner	Jesus	E. Ashmead-Bartlett	Ch. Ch.

1873–4

M.	A. K. Cook	New Coll.	R. G. C. Mowbray	Balliol
H.	A. K. Cook	New Coll.	M. H. Gould	Trinity
E.	J. Ashton Cross	Balliol	H. H. Asquith	Balliol

OFFICERS FROM 1841

1874–5

M.	S. H. Leonard	*Lincoln*	T. Raleigh	*Balliol*
H.	R. S. Mylne	*Oriel*	T. Raleigh	*Balliol*
E.	H. C. Wright	*Pembroke*	A. Milner	*Balliol*

1875–6

M.	J. M. Rigg	*St. John's*	A. Milner	*Balliol*
H.	E. G. O'Donoghue	*Exeter*	A. Milner	*Balliol*
E.	E. C. Lefroy	*Keble*	D. P. Barton	*Corpus*

1876–7

M.	R. A. Germaine	*Brasenose*	D. P. Barton	*Corpus*
H.	A. C. Stephen	*New Coll.*	A. A. Baumann	*Balliol*
E.	S. M. Burrows	*Exeter*	R. A. Germaine	*Brasenose*

1877–8

M.	O. R. Vassall	*Balliol*	R. A. Germaine	*Brasenose*
H.	R. Dawson	*Hertford*	R. A. Germaine	*Brasenose*
E.	B. C. Skottowe	*New Coll.*	F. R. Burrows	*Trinity*

1878–9

M.	A. W. Stirling	*Lincoln*	F. R. Burrows	*Trinity*
H.	A. H. Hardinge	*Balliol*	F. R. Burrows	*Trinity*
E.	H. C. C. Macleod	*Balliol*	A. W. Ready	*Wadham*

1879–80

M.	C. Arnold White	*New Coll.*	A. W. Ready	*Wadham*
H.	E. L. S. Horsburgh	*Queen's*	A. W. Ready	*Wadham*
E.	C. B. Lucas	*Brasenose*	C. Arnold White	*New Coll.*

1880–1

M.	F. S. Webster	*Pembroke*	C. Arnold White	*New Coll.*
H.	J. C. Cawood	*St. Alban Hall*	C. Arnold White	*New Coll.*
E.	H. J. Mackinder	*Ch. Ch.*	J. A. Hamilton	*Balliol*

1881–2

M.	T. B. Saunders	*University*	A. N. Cumming	*Balliol*
H.	W. H. Shaw	*Balliol*	A. N. Cumming	*Balliol*
E.	W. H. Devenish	*Brasenose*	H. J. Mackinder	*Ch. Ch.*

OFFICERS FROM 1841

1874–5

M.	E. C. Thomas	*Trinity*	H. A. Venables	*New Coll.*
H.	E. C. Thomas	*Trinity*	A. Sloman	*Pembroke*
E.	W. E. Russell	*Corpus*	T. Raleigh	*Balliol*

1875–6

M.	T. H. Warren	*Balliol*	H. W. Paul	*Corpus*
H.	T. H. Warren	*Balliol*	G. M. Savery	*Lincoln*
E.	T. H. Warren	*Balliol*	A. Milner	*Balliol*

1876–7

M.	R. H. Chambers	*Corpus*	R. H. Hadden	*Merton*
H.	B. F. C. Costelloe	*Balliol*	D. P. Barton	*Corpus*
E.	B. F. C. Costelloe	*Balliol*	A. A. Baumann	*Balliol*
			Viscount Lymington	*Balliol*

1877–8

M.	E. B. Poulton	*Jesus*	R. F. Horton	*New Coll.*
H.	E. B. Poulton	*Jesus*	Hon. W. St. John Brodrick	*Balliol*
E.	E. B. Poulton	*Jesus*	R. A. Germaine	*Brasenose*

1878–9

M.	R. Dawson	*Hertford*	N. Micklem	*New Coll.*
H.	R. Dawson	*Hertford*	E. B. Poulton	*Jesus*
E.	R. Dawson	*Hertford*	F. R. Burrows	*Trinity*

1879–80

M.	J. Sargeaunt	*University*	E. T. Cook	*New Coll.*
H.	J. Sargeaunt	*University*	R. Dawson	*Hertford*
E.	J. Sargeaunt	*University*	B. R. Wise	*Queen's*

1880–1

M.	E. L. S. Horsburgh	*Queen's*	Hon. G. N. Curzon	*Balliol*
H.	E. L. S. Horsburgh	*Queen's*	J. Sargeaunt	*University*
E.	E. L. S. Horsburgh	*Queen's*	C. Arnold White	*New Coll.*

1881–2

M.	C. H. Griffith	*Exeter*	E. L. S. Horsburgh	*Queen's*
H.	J. S. G. Pemberton	*New Coll.*	J. A. Hamilton	*Balliol*
E.	J. S. G. Pemberton	*New Coll.*	A. N. Cumming	*Balliol*

TERM	SECRETARY		TREASURER	

1882–3

M.	H. L. W. Lawson	*Balliol*	H. J. Mackinder	*Ch. Ch.*
H.	C. E. Mallet	*Balliol*	H. J. Mackinder	*Ch. Ch.*
E.	C. G. Lang	*Balliol*	A. Dyson Williams	*Corpus*

1883–4

M.	G. O. Bellewes	*Brasenose*	W. H. A. Worsley	*New Coll.*
H.	H. D. Leigh	*New Coll.*	W. H. A. Worsley	*New Coll.*
E.	M. H. Temple	*Keble*	G. S. S. Vidal	*New Coll.*

1884–5

M.	Lord Robert Cecil	*University*	G. S. S. Vidal	*New Coll.*
H.	H. J. Newbolt	*Corpus*	Lord Robert Cecil	*University*
E.	J. M. Walker	*Wadham*	C. Emmott	*Ch. Ch.*

1885–6

M.	A. E. W. Mason	*Trinity*	C. Emmott	*Ch. Ch.*
H.	E. Cecil	*New Coll.*	C. Emmott	*Ch. Ch.*
E.	A. D. Tupper-Carey	*Ch. Ch.*	C. J. Blacker	*Merton*

1886–7

M.	W. R. W. Peel	*Balliol*	C. J. Blacker	*Merton*
H.	A. S. T. Griffith-Boscawen		C. J. Blacker	*Merton*
		Queen's		
E.	E. de L. Collinson	*New Coll.*	H. M. Godfray	*Exeter*
			W. R. W. Peel	*Balliol*

1887–8

M.	R. R. Marett	*Balliol*	A. S. T. Griffith-Boscawen	*Queen's*
	H. G. Snowden	*Lincoln*		
H.	F. Russell	*Oriel*	A. S. T. Griffith-Boscawen	*Queen's*
E.	S. C. Parmiter	*Oriel*	A. S. T. Griffith-Boscawen	*Queen's*

1888–9

M.	J. A. V. Magee	*Merton*	A. G. V. Peel	*New Coll.*
H.	R. B. S. Blakelock	*Queen's*	A. G. V. Peel	*New Coll.*
E.	W. H. Cozens-Hardy	*New Coll.*	A. G. V. Peel	*New Coll.*

1889–90

M.	W. Knox Johnson	*Merton*	C. T. Knaus	*Trinity*
H.	H. Maynard Smith	*Trinity*	C. T. Knaus	*Trinity*
E.	J. F. W. Galbraith	*Oriel*	C. T. Knaus	*Trinity*

OFFICERS FROM 1841

1882–3

M.	W. H. Devenish	*Brasenose*	M. E. Sadler	*Trinity*
H.	C. W. C. Oman	*New Coll.*	W. H. Shaw	*Balliol*
E.	C. W. C. Oman	*New Coll.*	H. J. Mackinder	*Ch. Ch.*

1883–4

M.	C. E. Mallet	*Balliol*	J. S. G. Pemberton	*New Coll.*
H.	C. E. Mallet	*Balliol*	A. Dyson Williams	*Corpus*
E.	C. E. Mallet	*Balliol*	W. H. A. Worsley	*New Coll.*

1884–5

M.	G. O. Bellewes	*Brasenose*	C. G. Lang	*Balliol*
H.	G. O. Bellewes	*Brasenose*	G. S. S. Vidal	*New Coll.*
E.	W. J. Seton	*New Coll.*	G. O. Bellewes	*Brasenose*

1885–6

M.	A. H. Cruickshank	*New Coll.*	Lord Robert Cecil	*University*
H.	A. H. Cruickshank	*New Coll.*	A. H. Hawkins	*Balliol*
E.	C. A. H. Green	*Keble*	C. Emmott	*Ch. Ch.*

1886–7

M.	A. J. McGregor	*Oriel*	W. A. Phillips	*St. John's*
H.	A. J. McGregor	*Oriel*	C. A. H. Green	*Keble*
E.	A. J. McGregor	*Oriel*	C. J. Blacker	*Merton*

1887–8

M.	E. de L. Collinson	*New Coll.*	H. M. Godfray	*Exeter*
H.	E. de L. Collinson	*New Coll.*	A. J. McGregor	*Oriel*
E.	E. de L. Collinson	*New Coll.*	A. J. Carlyle	*Exeter*

1888–9

M.	G. F. Mortimer	*Balliol*	A. S. T. Griffith-Boscawen	*Queen's*
H.	G. F. Mortimer	*Balliol*	S. C. Parmiter	*Oriel*
E.	F. H. Coller	*Ch. Ch.*	H. G. Snowden	*Lincoln*

1889–90

M.	F. H. Coller	*Ch. Ch.*	G. F. Mortimer	*Balliol*
H.	F. H. Coller	*Ch. Ch.*	A. G. V. Peel	*New Coll.*
E.	J. H. Peachey	*Queen's*	F. H. Coller	*Ch. Ch.*

OFFICERS FROM 1841

TERM	LIBRARIAN		PRESIDENT	

1890–1

M.	J. H. Peachey	*Queen's*	C. T. Knaus	*Trinity*
H.	J. H. Peachey	*Queen's*	W. H. Cozens-Hardy	*New Coll.*
E.	J. F. W. Galbraith	*Oriel*	Lord Ampthill	*New Coll.*

1891–2

M.	J. F. W. Galbraith	*Oriel*	A. E. Ripley	*Trinity*
H.	J. F. W. Galbraith	*Oriel*	J. A. V. Magee	*Merton*
E.	H. W. Liversidge	*Hertford*	J. F. W. Galbraith	*Oriel*

1892–3

M.	H. W. Liversidge	*Hertford*	R. C. Phillimore	*Ch. Ch.*
H.	H. W. Liversidge	*Hertford*	C. H. Eliot	*Merton*
E.	P. J. Macdonell	*Brasenose*	Earl Beauchamp	*Ch. Ch.*

1893–4

M.	P. J. Macdonell	*Brasenose*	H. W. Liversidge	*Hertford*
H.	P. J. Macdonell	*Brasenose*	Lord Balcarres	*Magdalen*
E.	H. Belloc	*Balliol*	F. E. Smith	*Wadham*

1894–5

M.	H. Belloc	*Balliol*	H. A. Morrah	*St. John's*
H.	J. S. Bradbury	*Brasenose*	H. Belloc	*Balliol*
E.	J. S. Bradbury	*Brasenose*	P. J. Macdonell	*Brasenose*

1895–6

M.	J. S. Bradbury	*Brasenose*	J. S. Phillimore	*Ch. Ch*
H.	F. W. Hirst	*Wadham*	J. A. Simon	*Wadham*
E.	F. W. Hirst	*Wadham*	A. Boyd-Carpenter	*Balliol*

1896–7

M.	J. W. Cleland	*Balliol*	F. W. Hirst	*Wadham*
H.	J. W. Cleland	*Balliol*	R. A. Johnson	*New Coll.*
E.	E. C. Bentley	*Merton*	J. W. Cleland	*Balliol*

1897–8

M.	E. C. Bentley	*Merton*	F. Lenwood	*Corpus*
H.	L. R. F. Oldershaw	*Ch. Ch.*	E. C. Bentley	*Merton*
E.	J. Buchan	*Brasenose*	C. F. Garbett	*Keble*

OFFICERS FROM 1841

TERM	SECRETARY		TREASURER	

1898–9

M.	G. Gathorne-Hardy	*New Coll.*	S. Armitage-Smith	*New Coll.*
H.	J. G. Jameson	*Balliol*	A. H. D. Steel	*Balliol*
E.	R. C. K. Ensor	*Balliol*	G. Gathorne-Hardy	*New Coll.*

1899–1900

M.	A. Cecil	*New Coll.*	R. C. K. Ensor	*Balliol*
H.	T. Cuthbertson	*Corpus*	A. Cecil	*New Coll.*
E.	E. T. Nelson	*St. John's*	T. Cuthbertson	*Corpus*

1900–1

M.	G. J. F. Tomlinson	*University*	E. T. Nelson	*St. John's*
H.	Hon. A. Herbert	*Balliol*	E. T. Nelson	*St. John's*
E.	A. D. Lindsay	*University*	Hon. A. Herbert	*Balliol*

1901–2

M.	H. du Parcq	*Exeter*	A. D. Lindsay	*University*
H.	F. W. Curran	*Lincoln*	H. Asquith	*Balliol*
E.	Hon. E. Cadogan	*Balliol*	H. du Parcq	*Exeter*

1902–3

M.	H. Thorp	*Wadham*	J. R. Brooke	*Corpus*
H.	W. Temple	*Balliol*	H. Thorp	*Wadham*
E.	A. S. Comyns-Carr	*Trinity*	E. Walls	*Corpus*

1903–4

M.	J. St. G. C. Heath	*Corpus*	M. H. Woods	*Trinity*
H.	C. P. Blackwell	*Wadham*	W. A. Moore	*St. John's*
E.	Hon. H. Lygon	*Magdalen*	A. Shaw	*Trinity*

1904–5

M.	J. H. N. Taylor	*Hertford*	Hon. H. Lygon	*Magdalen*
H.	A. H. Paterson	*University*	H. M. Paul	*New Coll.*
E.	E. M. C. Denny	*Jesus*	A. H. Paterson	*University*

1905–6

M.	G. S. C. Rentoul	*Ch. Ch.*	R. C. Bonnerjee	*Balliol*
H.	N. S. Talbot	*Ch. Ch.*	G. S. C. Rentoul	*Ch. Ch.*
E.	W. G. C. Gladstone	*New Coll.*	A. H. Villiers	*Magdalen*

1906–7

M.	G. B. Allen	*Wadham*	W. G. C. Gladstone	*New Coll.*
H.	H. I. P. Hallett	*Ch. Ch.*	W. S. Armour	*Jesus*
E.	S. F. S. Johnston	*Trinity*	Viscount Wolmer	*University*

OFFICERS FROM 1841

TERM	LIBRARIAN		PRESIDENT	

1898–9

M.	J. Buchan	*Brasenose*	L. R. F. Oldershaw	*Ch. Ch.*
H.	R. Asquith	*Balliol*	J. Buchan	*Brasenose*
E.	R. Asquith	*Balliol*	A. H. D. Steel	*Balliol*

1899–1900

M.	S. A. Gillon	*New Coll.*	G. Gathorne-Hardy	*New Coll.*
H.	H. T. Baker	*New Coll.*	R. C. K. Ensor	*Balliol*
E.	H. T. Baker	*New Coll.*	R. Asquith	*Balliol*

1900–1

M.	A. Cecil	*New Coll.*	H. T. Baker	*New Coll.*
H.	T. Cuthbertson	*Corpus*	A. Cecil	*New Coll.*
E.	G. J. F. Tomlinson	*University*	T. Cuthbertson	*Corpus*

1901–2

M.	Hon. A. Herbert	*Balliol*	G. J. F. Tomlinson	*University*
H.	E. Macfadyen	*Wadham*	A. D. Lindsay	*University*
E.	H. Asquith	*Balliol*	E. Macfadyen	*Wadham*

1902–3

M.	F. W. Curran	*Lincoln*	H. du Parcq	*Exeter*
H.	J. R. Brooke	*Corpus*	H. Asquith	*Balliol*
E.	H. Thorp	*Wadham*	F. W. Curran	*Lincoln*

1903–4

M.	W. Temple	*Balliol*	J. R. Brooke	*Corpus*
H.	J. St. G. C. Heath	*Corpus*	W. Temple	*Balliol*
E.	M. H. Woods	*Trinity*	W. A. Moore	*St. John's*

1904–5

M.	A. Shaw	*Trinity*	E. S. Jose	*Hertford*
H.	R. S. H. Noble	*Lincoln*	J. St. G. C. Heath	*Corpus*
E.	H. M. Paul	*New Coll.*	A. Shaw	*Trinity*

1905–6

M.	E. M. C. Denny	*Jesus*	M. H. Woods	*Trinity*
H.	A. H. Paterson	*University*	H. M. Paul	*New Coll.*
E.	N. S. Talbot	*Ch. Ch.*	Hon. H. Lygon	*Magdalen*

1906–7

M.	A. H. Villiers	*Magdalen*	G. S. C. Rentoul	*Ch. Ch.*
H.	W. G. C. Gladstone	*New Coll.*	N. S. Talbot	*Ch. Ch.*
E.	W. S. Armour	*Jesus*	W. G. C. Gladstone	*New Coll.*

OFFICERS FROM 1841

1907-8

	SECRETARY		TREASURER	
M.	M. H. Richmond	*New Coll.*	H. I. P. Hallett	*Ch. Ch.*
H.	R. A. Knox	*Balliol*	M. H. Richmond	*New Coll.*
E.	E. P. Swain	*St. John's*	W. M. Ogilvy	*University*

1908-9

M.	L. J. Stein	*Balliol*	R. G. D. Laffan	*Balliol*
H.	Hon. R. S. A. Palmer		L. J. Stein	*Balliol*
		University		
E.	A. H. M. Lunn	*Balliol*	R. H. W. Brinsley-Richards	
				Hertford

1909-10

M.	A. W. Cockburn	*New Coll.*	N. Micklem	*New Coll.*
H.	F. K. Griffith	*Balliol*	A. W. Cockburn	*New Coll.*
E.	G. S. Woodhouse	*Lincoln*	P. Guedalla	*Balliol*

1910-11

M.	L. N. G. Montefiore	*Balliol*	F. K. Griffith	*Balliol*
H.	S. H. Wall	*Lincoln*	G. S. Woodhouse	*Lincoln*
E.	R. M. Barrington-Ward	*Balliol*	L. N. G. Montefiore	*Balliol*

1911-12

M.	W. T. Monckton	*Balliol*	R. M. Barrington-Ward	*Balliol*
H.	W. J. Bland	*Lincoln*	W. T. Monckton	*Balliol*
E.	G. W. L. Talbot	*Ch. Ch.*	W. J. Bland	*Lincoln*

1912-13

M.	F. J. P. Richter	*New Coll.*	G. W. L. Talbot	*Ch. Ch.*
H.	A. H. M. Wedderburn	*Balliol*	G. P. Dennis	*Exeter*
E.	P. R. S. Nichols	*Balliol*	A. H. M. Wedderburn	*Balliol*

1913-14

M.	A. P. Herbert	*New Coll.*	P. R. S. Nichols	*Balliol*
			A. F. H. Wiggin	*Oriel*
H.	M. H. Macmillan	*Balliol*	H. G. Strauss	*Ch. Ch.*
E.	V. A. L. Mallet	*Balliol*	M. H. Macmillan	*Balliol*

1914-15*

M.	D. F. Jerrold	*New Coll.*	E. H. Davenport	*Queen's*

* During the period of the war no elections were held.

OFFICERS FROM 1841

1907–8

M.	C. T. Le Quesne	*Exeter*	W. S. Armour	*Jesus*
H.	Viscount Wolmer	*University*	C. T. Le Quesne	*Exeter*
E.	R. A. Knox	*Balliol*	H. I. P. Hallett	*Ch. Ch.*

1908–9

M.	E. P. Swain	*St. John's*	M. H. Richmond	*New Coll.*
H.	W. M. Ogilvy	*University*	R. A. Knox	*Balliol*
E.	Hon. R. S. A. Palmer		E. P. Swain	*St. John's*
		University		

1909–10

M.	L. J. Stein	*Balliol*	R. G. D. Laffan	*Balliol*
H.	N. Micklem	*New Coll.*	Hon. R. S. A. Palmer	*University*
E.	R. Bevir	*Hertford*	L. J. Stein	*Balliol*

1910–11

M.	P. Guedalla	*Balliol*	A. W. Cockburn	*New Coll.*
H.	F. K. Griffith	*Balliol*	N. Micklem	*New Coll.*
E.	G. S. Woodhouse	*Lincoln*	R. Bevir	*Hertford*

1911–12

M.	G. E. Dodds	*New Coll.*	P. Guedalla	*Balliol*
H.	R. M. Barrington-Ward	*Balliol*	F. K. Griffith	*Balliol*
E.	W. T. Monckton	*Balliol*	R. M. Barrington-Ward	*Balliol*

1912–13

M.	W. J. Bland	*Lincoln*	G. S. Woodhouse	*Lincoln*
H.	G. W. L. Talbot	*Ch. Ch.*	W. T. Monckton	*Balliol*
E.	E. H. G. Roberts	*Trinity*	W. J. Bland	*Lincoln*

1913–14

M.	G. P. Dennis	*Exeter*	G. W. L. Talbot	*Ch. Ch.*
H.	A. H. M. Wedderburn	*Balliol*	E. H. G. Roberts	*Trinity*
E.	A. F. H. Wiggin	*Oriel*	A. H. M. Wedderburn,	*Balliol*

1914–15*

M.	M. H. Macmillan	*Balliol*	A. F. H. Wiggin	*Oriel*

* During the period of the war no elections were held.

OFFICERS FROM 1841

OFFICERS FROM 1841

1919

T.	J. B. S. Haldane	*New Coll.*	L. Hore Belisha	*St. John's*

1919–20

M.	J. W. Russell	*New Coll.*	T. W. Earp	*Exeter*
H.	J. Beverley Nichols	*Balliol*	C. Gallop	*Balliol*
T.	N. A. Beechman	*Balliol*	J. W. Russell	*New Coll.*

1920–1

M.	N. A. Beechman	*Balliol*	J. Beverley Nichols	*Balliol*
H.	J. Victor Evans	*St. John's*	N. A. Beechman	*Balliol*
T.	J. Victor Evans	*St. John's*	C. B. Ramage	*Pembroke*

1921–2

M.	J. B. Herbert	*Ch. Ch.*	K. M. Lindsay	*Worcester*
H.	E. Marjoribanks	*Ch. Ch.*	J. Victor Evans	*St. John's*
T.	J. G. Morgan	*St. John's*	R. M. Carson	*Oriel*

1922–3

M.	J. D. Woodruff	*New Coll.*	E. Marjoribanks	*Ch. Ch.*
H.	M. C. Hollis	*Balliol*	J. D. Woodruff	*New Coll.*
T.	C. H. O. Scaife	*St. John's*	A. G. Bagnall	*St. John's*

1923–4

M.	H. J. S. Wedderburn	*Balliol*	M. C. Hollis	*Balliol*
H.	H. J. S. Wedderburn	*Balliol*	C. H. O. Scaife	*St. John's*
T.	R. de C. Matthews	*New Coll.*	G. A. Gardiner	*Magdalen*

1924–5

M.	R. H. Bernays	*Worcester*	H. J. S. Wedderburn	*Balliol*
H.	H. V. Lloyd-Jones	*Jesus*	R. H. Bernays	*Worcester*
T.	A. H. E. Molson	*New Coll.*	H. V. Lloyd-Jones	*Jesus*

1925–26

M.	G. Isham	*Magdalen*	A. H. E. Molson	*New Coll.*
H.	L. M. Fraser	*Balliol*	G. Isham	*Magdalen*
T.	A. T. L. Lennox-Boyd	*Ch. Ch.*	L. M. Fraser	*Balliol*

1926–7

M.	J. P. Price	*New Coll.*	A. T. L. Lennox-Boyd	*Ch.Ch.*
H.	C. S. M. Brereton	*Balliol*	R. T. B. Fulford	*Worcester*
T.	R. T. D. Acland	*Balliol*	J. P. Price	*New Coll.*

OFFICERS FROM 1841

OFFICERS FROM 1841

TERM	LIBRARIAN		PRESIDENT	

1927–8

M.	A. Herbert	*University*	C. S. M. Brereton	*Balliol*
H.	E. Shackleton Bailey	*Worcester*	D. M. Foot	*Balliol*
T.	R. C. Wilson	*Queen's*	A. Herbert	*University*

1928–9

M.	Hon. Q. McGarel Hogg		S. Stopford Brooke	*Balliol*
		Ch. Ch.		
H.	B. J. M. McKenna	*New Coll.*	R. C. Wilson	*Queen's*
T.	F. Correia-Afonso	*Non.-Coll.*	Hon. Q. McGarel Hogg	*Ch. Ch.*

1929–30

M.	J. A. Boyd-Carpenter	*Balliol*	R. M. M. Stewart	*St. John's*
H.	J. E. MacColl	*Balliol*	E. M. Lustgarten	*St. John's*
T.	J. M. Foot	*Balliol*	J. P. W. Mallalieu	*Trinity*

1930–1

M.	E. D. O'Brien	*Exeter*	J. A. Boyd-Carpenter	*Balliol*
H.	G. M. Wilson	*Oriel*	J. M. Foot	*Balliol*
T.	H. Z. A. Kabir	*Exeter*	G. M. Wilson	*Oriel*

1931–2

M.	A. J. Irvine	*Oriel*	E. D. O'Brien	*Exeter*
H.	J. C. Smuts	*University*	A. J. Irvine	*Oriel*
T.	A. W. J. Greenwood	*Balliol*	B. Davidson	*New Coll.*

1932–3

M.	F. M. Hardie	*Ch. Ch.*	J. C. Smuts	*University*
H.	D. M. Graham	*Balliol*	F. M. Hardie	*Ch. Ch.*
T.	M. M. Foot	*Wadham*	A. W. J. Greenwood	*Balliol*

1933–4

M.	D. F. Karaka	*Lincoln*	M. M. Foot	*Wadham*
H.	K. R. F. Steel-Maitland	*Balliol*	D. F. Karaka	*Lincoln*
				Balliol
T.	W. G. Murray	*Balliol*	K. R. F. Steel-Maitland	*Balliol*

1934–5

M.	J. P. Hickerton	*St. Cath's.*	W. G. Murray	*Balliol*
H.	L. A. Larson	*Pembroke*	D. Lewis	*Lincoln*
T.	B. A. Farrell	*Balliol*	J. P. Hickerton	*St. Cath's.*

TERM	SECRETARY		TREASURER	

1935–6

M.	J. A. Brown	*Balliol*	M. Beloff	*Corpus*
H.	R. McM. Bell	*Magdalen*	J. A. Brown	*Balliol*
T.	W. A. Nield	*St. Edm. Hall*	R. McM. Bell	*Magdalen*

1936–7

M.	M. P. Solomon	*Magdalen*	P. J. Anderson	*Worcester*
H.	L. Wilkes	*Balliol*	M. P. Solomon	*Magdalen*
T.	R. H. Walton	*Balliol*	A. M. Fyfe	*Balliol*

1937–8

M.	P. T. Toynbee	*Ch. Ch.*	E. Jones	*St. Peter's Hall*
H.	E. R. G. Heath	*Balliol*	P. T. Toynbee	*Ch. Ch.*
T.	J. R. J. Kerruish	*Magdalen*	A. W. Wood	*Balliol*

1938–9

M.	Hon. Hugh Fraser	*Balliol*	E. A. Bramall *	*Magdalen*
			C. M. Cadogan	*Magdalen*
H.	A. F. Giles	*Balliol*	Hon. Hugh Fraser	*Balliol*
T.	P. A. O'Donovan	*Ch. Ch.*	E. P. Street	*Exeter*

1939–40

M.	J. R. C. Symonds *	*Corpus*	P. A. O'Donovan *	*Ch. Ch.*
	J. M. Kershaw	*Magdalen*	R. M. Seligman	*Balliol*
H.	R. H. Jenkins	*Balliol*	C. A. R. Crosland	*Trinity*
T.	I. J. Bahadoorsingh	*St. Cath's.*	J. G. P. Comyn	*New Coll.*

1940–1

M.	K. W. Riddle	*St. Cath's.*	L. F. Crisp*	*Balliol*
			R. I. Gray	*Queen's*
H.	M. A. Ashcroft	*Magdalen*	K. G. I. Jones	*University*
T.	G. Hirsch	*Brasenose*	J. A. T. Douglas	*New Coll.*

1941–2

M.	F. P. R. Hinchliffe	*New Coll.*	B. T. Wigoder	*Oriel*
H.	Hon. D. J. H. Mond	*Ch. Ch.*	G. Knight	*St. Cath's.*
T.	J. S. Smith	*St. Cath's.*	J. C. Tudor	*Keble*

1942–3

M.	J. F. Blitz *	*Magdalen*	J. H. Davies *	*Wadham*
	F. A. Reid	*Magdalen*	H. L. Clarke	*Jesus*
H.	E. B. C. Clifford	*Ch. Ch.*	J. P. Honour	*Ch. Ch.*
T.	A. H. Head	*Magdalen*	J. G. Le Quesne	*Exeter*

* Elected but did not hold office owing to war service or other causes.

OFFICERS FROM 1841

1935–6

M.	I. D. Harvey	*Ch. Ch.*	B. A. Farrell	*Balliol*
H.	M. Beloff	*Corpus*	I. D. Harvey	*Ch. Ch.*
T.	J. A. Brown	*Balliol*	W. G. C. Shebbeare	*Ch. Ch.*

1936–7

M.	C. P. Mayhew	*Ch. Ch.*	J. A. Brown	*Balliol*
H.	P. J. Anderson	*Worcester*	C. P. Mayhew	*Ch. Ch.*
T.	C. G. P. Smith	*Wadham*	P. J. Anderson	*Worcester*

1937–8

M.	R. H. Walton	*Balliol*	A. M. Fyfe	*Balliol*
H.	E. Jones	*St. Peter's Hall*	R. H. Walton	*Balliol*
T.	E. R. G. Heath	*Balliol*	P. T. Toynbee	*Ch. Ch.*

1938–9

M.	J. R. J. Kerruish	*Magdalen*	A. W. Wood	*Balliol*
H.	C. M. Cadogan	*Magdalen*	E. R. G. Heath	*Balliol*
T.	A. F. Giles	*Balliol*	Hon. Hugh Fraser	*Balliol*

1939–40

M.	E. P. Street*	*Exeter*	A. F. Giles*	*Balliol*
	M. Evans	*Hertford*	J. N. Henderson	*Hertford*
H.	R. H. G. Edmonds	*Brasenose*	R. M. Seligman	*Balliol*
T.	R. H. Jenkins	*Balliol*	R. G. H. Edmonds	*Brasenose*

1940–1

M.	I. J. Bahadoorsingh	*St. Cath's.*	J. G. P. Comyn	*New Coll·*
H.	K. W. Riddle	*St. Cath's.*	I. J. Bahadoorsingh	*St. Cath's.*
T.	M. Kinchin-Smith	*Ch. Ch.*	K. W. Riddle	*St. Cath's.*

1941–2

M.	G. Hirsch	*Brasenose*	M. Kinchin-Smith	*Ch. Ch.*
H.	F. P. R. Hinchliffe	*New Coll.*	G. Hirsch	*Brasenose*
T.	Hon. D. J. H. Mond	*Ch. Ch.*	F. P. R Hinchliffe	*New Coll.*

1942–3

M.	J. S. Smith	*St. Cath's.*	J. C. Tudor	*Keble*
H.	C. T. G. Blackmore	*Keble*	H. L. Clarke	*Jesus*
T.	E. B. C. Clifford	*Ch. Ch.*	C. T. G. Blackmore	*Keble*

* Elected but did not hold office owing to war service or other causes.

TERM	SECRETARY		TREASURER	

1943-4
M.	J. A. F. Pickford	*Oriel*	Hon. K. H. L. Lamb	*Trinity*
H.	A. G. F. Rippon	*Brasenose*	F. Henriques	*Brasenose*
T.	N. A. S. Gibson	*Queen's*	F. J. Long	*Queen's*

1944-5
M.	A. M. Walton	*Hertford*	R. L. Weisweiller	*New Coll.*
H.	R. F. Brown	*Brasenose*	W. H. Taylor	*Ch. Ch.*
T.	H. J. Fairlie	*Corpus*	R. F. Brown	*Brasenose*

1945-6
M.	A. Hever	*Queen's*	J. Pickles	*Ch. Ch.*
H.	A. A. Whitaker	*Ch. Ch.*	N. Labovitch	*Brasenose*
T.	Hon. G. E. Noel	*Exeter*	A. A. Whitaker	*Ch. Ch.*

1946-7
M.	Hon. A. N. Wedgwood Benn	*New Coll.*	Hon. G. E. Noel	*Exeter*
H.	Sir E. Boyle, Bt.	*Ch. Ch.*	Hon. A. N. Wedgwood Benn	*New Coll.*
T.	C. Wigram	*Oriel*	P. E. Kroyer	*Ch. Ch.*

1947-8
M.	H. J. E. Nelson-Williams	*Brasenose*	J. A. Baker	*Wadham*
H.	S. H. Hills	*St. Cath's.*	J. N. L. Stobbs	*Pembroke*
T.	P. M. Kirk	*Trinity*	A. L. Price	*Keble*

1948-9
M.	K. P. Tynan	*Magdalen*	G. C. Jackson	*St. John's*
H.	R. Day	*St. Edm. Hall*	R. S. Faber	*Ch. Ch.*
T.	A. L. Mildon	*Wadham*	R. S. Arthur	*Keble*

1949-50
M.	D. Taverne	*Balliol*	G. N. L. Dalzell-Payne	*Brasenose*
H.	G. S. Smith	*Worcester*	D. Taverne	*Balliol*
T.	S. Booth-Clibborn	*Oriel*	G. S. Smith	*Worcester*

1950-1
M.	J. K. Kyle	*Magdalen*	J. J. Thorpe	*Trinity*
H.	H. E. Shuman	*New Coll.*	I. M. Yates	*Pembroke*
T.	Hon. D. Wedgwood Benn	*Balliol*	O. Kerensky	*Ch. Ch.*

TERM	LIBRARIAN		PRESIDENT	

1943–4

M.	A. H. Head	Magdalen	J. G. Le Quesne	Exeter
H.	J. A. F. Pickford	Oriel	Hon. K. H. L. Lamb	Trinity
T.	A. G. F. Rippon	Brasenose	F. Henriques	Brasenose

1944–5

M.	N. A. S. Gibson	Queen's	J. A. F. Pickford	Oriel
H.	A. M. Walton	Hertford	N. A. S. Gibson *	Queen's
			R. L. Weisweiller	New Coll.
T.	F. J. Long	Queen's	A. M. Walton	Hertford

1945–6

M.	R. F. Brown	Brasenose	F. J. Long	Queen's
H.	A. Hever	Queen's	B. T. Wigoder	Oriel
T.	J. Pickles	Ch. Ch.	C. A. R. Crosland	Trinity

1946–7

M.	A. A. Whitaker	Ch. Ch.	R. F. Brown	Brasenose
H.	Hon. G. E. Noel	Exeter	R. I. Gray	Queen's
T.	Sir E. Boyle, Bt.	Ch. Ch.	Hon. A. N. Wedgwood Benn	
				New Coll.

1947–8

M.	C. Wigram	Oriel	P. E. Kroyer	Ch. Ch.
H.	H. J. E. Nelson-Williams		C. Wigram	Oriel
		Brasenose		
T.	S. H. Hills	St. Cath's.	Sir E. Boyle, Bt.	Ch. Ch.

1948–9

M.	P. M. Kirk	Trinity	S. H. Hills	St. Cath's.
H.	R. S. C. Donald	Ch. Ch.	P. M. Kirk	Trinity
T.	R. Day	St. Edm. Hall	R. S. C. Donald	Ch. Ch.

1949–50

M.	U. Kitzinger	New Coll.	R. S. Faber	Ch. Ch.
H.	P. F. H. Emery	Oriel	U. Kitzinger	New Coll.
T.	D. Taverne	Balliol	R. Day	St. Edm. Hall

1950–1

M.	W. Rees-Mogg	Balliol	G. S. Smith	Worcester
H.	G. N. L. Dalzell-Payne		J. J. Thorpe	Trinity
		Brasenose		
T.	H. E. Shuman	New Coll.	W. Rees-Mogg	Balliol

* Elected but did not hold office owing to war service or other causes.

OFFICERS FROM 1841

1951–2

M.	P. Hutber	*New Coll.*	P. A. R. Blaker	*New Coll.*
H.	N. St. John-Stevas	*Ch. Ch.*	P. B. B. Mayhew	*Balliol*
T.	B. E. Magee	*Keble*	R. N. Iyer	*Magdalen*

1952–3

M.	J. Ryman	*Pembroke*	B. E. Magee	*Keble*
H.	N. G. Barnett*	*St. Edm. Hall*	Sir A. Cuninghame, Bt.	*Worcester*
	J. D. Stewart	*Balliol*		
T.	T. E. Burgess	*Keble*	J. D. Stewart	*Balliol*

1953–4

M.	R. O. S. Booth	*Jesus*	T. E. Burgess	*Keble*
H.	M. R. D. Heseltine	*Pembroke*	R. O. S. Booth	*Jesus*
T.	B. E. Burton	*Jesus*	M. R. D. Heseltine	*Pembroke*

1954–5

M.	J. King-Farlow	*Ch. Ch.*	A. M. Howard	*Ch. Ch.*
H.	S. D. Watkins	*Keble*	R. W. B. Dickson	*Exeter*
T.	R. F. B. Greig	*Ch. Ch.*	S. D. Watkins	*Keble*

1955–6

M.	K. Thompson	*New Coll.*	M. Brown	*Wadham*
H.	P. Somerset Fry	*St. Cath's.*	E. Ions	*Merton*
T.	T. Bendhem	*St. Edm. Hall*	J. Lever	*University*

1956–7

M.	B. Ellis	*St. John's*	B. Walden	*Queen's*
H.	L. Athulathmudali	*Jesus*	P. Brooke	*Balliol*
T.	R. D'Mello	*Pembroke*	L. Athulathmudali	*Jesus*

1957–8

M.	S. Griffiths	*Magdalen*	R. D'Mello	*Pembroke*
H.	E. Langford	*University*	A. H. Newton	*Trinity*
T.	K. Baker	*Magdalen*	R. Owen	*Ch. Ch.*

1958–9

M.	J. Trattner	*St. Cath's.*	L. Kadirgamer	*Balliol*
H.	I. A. Lyon	*Oriel*	K. G. Garry	*Magdalen*
T.	A. G. B. Hazelhurst	*Oriel*	I. A. Lyon	*Oriel*

* Resigned in the first week of term.

OFFICERS FROM 1841

1951–2

M.	O. Kerensky	*Ch. Ch.*	I. M. Yates	*Pembroke*
H.	P. Hutber	*New Coll.*	P. A. R. Blaker	*New Coll.*
T.	P. B. B. Mayhew	*Balliol*	H. E. Shuman	*New Coll.*

1952–3

M.	R. N. Iyer	*Magdalen*	P. B. B. Mayhew	*Balliol*
H.	J. Ryman*	*Pembroke*	B. E. Magee	*Keble*
	J. Peters	*Balliol*		
T.	Sir A. Cuninghame, Bt.		J. Peters	*Balliol*
		Worcester		

1953–4

M.	P. H. B. Tapsell	*Merton*	Sir A. Cuninghame, Bt.	*Worcester*
H.	J. F. S. Boswell	*New Coll.*	T. E. Burgess	*Keble*
T.	R. O. S. Booth	*Jesus*	R. N. Iyer	*Magdalen*

1954–5

M.	J. I. Isaacs	*Merton*	M. R. D. Heseltine	*Pembroke*
H.	J. King-Farlow	*Ch. Ch.*	J. I. Isaacs	*Merton*
T.	R. W. B. Dickson	*Exeter*	A. M. Howard	*Ch. Ch.*

1955–6

M.	A. A. A. Grant	*Merton*	S. D. Watkins	*Keble*
H.	K. Thompson	*New Coll.*	A. A. A. Grant	*Merton*
T.	E. Ions	*Merton*	R. W. B. Dickson	*Exeter*

1956–7

M.	J. Lever	*University*	E. Ions	*Merton*
H.	B. Evans	*Wadham*	J. Lever	*University*
T.	B. Walden	*Queen's*	P. Brooke	*Balliol*

1957–8

M.	L. Athulathmudali	*Jesus*	B. Walden	*Queen's*
H.	S. Griffiths	*Magdalen*	L. Athulathmudali	*Jesus*
T.	A. H. Newton	*Trinity*	S. Griffiths	*Magdalen*

1958–9

M.	A. Rowe	*Merton*	R. Owen	*Ch. Ch.*
H.	J. Trattner	*St. Cath's.*	L. Kadirgamer	*Balliol*
T.	P. Jay	*Ch. Ch.*	A. H. Newton	*Trinity*

* Resigned in first week of term.

OFFICERS FROM 1841

1959–60

M.	R. M. D. Rowland	*Keble*	A. G. B. Hazelhurst	*Oriel*
H.	P. M. Foot	*University*	R. M. D. Rowland	*Keble*
T.	P. Whitehead	*Exeter*	P. M. Foot	*University*

1960–1

M.	J. Hazelgrove	*Keble*	A. E. Arblaster	*Balliol*
H.	M. Mosley	*Ch. Ch.*	H. F. Preece	*Merton*
T.	J. B. W. McDonnell	*Balliol*	D. E. Prior-Palmer	*Ch. Ch.*

1961–2

M.	M. J. Beloff	*Magdalen*	H. A. Stephenson	*New Coll.*
H.	G. R. Karnad	*Magdalen*	N. J. C. B. Picarda	*Ch. Ch.*
T.	J. W. Hicks	*Ch. Ch.*	G. R. Karnad	*Magdalen*

1962–3

M.	J. R. M. Davies	*Ch. Ch.*	L. R. Reed*	*University*
H.	G. V. T. Pratt	*Corpus*	J. S. Jowell	*Hertford*
T.	Lord J. Douglas-Hamilton	*Balliol*	T. A. A. Hart	*New Coll.*

1963–4

M.	C. J. B. Mott	*Ch. Ch.*	T. A. A. Hart	*New Coll.*
H.	N. L. J. Montagu	*New Coll.*	R. J. Kirkwood	*Ch. Ch.*
T.	E. A. H. Abrahams	*St. Peter's*	T. Ali	*Exeter*

1964–5

M.	H. C. Q. Brownrigg	*New Coll.*	R. C. Floud	*Wadham*
H.	J. A. N. Bamfield	*Pembroke*	J. B. Beloff	*St. Cath's.*
T.	Hon. S. A. Head	*Ch. Ch.*	R. I. P. Bulkeley	*Exeter*

* Resigned in sixth week of term.

OFFICERS FROM 1841

1959–60

M.	I. A. Lyon	*Oriel*	J. Trattner	*St. Cath's.*
H.	A. G. B. Hazelhurst	*Oriel*	I. A. Lyon	*Oriel*
T.	R. M. D. Rowland	*Keble*	P. Jay	*Ch. Ch.*

1960–1

M.	P. Whitehead	*Exeter*	R. M. D. Rowland	*Keble*
H.	J. Hazelgrove	*Keble*	P. Whitehead	*Exeter*
T.	H. F. Preece	*Merton*	P. M. Foot	*University*

1961–2

M.	J. B. W. McDonnell	*Balliol*	H. F. Preece	*Merton*
H.	M. J. Beloff	*Magdalen*	H. A. Stephenson	*New Coll.*
T.	D. E. Prior-Palmer	*Ch. Ch.*	J. B. W. McDonnell	*Balliol*

1962–3

M.	G. R. Karnad	*Magdalen*	M. J. Beloff	*Magdalen*
H.	J. R. M. Davies	*Ch. Ch.*	G. R. Karnad	*Magdalen*
T.	G. V. J. Pratt	*Corpus*	J. S. Jowell	*Hertford*

1963–64

M.	Lord J. Douglas Hamilton		T. A. A. Hart	*New Coll.*
		Balliol		
H.	C. J. B. Mott	*Ch. Ch.*	G. V. J. Pratt	*Ch. Ch.*
T.	J. W. P. Aitken	*Ch. Ch.*	Lord J. Douglas Hamilton	*Balliol*

1964–5

M.	D. N. MacCormick	*Balliol*	E. A. H. Abrahams	*St. Peter's*
H.	D. M. Hogg	*Ch. Ch.*	D. N. MacCormick	*Balliol*
T.	J. A. N. Bamfield	*Pembroke*	T. Ali	*Exeter*

SENIOR TREASURER

Rev .T. H. Grose, M.A., *Queen's* Ex-President, 1888–1906
Sidney Ball, M.A., *St. John's*, 1906–18
R. S. Rait, M.A., *New College*, Trinity Term to Michaelmas Term, 1918
Sir C. Grant Robertson, C.V.O., M.A., *All Souls*, 1919–20
E. Barker, M.A., *New College*, 1920
Rev. Dr. A. J. Carlyle, *University*, Ex-President, 1921–30
J. F. Stenning, M.A., *Warden of Wadham*, 1930–4
Rt. Rev. C. M. Chavasse, O.B.E., M.C., M.A., *St. Peter's Hall*, 1934–9
Rev. N. Micklem, M.A., *New College*, Ex-President, 1940–2
M. L. Jacks, M.A., *Wadham*, 1942–4
Rev. R. H. Lightfoot, D.D., *New College*, 1945–50
Asa Briggs, M.A. B.SC., *Worcester*, 1950–3
G. B. Richardson, M.A., *St. John's*, 1953–4
M. Shock, M.A., *University*, 1954–

SENIOR LIBRARIAN

R. S. Rait, M.A., *New College*, 1907–13
W. H. Moberly, D.S.O., M.A., *Lincoln*, 1913–21
A. D. Lindsay, C.B.E., M.A., *Balliol*, Ex-President, 1921–2
E. L. Woodward, M.A., *All Souls*, 1922–9
H. R. F. Harrod, M.A., *Christ Church*, 1929–39
Rev. Canon Claude Jenkins, D.D., *Christ Church*, 1939–59
M. Maclagan, M.A., *Trinity*, 1959–

INDEX

S = Secretary: T = Treasurer: L = Librarian: P = President:
ST = Senior Treasurer

273

BIBLIOGRAPHY

L. S. Amery. *My Political Life.*
Dacre Balsdon. *Oxford Life.*
Dacre Balsdon. *Freshman's Folly.*
Earl of Birkenhead. *Life of the First Earl of Birkenhead.*
Vera Brittain. *The Women at Oxford.*
G. V. Cox. *Recollections of Oxford.*
J. B. Firth. *The Minstrelsy of Isis.*
Roger Fulford. *The Right Honourable Gentleman.*
V. Gollancz. *My Dear Timothy.*
V. H. H. Green. *Oxford Common Room.*
G. B. Grundy. *Fifty-Five Years at Oxford.*
Christopher Hobhouse. *Oxford as it was and as it is To-Day.*
David Kelly. *The Ruling Few.*
Ronald Knox. *Spiritual Aeneid.*
Andrew Lang. *Oxford.*
S. P. B. Mais. *The True Story of Oxford.*
Sir C. E. Malet. *History of the University of Oxford.*
J. C. Masterman. *To Teach Their Senators Wisdom.*
Sir H. C. Maxwell Lyte. *History of the University of Oxford.*
Herbert Morrah. *Oxford Union.*
Sir Charles Oman. *Memories of Victorian Oxford.*
Rev. James Pyecroft. *Oxford Memories.*
Viscount Samuel. *Memoirs.*
T. Seccombe and H. S. Scott. *In Praise of Oxford.*
Viscount Simon. *Retrospect.*
Evelyn Waugh. *Life of Ronald Knox.*
Evelyn Waugh. *A Little Learning.*
A. R. Wooley. *Oxford, University and City.*